THE NARRATIVE WORKS OF GÜNTER GRASS

GERMAN LANGUAGE AND LITERATURE MONOGRAPHS

Wolfgang W. Moelleken, *General Editor*

Volume 12

Noel Thomas

The Narrative Works of Günter Grass

NOEL THOMAS

THE NARRATIVE WORKS
OF
GÜNTER GRASS

A CRITICAL INTERPRETATION

1982

Table of Contents

CHAPTER I

Die Blechtrommel: from the perspective of a child

Introduction

When in 1959 *Die Blechtrommel* was first published
it burst onto the literary scene like a bombshell, oc-
casioning loud cries of horror, disgust, enthusiasm and
admiration, according to the individual attitude of the
critic concerned. Hans Magnus Enzensberger was quick to
point out the uniqueness of Grass and of his first novel:
"Dieser Mann ist ein Störenfried, ein Hai im Sardinen-
tümpel, ein wilder Einzelgänger in unserer domestizierten
Literatur, und sein Buch ist ein Brocken wie Döblins *Berlin Alexanderplatz*, wie Brechts *Baal*, ein Brocken an dem
Rezenzenten und Philologen mindestens ein Jahrzehnt lang
zu würgen haben, bis es reif zur Kanonisation oder zur
Aufbewahrung im Schauhaus der Literaturgeschichte ist."[1]
Enzensberger was unduly optimistic in quoting ten years
as the minimum period of time which critics and academics
would require in order to come to terms with the novel.
The process of digestion is still underway and until digestion is complete, canonisation or storage still belongs

to a somewhat remote future. Theories abound as to how
the novel should be approached and how it should be interpreted. No single interpretation provides the ultimate
truth which would allow the final categorisation to take
place. One has rather the impression that each new ven-
ture into the still partially uncharted interior of the
novel complements but does not necessarily invalidate
other previous pronouncements. The process of digestion
is a literary communion in which all participate, from
which one day a collective assessment will emerge and per-
mit the novel to have an appropriate resting place in the
literary museum.

The Film of Die Blechtrommel

However, the production of Volker Schlöndorff's film
of *Die Blechtrommel*, twenty years after the publication
of the novel, allows a slightly different approach to the
novel and permits us to re-emphasize some of the statements which Grass himself has made and which sometimes
are partially or completely ignored by those who seek to
reduce the novel to a single, all-embracing formula. In
comparing film and novel we shall also become aware of
the correctness of Hans Magnus Enzensberger's response to
the novel dating from the year 1959. What is more important, however, is that in relating the film to the novel,

tne distinctive qualities of the two artistic products may emerge with greater clarity. Before commencing this comparison it is worth recalling that Grass had confidence in Schlöndorff's capacity to adapt material in keeping with the aesthetics of the film-producer: "erst als ich merkte, daß der Schlöndorff in der Lage ist, die Syntax des Schriftstellers in die Optik der Kamera zu übersetzen, da war die Sache für mich geklärt." (p. 24).[2] As a result of such confidence he felt justified in accepting Schlöndorff as a producer who could convert the novel into film.

One of the fundamental differences between the novel and the film is the change in narrative perspective. In the novel Oskar writes his memoires in the years from 1952 to 1954 and in so doing covers the lives of his immediate ancestors and thirty years of his own life, having been born in September 1924 and completing his autobiography on his thirteenth birthday in September 1954. Oskar tells the story of himself, the child who at the age of three consciously refuses to enter the adult world, and accordingly causes an accident, a fall down some cellar steps which arrests his growth. Oskar pretends to view the world through the eyes of a three-year-old child: his intellectual faculties remain unimpaired but he ceases to grow physically. The narrative perspec-

tive acquires a further complication by the fact that
Oskar writes his life-story as an inmate of a lunatic
asylum, having been confined there because he is suspected
of murder. The opening sentence of the novel casts its
shadow over the whole narrative: "Zugegeben: ich bin
Insasse einer Heil- und Pflegeanstalt, mein Pfleger beo-
bachtet mich, läßt mich kaum aus dem Auge..." (p. 9).[3] In
the film this qualification does not exist. The author,
producer and scriptwriter were in agreement that the situation of the narrator should be sacrificed: "Es hätte
sonst eine ständige Rückblende gegeben, umständlich und
dreimal um die Ecke; was man mit einem Semikolon beim
Schreiben machen kann, wird im Film umständlich." (p. 23).[2]
This change in the position of the narrator is the basic
difference between the film and the novel-- apart from
the obvious, more fundamental fact that the film and novel are two different artistic media. In the film everything is viewed through the eyes of the child, as though
he were experiencing the events at the time. The viewer
is presented with a series of tableaux or episodes with
Oskar acting as commentator, "doch nicht um Informationen
zu geben, sondern um seine Gedanken zu sich und dem Ge-
schehen zu formulieren." (p. 38).[2]

In the novel many of the difficulties which reader
experiences in interpreting it stem from the fact that

an apparent madman recapitulates the past from the perspective of a child. The alienation effect which is thus
produced coupled with the total amorality of the narrative viewpoint make it virtually impossible for the reader
to identify himself with Oskar or with any of the characters in the novel. In the film, however, orientation is
much easier, for, as Schlöndorff maintains, the viewer
can identify himself with Oskar (p. 24).[2] The possibility
of our projecting ourselves into the situation of Oskar
is enhanced by the fact that Oskar is portrayed as a child,
and not as a gnome. Both Schlöndorff and Grass were of
the opinion that Oskar should be portrayed as a child
and Grass himself went so far as to maintain that the
difficulties would-be film producers experienced in assessing *Die Blechtrommel* originated in their misunderstanding the character of Oskar: "Es gab ja große
Schwierigkeiten in den Jahren davor bei den Leuten, die
Die Blechtrommel verfilmen wollten. Sie gingen immer davon aus-- das ist auch durch einen Teil der Literatur-
kritik mit verursacht--, sie sprachen immer von einem
häßlichen Zwerg, von einem Gnom. Dabei macht das Buch
deutlich: es ist ein Kind, das sein Wachstum eingestellt
hat." (p. 25).[2] Furthermore, David Bennent, the child
chosen by Schlöndorff to act the role of Oskar, is an
attractive-looking person, in no way to be considered as

a repulsive individual. Hence the credibility of Oskar
in the film is not seriously in doubt, in the way that
Oskar in the novel quickly brands himself as a thoroughly
unreliable narrator. This is not to say that the viewer
projects himself into the situation of Oskar as he shatters
glass, either in the sitting room or from the 'Stockturm',
but rather that we can comprehend and enjoy Oskar's impishness, when, for example, he hangs the drum on the figure
of Jesus in the 'Herz-Jesu-Kirche' or converts the party-
rally into a festival of dance and we can share the grief
of Oskar at the loss of his mother. At the same time it
can scarcely be maintained that we have a clear-cut notion of Oskar as a character-- his principal attribute is
his childishness, the fact that he is a child and indulges
in childish activities. His attachment to his drum is
the clearest indication of this. As in the novel Oskar
is primarily a person through whose eyes we view a period
of German history. By his very childishness Oskar cannot
sit in judgement on that period of time which he exposes
to our gaze. Oskar perceives an amoral world in the a-
moral and egocentric terms of a child.

In identifying ourselves with Oskar, we can share his
grief at the destruction and loss of his native city--
the film covers the first two books of the novel and ends
with the train departing for the West with its load of

refugees. The child who yearns to remain a child loses
the place in which his childhood was spent. A number of
critics-- though not Hans Magnus Enzensberger-- seem to
ignore the historical fact which forms the core of the
novel-- and obviously of the film-- ie. the expulsion
of the Germans from Danzig. The film emerges quite clearly as a lament-- it ends with a painful sense of loss and
deprivation. This effect is achieved largely because of
what is presented usually by the camera, but also because
we share Oskar's sorrow. In seeing the film we are reminded of Enzensberger's statement about the novel: "In
der Tat ist *Die Blechtrommel* unter anderem auch ein his-
torischer Roman aus dem zwanzigsten Jahrhundert, eine
Saga der untergegangenen Freien Stadt Danzig, eine po-
etische Rettung jener kleinen Welt, in der Deutsche und
Polen, Juden und Kaschuben zusammenlebten, vor dem Ver-
gessenwerden." (p. 12).[1]

This quotation also allows one to draw conclusions
about the nature of the German guilt, in other words why
Oskar is forced to leave his place of birth. The film
shows most empathetically how the community of Danzig was
systematically destroyed from within by the Germans. On
the screen we see how Sigismund Markus, the Jew, is force-
fully evicted from the cemetery where Anna Matzerath's
funeral is taking place, we witness the German attack on

the Polish Post Office and the breakdown of communication
between the two national groups and we are spectators at
the 'Kristallnacht' when Jewish shops and synagogues are
set ablaze and when Sigismund Markus, Oskar's supplier
of drums, commits suicide. Before Oskar and the remnants
of his family depart for the West, his grandmother com-
plains that the Kaschubs, being neither Germans nor Poles,
get it in the neck from both sides. The Germans shatter
the community of Danzig. What happens in the microcosm
or Oskar's native city happens elsewhere in Germany and
in Europe. The Germans burden themselves with guilt.
Oskar feels the need to be guilty and, in accordance with
need and fashion, he indulges in the fantasy of having
murdered mother, uncle, girl-friend (Roswitha Raguna) and
father. The cinema audience cannot take such childish
extravaganzas as seriously as do many readers when they
see Oskar's confessions in black and white. The film
allows one to gain at least some insight into what Grass
has in mind when, in talking of Oskar, he refers to "seine
fingierte Schuld" and "seine wirklichen Verschulden"
(p. 18).[4] The theme of guilt is one which occupies a central position in the Danzig Trilogy and throughout all
Grass's narrative works and one to which we shall return
shortly.

The film constitutes a historical survey as seen

through the eyes of a child who is himself located in
the petty-bourgeois environment of a shop-keeper's house-
hold. It consists of a series of episodes which achieve
a greater visual impact than their equivalents in the
novel but clearly cannot attain the level of subtlety
and complexity which exclusive concentration upon the
medium of language can and does reach. The film appears
in conventional terms to be more realistic than the novel,
whereas the novel can draw on elements of fantasy which
are not at the disposal of the film and, by intermingling
fantasy and reality, can achieve a greater degree of
stimulation than is the case with the film. Even though
the episodes of the film may be regarded as a kind of
tableaux, the film is forced, for reasons of condensation,
to dispense with the imagery which makes such a major
contribution to the total impact of the novel. Above all
the sacrifice of the narrator's position produces a simplified viewpoint, less ambivalence and ambiguity, and
allows at least some identification between the viewer
and Oskar, the commentator within the film. However, the
total impact which the film achieves is not dissimilar,
if one disregards the problems associated with the narrative perspective, from that which is achieved by the
novel. Like the novel, the film of *Die Blechtrommel* is
a lament which contains within it a critique of Germany's

social and political behavior.

The film is a simplified version of the novel, not
only because of the change in narrative perspective, the
reduced imaginative content, and the absence of imagery,
but also because it stops short at the year 1945. In
other words, the film is unable to convey the impression
of historical continuity which stretches across the big
divide of 1945 linking together the period of National
Socialism and the post-war era. The film assists us in
isolating the distinctive features of the novel, that is,
the narrative perspective, the narrative skill, the
imagery, and the chronological framework. Let us now
turn to an analysis of the novel and concern ourselves
in particular with these four aspects as well as with the
theme of guilt.

The Narrative Perspective

In discussing the narrative perspective in *Die Blechtrommel* it is useful to remind ourselves of the remarks
which Grass himself has made on the topic, to which Kurt
Lothar Tank refers in his book.[5] Grass describes how he
had originally written a cycle of poems entitled *Der
Säulenheilige*. It tells of a young man who suddenly gives
up his career as a mason and becomes a stylite. Grass
goes on to say that Oskar ultimately takes up an equally

eccentric viewpoint: "Aus Oskar ist dann später ein um-
gekehrter Säulenheiliger geworden.   Es erwies sich, daß
der Mann auf der Säule zu statisch ist, um ihn Prosa
sprechen zu lassen, und deswegen ist Oskar von der Säule
herabgestiegen.   Er blieb nicht bei der normalen Größe,
sondern ist noch ein bißchen mehr an die Erde gegangen
und hat dann einen Blickwinkel, der dem Blickwinkel des
Säulenheiligen entgegensetzt ist." (p. 59).   It is clear
then that Oskar, the narrator, is intended to view human
affairs from an unusual angle.   This perspective allows
Grass to describe human beings and events in a way in
which adults would not normally perceive them.   In the
same conversation with Bienek, Grass comments upon the
advantages which stem from the fact that his main figure
ceases growing at the age of three and yet from his birth
onwards possesses the intelligence and clear-sightedness
of the adult with all his faults and false speculations.
He states that Oskar is later not regarded as an adult by
those with whom he comes into contact, but always remains
the childish dwarf, the urchin who cannot belong to the
adult world.   From this eccentric point of view Oskar is
able to play the role of observer and narrator, viewing
not only the people who surround him but the whole epoch
in a manner which Grass describes as being "von unten nach
oben".   It is important to note that Oskar is described

as "seeing" the world around him: there is no suggestion
of his judging or criticising events and people, a thing
that one could scarcely expect of a child in any case.

The narrative perspective is complicated still further by another factor.   Idris Parry reminds us of a fundamental truth about fiction when he says that "what we
are reading is not actually happening, but is being recalled and put together for our benefit by a sentient
human being." (p. 102).[6]   This we automatically accept,
perhaps almost unconsciously.   In *Die Blechtrommel* the
past is certainly being conjured up, structured and re-
structured.   However, it is being recalled by a much
flawed sentient human being, in other words by a person
who admits that he is the inmate of a mental asylum.   This
huge qualification, as we have already stated earlier in
this chapter, is erected like a warning sign at the beginning of the novel, indicating in no uncertain terms
that an unreliable narrator is at work.   This first sentence of *Die Blechtrommel*, one of the few certainties in
the novel, affects our assessment of each individual
piece of information with which Oskar provides us.   We
are constantly forced to pose ourselves the question whether a given statement may be considered valid in view of
the fact that Oskar might be a madman-- Oskar does not
describe himself as being insane, he contents himself with

the observation that he is the inmate of a lunatic asylum.
Oskar's introductory remark contains within it a second
qualification: from it the reader gathers that the narrator is describing his own life after the passage of
what is in many cases a considerable amount of time. As
can be seen by examining the time-scale within the novel,
Oskar is not presenting us with a diary written day by
day and recounting the events of the immediate past. The
passage of time, we must presume, will have blurred some
of the details and perhaps even have allowed imagination
to reconstruct the past. We have to be satisfied with
Oskar's pious hope that he has an accurate memory (see
p. 10).

As we have already stated, Volker Schlöndorff was
forced to abandon the 'Erzählerposition' of the novel and
thus some identification is made possible between the
child Oskar and the viewer. In the novel ambiguity, ambivalence and disorientation reign supreme: the reader
has to contend with what is to all intents and purposes
a double perspective. An apparent or real madman recounts
the events of his life through the eyes of a child. The
"terrible fluidity of self-revelation", to use Henry James'
description of the first-person narrative, is complete.

Yet even the term 'self-revelation' is incorrect
when applied to Oskar, for the narrator does not reveal

himself. Oskar does not grant us any real insight into his personality and we have more or less no understanding of his motivation, apart from the fact that he refuses to assume responsibility, opting out of any moral obligations towards others. Oskar's unreliability as a purveyor of information is an indication of the fact that he is estranged from himself, and this is reinforced in a number of ways: his craving to return to the prenatal state is a sign of his alienation from the present whilst at the same time being a comment on the state of the world and his attitude to it. His attachment to his drum is also indicative of his fractured relationship to reality; the existence of 'two souls fighting within his breast', the Oskar who acts and the Oskar who observes, the one who feels and the one who thinks, such divisions are a sign of the narrator's schizophrenia. His attachment to the mask of a child, his assumed pose of innocence, his delight in falsehood and prevarication, his destruction of truth, all suggest that he has not broken away from the unhealthy and seductive world of childish-- and romantic-- inwardness. Oskar does not succeed in emerging from infantile subjectivism, in making the journey from childhood to adulthood, and at the same time exploits the possibilities of feigned innocence in order to prevent his transition from inwardness to maturity. So

fragmented is Oskar's personality that he does not emerge
as a character. His eccentric, highly imaginative viewpoint is a sign of the individual who has never acquired
a focal point for his existence and is hence subject to
the centrifugal forces at work within himself and within
society. He is a 'persona' and not a personality.

As a 'persona', as an inscrutable sentient human
being, Oskar acts solely as an observer in many instances
throughout the course of the novel without participating
actively in the events which are taking place. From his
vantage point under the table, for example, Oskar is able
to observe, "von unten nach oben", the manoeuvres of his
uncle's foot during the game of Skat (p. 75). This is
the classic instance of Oskar, the child, exploiting his
unique perspective to the full. Oskar is the willing or
unwilling witness of other equally interesting scenes. In
all such instances Oskar brings an unprejudiced eye to
the scenes which he witnesses. His descriptive powers
are not inhibited by any form of censorship. His attitude is not affected by the religious or sexual taboos of
the adult and it would be true to say that he is equally
open-minded about the subject of death. As Enzensberger
states, "Grass jagt nicht, wie Henry Miller, hinter dem
Tabu her: er bemerkt es einfach nicht."[1] Oskar is thus
able to enjoy a freedom of expression which the adult

observer could not enjoy at all. Much of the humour of
the novel-- albeit frequently of a black variety and unfolding within the context of the grotesque-- stems from
the fact that our narrator approaches adult affairs in
such an unjaundiced manner. He is not afraid to survey
the totality of the human experience. This totality includes, unfortunately, smells, some of which are ob-
noxious, sexual practices which may be disagreeable,
blasphemy, and instances of death, which do not accord
with an orderly, rigidly structured view of the universe.
Oskar, as may be expected, does not engage in any false
moralising; as a child or a madman assuming the guise
of a child he can take up a completely neutral attitude
to the happenings which take place around him-- or 'took
place' would be more appropriate since Oskar is conjuring
up events of the past. Oskar is absolved of the require-
ment which is automatically imposed upon a thirty-year
old, that of assessing the past in terms of an adult.
Such assessment inevitably involves a moral evaluation,
the statement that this is right or that is wrong, or it
involves slanting the 'facts' in keeping with the pattern associated with a given philosophical or ideological
attitude. Oskar can dispense with such encumbrances. He
presents us with the details of the scenes which unfold,
retrospectively, before his eyes though, of course, the

'facts' as seen through the eyes of a child or a madman.
They are tinged by the limitations-- or limitlessness--
of the child or the madman. Oskar recreates the past, or
attempts to do so, with the qualification that through
Oskar we receive a subjective perception of the event,
though normally we would expect a perception of the past
in light of the present.

As a result of this perspective it is possible to
find a large number of statements and actions in the novel which are an expression of the attitude of the child.
When, for example, Oskar visits the opera, he plunges
the theatre into darkness because he thinks the spotlight
is blinding the singer (p. 128). The brutality of the
'Kristallnacht' is described in the terms of the child
who is baffled by the nature of the events which he sees
happening. The whole chapter is punctuated by the phrase,
"Es war einmal...", which gives it the incomprehensible
flavour of a savage nursery tale (pp. 229-40). During
the defence of the Polish Post Office Oskar cannot understand why the adults are not bothered about his drum (p.
257). Many of Oskar's statements and actions are amusing
because they are those of a naive, unprejudiced, self-
centered child. He is concerned solely with his own interests and desires. Hence when Kobyella is wounded, Oskar describes this occurrence in the following terms:

"da hatte sich eine Granate einen Riesenspaß erlaubt."
(p. 274). Oskar's pronouncements may be interpreted on
two, if not three, levels: they may stem from the na-
turalness and simplicity of the child who is baffled by
the nominally adult affairs or, what is more likely, from
the deranged mind of an adult who has successfully pro-
jected himself into the mentality of a child or alter-
natively they may be based on the playfulness and the
tongue-in-cheek attitude of the person who is acting the
role of the child, stating on many occasions the opposite
of what he believes. Such an ironical point of view allows the author to describe the events of our age in a
detached manner, pervents him from degenerating into a
judge or a prosecutor.

Amidst so much ambiguity and ambivalence the reader
often finds himself bewildered. He is disconcerted by
the ever-changing fluidity of the narrative and of Oskar's pronouncements. He feels unsure of himself and
lacks confidence in his capacity to come to any firm conclusions. The narrative perspective engenders doubt in
his mind: doubt about himself and doubt about Oskar, the
source of the so-called information. The reader scarcely
knows when to take Oskar seriously: the narrator's humour, irony and impishness form a barrier behind which
Oskar conceals himself and make it all the more difficult

to know Oskar as a person. It is not merely the drum
which separates him from the adult world but also the
virtually impenetrable wall of derision, irony and doubt.
Oskar's ironic perspective leads to a debunking of political happenings and attitudes, often because his mind in-
terconnects details in a childish, inconsequential-- and
often irreverent manner: he links, for example, the defeat of the German army in North Africa with Kurt's recovery from whooping cough (p. 379). The ironic pose
characterises many of Oskar's observations about history
and politics. His comment on the partition of Poland is
a good example of this: "Der Friede zu Oliva:-- wie
hübsch und friedlich das klingt. Dort bemerkten die Groß-
mächte zum erstenmal, daß sich das Land der Polen wunder-
bar fürs Aufteilen eignet." (p. 476). The same sham seriousness is in evidence when Oskar refers to Marshal Ro-
kossovsky's arrival in Danzig: "Der erinnerte sich beim
Anblick der heilen Stadt an seine großen internationalen
Vorgänger, schoß erst einmal alles in Brand, damit sich
jene, die nach ihm kamen, im Wiederaufbau austoben konnten." (p. 476). The superficially humerous tone conceals an underlying bitterness and despair, which, if it
had to be categorized, is more the expression of the mind
of an adult than that of a child. Such a point of view--
whether this be the naivety of a child or the irony of an

adult-- allows a detached treatment of the events concerned, permits the reader to gain the necessary distance
towards an epoch in which he himself may be too emotionally involved, and demolishes all preconceived judgements.

There are other events in the novel in which Oskar
actively participates but in which he nevertheless still
preserves his dominant role as the naive or ironic observer. During the course of Oskar's lessons at the hands
of Gretchen Scheffler it is just as important for the
reader to be able to observe Gretchen and Agnes reacting
to Rasputin as it is for us to realise the nature of Oskar's upbringing. Oskar is the witness of this scene
which is meant to have a general validity-- at least with
reference to the German context-- and which we as readers
view through the eyes of Oskar. In the chapter entitled
'Schaufenster' (pp. 142-53), Oskar cuts holes in the
glass of shop-windows and thereby presents himself-- and
us-- with the opportunity of watching how others react to
temptation. In 'Glaube Hoffnung Liebe' the bewildered
child tells of his reaction to the events of the 'Kristallnacht'. Once again Oskar acts as the observer-- though
his is a flawed vision-- and in this last instance certainly does not take part in the happenings at all. In
his post-war career Oskar apparently adapts himself to
the demands of art students and in this sense seems to be

fashioned by them. Hence the 'Madonna 49' says as much
about the guilt-ridden complexes of the students and their
teacher as it does about Oskar. The situation is clearer
still with regard to Oskar's activities as a drummer in
the Onion Cellar and his later tours of West Germany.
Oskar certainly assumes an active role on these occasions
but it is the tearful breast-beating of the guests which
claims our attention and which is exposed to ridicule.
And we are told furthermore that they are intended to
represent West German society. Oskar is in effect the
fractured medium through which the activities of others
may be scrutinized. During the course of Oskar's performances in West German towns, the figure of Oskar is
once again the device which enables West German society
to be held up to our gaze.

Regarding Oskar as an observer needs to be undertaken
with caution, for allocating him this role is to oversim-
plify the situation. We are constantly reminded that he
is a thoroughly untrustworthy observer. He himself has
no illusions about his unreliability. Having located
himself in a lunatic asylum he emphasises that he indulges in telling lies in the process of relating the events
of his life to Bruno Münsterberg, his mental nurse: "Lieb-
gewonnen habe ich ihn, erzähle dem Gucker hinter der Tür,
sobald er mein Zimmer betritt, Begebenheiten aus meinem

Leben, damit er mich trotz des ihn hindernden Guckloches kennenlernt. Der Gute scheint meine Erzählungen zu schätzen, denn sobald ich ihm etwas vorgelogen habe, zeigt er mir, um sich erkenntlich zu geben, sein neustes Knotengebilde." (p. 9). Oskar thus emphasises his delight in falsehood from the outset. The desire to pretend, the child's inclination to lose itself in the inner world of imagination and to ignore the dividing line between the real and the fictional or merely the momentary wish to pull somebody's leg-- whether it be Münsterberg's or the reader's-- all this soon manifests itself in Oskar's life. Even on the day of his birth Oskar would have us believe that he plays at being a baby (p. 49). Acting as a child, playing a role, becomes a permanent feature of Oskar's behaviour. Throughout the novel, Oskar constantly refers to his need to maintain a façade of pretence and deceit between himself and grown-ups. A person who has elevated make-believe into an essential principle of his life cannot, as one might expect, be considered as a reliable narrator whose judgement can be trusted and whose statements are always in focus. Oskar is to be regarded rather as a narrative device or ironical viewpoint than as a person whose character can be understood in psychological terms and whose statements give us insight into his personality. Jochen Rohlfs explains the role of the

narrator in the following way: "Dabei kommt es Grass
weniger darauf an, den Erzähler selbst menschlich-über-
zeugend zu gestalten, als ihm vielmehr eine Perspektive
abzugewinnen, aus der das Zeitgeschehen realistischer als
gemeinhin in Geschichtsbüchern dargestellt werden kann."
(p. 52).[7]

In discussing irony it is frequently emphasised that
a sense of dissembling that is meant to be seen through
is a fundamental element of irony.[8] Since Oskar is telling his story from an assumed point of view, pretence can
be said to be one of Oskar's basic principles. He tries
to observe the world through the innocent or naive eyes
of the child, or from the point of view of the madman.
Grass, however, allows Oskar to be only partly successful in his attempts to disguise. The reader is permitted
to see through the narrator's camouflage. Hence a contrast emerges between what the narrator appears to be
saying and what the situation might well be. We are certainly made aware that Oskar's world of make-believe is
not to be taken at its surface value. We know, in other
words, that Oskar does not present us with a true picture
of reality because he intermingles fact and fiction. We
are not, however, made aware of those objective criteria
by which we could gain an insight into the nature of the
reality which Oskar is attempting to conceal. Only in

this negative sense is it possible to speak of a contrast
in the novel between appearance and reality, a contrast
which, according to D. C. Muecke, is a basic feature of
irony. Admittedly the framework of political and historical references constitutes a stabilising factor within
the novel, provides, along with the reader's knowledge
of the period of history concerned, a set of verifiable
external relationships and hence forms a link with the
reality of the time. As would be expected, the irony is
meant to be detected. As D. C. Muecke asserts, "the
half-concealment is part of the ironist's artistic purpose and the detection and appreciation of the camouflage
is a large part of the reader's pleasure." (pp. 52-53).
The other characteristics of irony which Muecke mentions
in his book can easily be found in the style of *Die Blechtrommel*: a comic element, an element of detachment, and
what he refers to as an aesthetic element (see p. 48).

In a sense it is true to say that the reader is presented with two levels of irony in *Die Blechtrommel*. He
knows that there is a supreme God-like ironist in the
background and by turning to the cover of the book he
learns that the ironist in question bears the name of
Günter Grass. The latter opts out of the reality he wishes to depict and leaves the reader without any instruction, direct or indirect, for understanding his creation.

The reader is left to judge the characters and situations
in the novel, unable to rely on the advice of its maker.
Meanwhile Grass hands over the task of narrating to Oskar, who as an ironist is himself cast, in the same mould
as his creator, who simulates innocence or madness and
sees the world darkly through this glass of dissembling.
Our only contact with reality in the novel-- apart from
the chronological framework of history-- is through the
troubled vision of Oskar, who makes it his purpose to de-
ceive us, fortunately inconsistently, and perhaps on occasions he even deceives himself. We are hence confronted
with the kind of situation which, according to Wayne C.
Booth, readers face in coming to terms with the novels of
Henry James.[9] The latter, he tells us, "fails to provide
any theory relevant to one large segment of his own work--
those stories narrated, whether in the first or third person, by a profoundly confused, basically self-deceived,
or even wrong-headed or vicious reflector." (p. 340). Grass
similarly does not supply any theories, instructions or
even hints for interpreting the statements of his narrator.
Like Henry James, Günter Grass shrouds his narrator in
ambiguity and ambivalence.

In his discussion of irony (p. 63), D. C. Muecke
claims that "verbal irony is employed principally (i) as
a rhetorical device-- the ironist asserts a 'falsehood'

knowing he can rely upon the listener to contradict it
mentally by an indignant or amused counter-assertion,
this counter-assertion with all its emphasis being the
ironist's real meaning, (ii) as solemn foolery..., (iii)
as a weapon of satire, or, more broadly, in the interests
of morality. As a satirist or moralist, the ironist may
... present situational ironies, particularly ironies of
self-betrayal or incongruity." All four types of irony
may be found throughout the course of *Die Blechtrommel*.
Satirical elements are present in all parts of the novel,
though perhaps more especially in the third book in which
Grass deals with the post-war period eg. in the chapters
entitled 'Madonna 49' and 'Im Zwiebelkeller'. Günter
Grass has been described as a satirist and Grass himself
refers to the satiric element in his novel.[10] Nevertheless, Wayne C. Booth's observation that extensive ambiguity in a novel will be paid for by a loss of satiric
force is, I think, relevant in discussing *Die Blechtrommel* as a work of satire. Examples of solemn foolery--
the pronouncements of the clown or of the impish child--
abound throughout the novel and are placed like traps in
the path of the critic who wishes to prod them in search
of the elusive truth. In referring to irony as a rhetorical device Muecke touches upon one of the fundamental
problems which arises in the analysis of *Die Blechtrommel*.

It is clear from what has already been said that it is
impossible for the reader to identify himself with the
narrator or his characters and that there is a gulf between Oskar's set of values-- or non-values-- and those
of the reader. In commenting upon the opening words of
the novel Georg Just makes the following observation:
" 'Identifikationsverweigerung' bzw. 'Wertesystemkonflikt'
bezeichnet die Struktur dieses Textes." (p. 33).[11] In
the same article he comes to the conclusion that the inadequacy of Oskar's actions provokes the reader into setting up his own criteria, examining the situation and
condemning what behaviour might have been appropriate:
"Die Inadäquatheit von Oskars Handeln gibt nicht Anweis-
ung zu allegorischer Ausdeutung-- Ergebnis einer solchen
könnten immer nur willkürliche Spekulationen sein-- sondern zur Reflexion der eigenen Einstellung. D.h. die
Handlungsanweisung, die davon ausgeht, richtet sich nicht
unmittelbar auf die damalige Situation: so und so hättest
du handeln sollen, sondern an die Reflexion des Lesers:
überleg dir, welches Handeln der damaligen Situation adä-
quat gewesen wäre, wenn (a) Oskars Handeln, (b) das Handeln der dargestellten Zeitgenossen-- wenn auch auf ver-
schiedenen Ebenen-- als inadäquat gelten muß." (p. 42).
Georg Just is certainly correct in stating that *Die Blechtrommel* cannot be satisfactorily interpreted in allegor-

ical terms, but this only confirms what Grass himself
has said. Both Muecke and Just are analysing a similar
situation in that both stress the importance of the reader's response; the reader is provoked into reacting
against the narrator's actions and statements. Georg
Just is rather too restrictive in stressing the idea that
the reader should reflect on the characters' actions. It
is frequently the case that we are stimulated into for-
mulating our own attitude as a counterweight to Oskar's
attitude and pondering upon the totality of Oskar's be-
haviour-- and of the German situation-- especially when
one bears in mind Grass's avowed intention: "ich will
nur die Strömungen der Zeit umfangen." (p. 198).[12] In
approaching the novel the reader is thrust back upon himself, is dependent on his own resources, must provide his
own criteria, for there are no guide lines within the
novel, he must formulate his own response and come to his
own conclusions. Irony, however, can take on various
forms, as we have already seen. Furthermore Oskar's dis-
sembling-- the pretence which is the basic ingredient of
Oskar's ironic pose-- may assume an equally wide range of
forms: the narrator indulges in exaggeration, prevarication, flights of fancy, bravado, self-pity, melodrama,
loss of perspective, unrealistic statements, fibs, indeed
downright lies and many other tricks. Oskar twists and

turns like an eel. The confidence trickster is never
still-- one pose is rapidly supplanted by another. His
lack of seriousness constantly diverts attention from
himself. In addition Oskar draws comparisons between the
events and characters of his stories and the events and
characters in literary and religious contexts. Parody is
yet another aspect of the histrionics which Oskar enjoys
so much. The narrator produces a rich kaleidoscopic effect in order to preserve his facelessness. In short, the
reader must be as agile as the impostor and no single,
stock response can cope with the ever-shifting fluidity
of Oskar's phantasmagoria. Given the fact that Grass
attempts to do battle with the totality of the human
scene, this can scarcely be done otherwise.

If Oskar creates a wild unfathomable world of fantasy, what prevents the reader from plunging into this
dark abyss of romance and disappearing without trace? At
least four elements serve as a counterweight to the ambivalence and ambiguity created by the unreliability of
Oskar as a narrator: firstly, the narrative zest of the
author; secondly, his attachment to the world of sensuous detail; thirdly, the imagery; and, fourthly, the
framework of historical and political events. Let us now
look at each of these items in turn.

Narrative Skill

What attracts us to the novel in the first instance
is the author's highly developed capacity for story-telling. This provides the momentum which keeps the craft of
the novel in flight. From the first chapter onwards we
are fascinated by the series of episodes which are connected directly or indirectly with the central figure of
the novel. The first chapter sets the tone: Oskar's
grandfather, Joseph Koljaiczek, is attempting to escape
from the clutches of the German police and takes refuge
from his pursuers under the voluminous Kaschubian skirts
of Anna Bronski, who is conveniently sitting by the side
of a fire in a potato field. Having entered the sanctu-
ary formed by Anna's four skirts, he puts them to good
use by founding a dynasty. Within hours the two of them
are united in marriage. The episode is not untypical:
the narrative concentrates upon the actions and the general behaviour of the characters concerned. There is no
sense in which the author concerns himself with the in-
ward world of man. Rather does the converse seem to be
true: feelings and thoughts are objectivized, i.e. they
are reflected in the objects which comprise the external
world. A stream of consciousness does not retard the
momentum of the narrative: rarely does the tension created by the story-telling slacken. Sometimes the novel

perspective of the narrative adds a special flavour to
the episodes. The absurd and the grotesque both heighten
the narrative élan. And it must be admitted that-- in
conventional terms-- a pinch of blasphemy or obscenity
adds spice to Grass's literary recipe. Oskar's amorous
adventures are especially intriguing and grip the reader's attention whilst at the same time being rich in comic effect. A number of these stand out in the reader's
mind: Oskar's and Maria's adolescent love for each other
erupts with volcanic fury under the influence of sherbet;
in order to escape Maria's insidious spell Oskar falls
victim to Frau Greff whose stench bludgeons our hero's
senses into submission-- we learn how he joins her in bed
fully clothed with his shoes on and appreciates the wash-
ing facilities which the husband supplies after the oper-
ations have been completed; another amorous interlude
is provided by Oskar's gymnastics on the coconut matting
which, placed between him and the lady of his choice,
constitutes an effective but rather itchy form of insu-
lation. Such episodes-- and probably the majority of the
novel-- can be enjoyed for their own sake without reference to previous events and without any need to occupy
oneself with the background political happenings and without any awareness of the significance-- of even presence--
of the imagery. One can be entertained by the anecdotes

without being unduly troubled by Oskar's unreliability as
a narrator, such is the gusto with which such stories are
told. One enters into Oskar's world of fantasy and is
delighted by the imaginative inventiveness which gives
shape to the series of incidents within the narrative.
In this way we frequently find that our disbelief is sus-
pended and our doubt made to look superfluous. Henri
Plard has summarised Günter Grass's skill as a story-
teller in the following terms: "Ich wüßte keinen von den
jüngeren deutschen Erzählern zu nennen, der so unmittelbar und primitiv packend wie Günter Grass zu berichten
wüßte. Gemeint ist hier die einfache Kunst, den Leser in
Atem zu halten wie bei einem Krimi von Klasse." (p. 48).[13]

In describing how he came to write *Die Blechtrommel*,
Grass refers to his obsession with detail (p. 18)[4] and
constantly throughout the novel we encounter examples of
his meticulous preoccupation with detail, as though he
wanted to gather into his novel the multi-faceted range
of all created things. One is not surprised to read
Grass's remark: "Sprache hatte mich als Durchfall er-
wischt." (p. 15).[4] His insistence on precision in the
description of Oskar's external world manifests itself
in a number of ways. The actions and events in each episode are recounted in a systematic manner, even if the
content stems from the realm of fantasy, whether this be

the history of Niobe, the drumming machine on which Greff
commits suicide, the unearthing of a corpse (in the chapter entitled 'Fortuna Nord') or Oskar's antics on the
coconut matting. On other occasions Grass's obsession
with detail is evident in the location of the action in
a quite specific environment and this may take the form
of listing facts or pseudo-facts. The description of
Danzig as an inferno following air raids and artillery
attack is a case in point: "Es brannten die Häkergasse,
Langgasse, Breitgasse, Große und Kleine Wollwebergasse,
es brannten die Tobiasgasse, Hundegasse, der Altstädtische
Graben, Vorstädtische Graben, the Wälle brannten und die
Lange Brücke. Das Krantor war aus Holz und brannte besonders schön. In der kleinen Hosennähergasse ließ sich
das Feuer für mehrere auffallend grelle Hosen Maß neh-
men. Die Marienkirche brannte von innen nach außen und
zeigte Festbeleuchtungen durch Spitzbogenfenster." (p.
468). In the final pages of the book the reader is presented with a series of reminiscences which take the
form of objects and events with which Oskar has been associated. The narrator conjures up the past by collecting and recollecting the things, which have been for him
nodes of experience. In both these examples-- the burning down of Danzig and Oskar's review of his life-- the
reader is aware of the author's delight in sensuous detail.

Such cataloguing serves the remembrance of things past
and it is as though the readers were exposed to the onslaught of life itself in all its visual immediacy. Sometimes a single word is sufficient to unleash a torrent
of associated words and correspondences, as is the case
when Oskar prods the word 'cross' into feverish activity
(pp. 160-61). The phrase "Der Falter trommelte' provokes Oskar on another occasion into engaging in linguistic acrobatics, whilst at the same time giving added substance and significance to what appears at first sight to
be quite a simple sentence (p. 48). The totality of the
external world in all its varied manifestations, or so it
would seem, assails our senses. Grass's universal embrace anchors us to terra firma and rescues us from the
dark abyss of romance into which Oskar's fantasy and un-
trustworthiness would plunge us. In this context the
reader may well recall Grass's observations about Döblin,
his literary mentor: "Der Gegenstand des Romans ist die
entfesselte Realität... Im Roman heißt es schichten,
häufen, wälzen, schieben; im Drama, dem jetzigen, auf
die Handlung hin verarmten, handlungsverbohrten: "vor-
an!" Vorwärts ist niemals die Parole des Romans." (p.
11). In *Die Blechtrommel* Grass certainly unleashes reality of the external world upon the reader who is then
subjected to wave upon wave of attack. This reality

constitutes, paradoxically, in all its complexity a stabilising factor within the novel.

Imagery

Imagery also contributes to the coherence of *Die
Blechtrommel* as a whole-- though much of it is not acces-
sible to the reader when he approaches the novel for the
first time. In examining the imagery in *Die Blechtrommel*-- and for that matter in other narrative works of
Grass-- it is appropriate to recall that Grass has said
that poetry is the art form which suits him most and that
he started his literary career as a lyricist (p. 17).[7]
Hence one may expect that the poetic usage will be of
significance in Grass's works. It is obvious, even from
a superficial reading of the novel, that certain words
occur frequently within the text, reinforcing already
existent associations and gathering fresh ones in the
process. They constitute nodes of experience and present "an intellectual and emotional complex in an in-
stant of time."[15]   The images are allowed to stand alone,
"teasing our understanding by nondiscursive relationship
with what surrounds them."[16]   In that Grass provides no
theoretical explanation of their meaning, they force the
reader to come to his own conclusions. As has been stated elsewhere, Grass presents us with a series of stories

which have a partial independence of their own and can be enjoyed in their own right. Nevertheless the concrete particulars and the arrangement of the stories carry meanings beyond immediate significance. As with Joyce's *Ulysses*, imagery and juxtaposition-- both devices which are more frequently encountered in poetry-- supplement the narrative. Imagery may even form the starting-point from which the episode develops. It is not coincidental that many of the titles of the chapters refer not to people or actions, but to objects, eg. 'Der weite Rock', 'Unterm Floß', 'Falter und Glühbirne', 'Die Tribune', 'Das Kartenhaus', 'Brausepulver', 'Die Ameisenstraße', 'Der Ringfinger' etc. In an interview with Burton Pike, Grass has stated that he is not interested in psychological characterization, but rather in presenting a character surrounded by the objects of his milieu.[17] "The characters," so he maintains, "don't explain themselves by means of the inner monolog or lectures about their tensions, but through quite simple relationships: what they do with food and furniture for instance." (p. 307). It is true that the objects with which Grass surrounds his characters and which take the role of Eliot's 'objective correlative' are allusive and not always totally explicable. Nevertheless, the strange paradox arises in *Die Blechtrommel*, that, though the narrator is

untrustworthy and engenders an atmosphere of doubt, the
objects, their associations and their correspondences
sometimes, though not necessarily, speak a clearer language and may unmask the ironic narrator. The accumula-
tion of associations knits the narrative together and as
Jochen Rohlfs has stated with regard to the chapter entitled 'Glaube Hoffnung Liebe' (p. 238), "Die Vergangenheit fließt in die Gegenwart der 'Ich weiß nicht'-Kette
ein, die Begriffe verlieren ihre klar umrissene Bedeutung,
an Stelle unmittelbarer sprachlicher Logik tritt Logik
des assozierenden Bewußtseins." (p. 57).[18] There are underlying trails of associations throughout the novel and
Grass is frequently at pains to make evident the links
between the objects which perform a similar evocative
function.

As is the case with *Katz und Maus* and *Hundejahre*
the title of the book-- and the dust-cover-- force the
central image or symbol into the forefront of the reader's consciousness from the outset. Grass observes the
same convention with this title as he does with the titles of the individual chapters: the novel is called 'Die
Blechtrommel' and not 'Der Blechtrommler', even though
the poem which Grass wrote as a kind of experiment in
narrative perspective was called 'Der Säulenheilige' and
even though the dust-cover shows a drum along with the

drummer. A number of associations which are attached to
the drum and the drummer are apparent on the cover of the
book. We see the grotesque figure of a boy with drumsticks raised, presumably about to strike a drum. His
body is strangely extended to form the background for the
drum. The hat he wears is the kind a child might wear at
a party and perhaps during carnival. The drummer is
drawn in black and white apart from his eyes which are
bright blue. The drum is coloured red and white. When
we come to read the novel, we find that the suggestiveness of the various colours is extended and reinforced:
black is a sign of mourning and of evil, it has a menac-
ing quality; blue recalls the fact that the typical German during the Nazi period was supposed to be blue-eyed
and blond-haired, it is the favorite colour of the ro-
mantics and is suggestive of physical-- and spiritual--
intoxication; red and white are the national colours of
Poland, whilst red in isolation is reminiscent of blood,
transgression, rebelliousness, and white is traditionally
the colour of innocence. There is a symbolism of colour
within the novel-- in the same way that Catholicism attaches specific meanings to various colours-- though it
would be wrong to think that each colour when it occurs
in the text has an inevitable symbolical significance.
The world Grass depicts in his novel is not transparent

with meaning: the objects of sensory perception have their own colours and cannot be forced into a symbolical or allegorical pattern. The drum has at least two as- sociations, even before we start reading the book: it is emblematic of war, for it can produce the rhythm which, as Oskar says, all men had to obey in 1914 (p. 39), and yet it also conjures up the atmosphere of lamentation and of mourning. At the funeral of his mother, for instance, Oskar wants to express his grief by drumming on her cof- fin. And in Schlöndorff's film Oskar intones a doleful rhythm on his drum which takes on almost the quality of a funeral march. The student of history will recall that Hitler was proud to be referred to as a drummer and re- garded this activity as his highest aspiration,[19] though no link of this kind is established between Hitler and Oskar in the novel. In *Die Blechtrommel* (and presumably the word 'Blech' benefits from the fact that it has two meanings, i.e. 'tin' and 'rubbish or nonsense') Oskar Matzerath makes use of the drum as a means by which he can preserve his status as a three-year old. This cen- tral function of the drum is one which Oskar emphasises on a number of occasions-- on this point the reader is left in no doubt as to how the drum should be regarded. When, for example, Matzerath wants to question his son about the robberies that have been taking place in the jeweller's shop, Oskar refuses to give any information "und versteckte mich mit immer größerem Geschick hinter meiner Blechtrommel und der permanenten Größe des zurück- gebliebenen Dreijährigen." (p. 149). In this way Oskar can erect a barrier between himself and the adults who surround him, prevent their intrusion into his own world of childish fantasy and in this way he can evade any re- sponsibility. The drum allows Oskar to indulge in pre- tence which is the precondition for his viewing the out- side world in ironic and grotesque terms. By means of the drum he can beat the retreat from reality and avoid having to follow in his father's footsteps as a shop- keeper: he can turn to art rather than to business and thus parodies the dilemma with which many of Thomas Mann's characters are confronted. He is a grotesque dis- tortion of Adrian Leverkühn, the musician who enters into a pact with the devil and whose life is compared oblique- ly with Germany's headlong plunge into destruction. The drum epitomises Oskar's fundamental attitude of withdraw- al from the world of reality and is employed at the same time, as we have indicated earlier in this chapter, as a narrative device by means of which a period of history may be surveyed.

Oskar would have us believe that the drum is his mode of expression, and that it is as it were part of his

flesh and blood as he himself suggests (see p. 253)--
the picture on the front of the book almost creates
the impression that the drum is part of Oskar's body.
The drum is hence Oskar's constant companion and, apart
from a brief respite during the post-war period, it
witnesses all the major events of his life, for the two
of them are virtually inseparable. He even describes it
on one occasion as the witness of his shame (p. 305).
Accordingly the drum is indicative of an attitude of mind,
serves, according to Oskar, as a narrative device but
draws the strands of the narrative together: in this
sense it fulfills a recapitulatory function. Oskar introduces us to the drum in the second chapter of the novel; his mother promises hin a drum for his third birthday (p. 47); he develops his glass-shattering voice as
a means of protecting his drum (in 'Glas, Glas, Gläß-
chen'); the drum accompanies him on his one and only day
in school; it helps him to break up a party-rally (in
'Die Tribüne'); he hangs it round the neck of Jesus hoping that the saviour will produce a miracle of drumming
(in 'Kein Wunder'); and he loses his supplier of drums
when Sigismund Markus commits suicide during the course
of the 'Kristallnacht'. All these are events in the
first book of the novel. The other two books of the novel are equally well strewn with references to the drum

and its associations. This symbol acquires a multi-faceted, allusive quality which constantly provokes the
reader into discovering new and stimulating relationships
between the various objects, characters and episodes in
novel. The reader comes to realise, as has been pointed
out by Manfred Jurgensen, that the metaphorical language
of Grass's literary works possesses "einen argumentativen
Grundzug." (p. 6).[20] At the same time a symbol such as
the drum-- or for that matter the cat and mouse in Grass's
'Novelle' or the dog in *Hundejahre*-- achieve a cohesive
effect within the novel and in conjunction with Grass's
narrative skill act as a counterweight to the ambivalence and ambiguity which are characteristic of Oskar's
narrative perspective. Oskar speaks the language of
doubt; the metaphorical language, despite Oskar and as
it were unbeknown to Oskar, sometimes reveals more than
the narrator himself.

The imagery of 'Kopf' and 'Schwanz' is another example of metaphorical language which assumes an argumen-
tative quality. This imagery and its related words occur
sufficiently frequently for the reader to be tempted to
think of them in terms of symbolism. René Wellek and
Austin Warren remind us that "an 'image' may be invoked
as a metaphor, but if it persistently recurs, both as
presentation and representation, it becomes a symbol, may

even become part of a symbolic (or mythic) system." (p.
189).[21] The recurrent images in *Die Blechtrommel* operate,
however, more in the no man's land which exists between
imagery and symbolism in that, though they form nodes of
hints and allusions, they may only seldom be considered
fully-fledged symbols, in other words, they rarely reach
the stage of actually standing for or representing something else quite specific. The words 'Kopf' and 'Schwanz'
certainly come close to assuming the function of symbols
in that, through the extension of already existent associations, the word 'Kopf' is developed as an allusive
pointer to the values of reason and moderation which have
been undermined by lustful passion and physical and political intoxication, as represented by the word 'Schwanz'
with its sexual suggestiveness. This somewhat syphilitic
imagery with its Nietzschean overtones occurs with particular force in the chapter entitled 'Karfreitagskost'.
In this chapter Oskar describes how the sexual triangle
of Agnes, Matzerath and Jan Bronski observe eels-- by implication the equivalent of 'Schwanz'-- devouring a
horse's head. Agnes is nauseated by what she sees, for
she regards it instinctively as the objectivisation of
the passionate love-affair in which she has been engaged
with Jan Bronski. So sickened is she by the sight of the
eels that she seeks to escape from her adulterous

relationship by poisoning herself with fish-- yet another
sexual image. In the same chapter Oskar retreats into
his parents' wardrobe and in a dream he visualises the
sanctification of an eel, as part of what appears to be
a grotesque communion service. He imagines seagulls set-
tling on the sacrifice, an eel, and throwing it to Sister
Inge, a nurse, "die fing ihn auch, feierte ihn und wurde
zur Möwe, nahm Gestalt an, nicht Taube, wenn schon heil-
iger Geist, dann in jener Gestalt, die da Möwe heißt,
sich als Wolke aufs Fleisch senkt und Pfingsten feiert."
(p. 183). The picture of the eels eating the horse's
head can be viewed as the re-enactment of Agnes' personal
predicament. As David Roberts observes, it can be regarded as an example of "the grotesque vision of life as
the eternal cycle of the flesh that feeds and is fed
upon." (p. 52).[22] At the same time the imagery of head
and tail adumbrates the triumph of passion and lust over
reason and moderation which has implications on the personal and on the political level. The same confrontation
between reason and unreason can be found in the juxtaposition of Goethe and Rasputin on whom, so Oskar would
have us believe, his education is based. However, it is
plain, in the chapter concerned-- 'Rasputin und das ABC'--
where Goethe does not even figure in the title that lust,
the 'Schwanz'-like principle of Rasputin, emerges

victorious over Goethe. This is evident in equal measure
elsewhere in the book, for example in the effervescent
explosion of feeling in which Maria and Oskar indulge:
"Da brach der Waldmeister wie ein Vulkan aus. Da kochte,
ich weiß nicht, wessen Volkes grünliche Wut." (p. 324).
Oskar develops a 'third drumstick' and he asks himself
the question: "Hatte der Herr da unten seinen eigenen
Kopf, eigenen Willen?" (p. 332).

In the post-war period reason is still vanquished by
unreason and this is made evident by the continued sexual
dislocation of Oskar and the characters who form his environment and by the recurrent imagery. By now it will
be clear that one image is made to link up with another
so much so that the one almost acts as the substitute for
the other, though obviously they are conditioned by the
context in which they occur. Freudian similarities
emerge between tails, eels, fish, drumsticks, and even
patent-leather belts. The occurrence of one motif suggests all the occurrences of all the other motifs, as W.
L. Scharfman has indicated.[23] A pattern of episodes also
re-echoes throughout the novel. Now established, in West
Germany, for example, Oskar finds another cupboard and
retreats into it, the cupboard in question belonging to
Nurse Dorothea ('Im Kleiderschrank'). Oskar is reminded
of the eels and the horse's head, and a patent-leather

belt stimulates him into self-abuse (p. 597). After the war Oskar makes a second visit to the fortifications on the Atlantic coast of France and the title of the chapter itself ('Am Atlantikwall oder es können die Bunker ihren Beton nicht loswerden') suggests that the attitudes and situations of the past are still to be encountered. Lankes, the former soldier, who has now turned commercial artist, and Oskar 'celebrate' a meal of fish, whilst seated behind the bunker. Once again a sexual image-- like that of eels in 'Karfreitagskost'-- is employed. Inevitably Oskar is reminded of a previous meal which he and members of the circus company enjoyed shortly before the Allied invasion. The two companions, Oskar and Lankes, enter into a dispute about who should have the head or tail of the fish. The brutality in which Lankes indulged during the war has its counterpart in other acts of senseless cruelty which he now commits: he assaults his former lieutenant and rapes a nun. One comment which Oskar makes on Lankes' character and behaviour is particularly revealing: "Er kannte nur entweder oder, Kopf oder Schwanz, ertrunken oder gefallen. Mir nahm er die Zigaretten ab, den Oberleutnant warf er von der Düne, von meinem Fisch aß er, und einem Kind, das eigentlich dem Himmel geweiht war, zeigte er das Innere unseres Bunkers, malte, während sie noch in die offene See hinausschwamm,

mit großem, knolligem Fuß Bilder in die Luft..." (p. 664).
Lankes then goes on to make a profit out of his amorality
by painting a series of pictures of nuns. Oskar condemns
the actions of Lankes, though he shows a childish lack of
differentiation by placing scrounging cigarettes and rape
in the same category of criminality. What appear initially to be alternatives, emerge on closer analysis to
be equally abhorrent extremes. Through the mouth of Oskar Grass condemns such extremism and in this way Lankes
joins the long line of characters in Grass's works,
whether this be Augst in *Aus dem Tagebuch einer Schnecke*
(see p. 192) or the 'Endzielmänner' described in *Der Butt*
(p. 44). Grass has referred to this kind of character in
his essay entitled significantly 'Begegnungen mit Kohlhaas' in his book *Der Bürger und seine Stimme*. The sexual activities of Lankes are reminiscent of the perverted
personal relationships of the various characters in the
novel whether this be between Oskar and Maria or Frau
Greff or Schwester Dorothea, or between Alexander Greff
and his boy scouts or between Maria and Matzerath. What
applies to Jan Bronski and Agnes Matzerath, is also ap-
plicable to many of the characters in the novel: "Die
aßen alles selbst auf. Die hatten den großen Appetit, der
nie aufhört, der sich selbst in den Schwanz beißt." (p.
114).

It is not coincidental that in the final chapters of
the novel Oskar finds a ring-finger, places it in a pre-
serving jar and proceeds to worship it, as though it were
a holy shrine. Grass makes plain the links between the
various phallic symbols at a previous stage in the novel,
though he never supplies an unambiguous interpretation
of the imagery he employs: "Gleichfalls versprachen mir
die Zeichen auf Herberts Rücken zu jenem frühen Zeit-
punkt schon den Ringfinger, und bevor mir Herberts Narben Versprechungen machten, waren es die Trommelstöcke,
die mir vom dritten Geburtstag an die Narben, Fort-
pflanzungsorgane und endlich den Ringfinger versprachen.
Doch muß ich weiter zurückgreifen: schon als Embryo,
als Oskar noch gar nicht Oskar hieß, verhieß mir das
Spiel mit meiner Nabelschnur nacheinander die Trommelstöcke, Herberts Narben, die gelegentlich aufbrechenden
Krater jüngerer und älterer Frauen, schließlich den Ring-
finger und immer wieder, vom Gießkännchen des Jesusknaben
an, mein eigenes Geschlecht, das ich unentwegt, wie das
launenhafte Denkmal meiner Ohnmacht und begrenzten Möglichkeiten, bei mir trage." (p. 206). Such images ful-
fulfil a prefigurative, configurative and recapitulatory
function within the novel and help to form a thematic
structure. They convey the subtlest of meaning, not
through explanatory discourses, but through association

with various episodes, interconnection, juxtaposition and amplification. 'Kopf' and 'Schwanz' and the images which cluster round them are examples of what Wellek and Warren choose to call 'figuration', the 'oblique' discourse which "Partially compares worlds, precising its themes by giving them translations into other idioms." (p. 186).[15] They give shape to the amorality and immorality or the age through which Oskar lives. The perverted sexuality is emblematic of the fractured relationship between individuals and suggests that unreason is being celebrated as the dominant force in the age through which Oskar has been and is living. Oskar's fantasies are revelatory of the unconscious mind of the narrator, and the characters he describes, as well as reflecting the collective unconscious of the people to which he belongs. The imagery of head and tail conjures up the idea that the values of Western civilisation and those of Christianity have been corrupted and perverted: Goethe has been undermined by Rasputin.

Another symbol which occurs in the novel is that of the unicorn, though it was prepared and prepacked as a symbol long before Grass chose to make use of it. Since the unicorn is a fabulous animal with a horse's body and a single horn, the associations connected with it also play a part in the network of correspondences surrounding

the imagery of head and tail (it is a horse's head which
is eaten away by the eels, it must be remembered). The
Duden-Lexikon provides the following rather interesting
definition of the unicorn: "Das Motiv der Einhornjagd
(das Einhorn ist nur zu fangen, wenn es in den Schoß
einer Jungfrau flüchtet) versinnbildlicht die Menschwer-
dung und jungfräuliche Geburt Christi. Als Sinnbild der
Keuschheit ist das Einhorn auch Attribut für Maria." As
is evident from a close examination of the text, the women with whom Oskar comes into contact are all allusively
linked with the Virgin Mary, either by direct reference
or by their function in Oskar's life. They are all "ladies on carpets who educate unicorns." (p. 458). In perverted fashion, Oskar fulfils all the conditions demanded
of a unicorn. He takes flight into the womb of a succession of virgins and is trapped. Oskar embodies his
needs in the image of a woman. She flatters his irresponsibility and gratifies his desire for retreat, support and centre. She serves as a symbol of his evasion
of responsibility and of his attempt to rid himself of
feelings of guilt. In this sense Oskar may well be mirroring once again a basic attitude of his own time.

It is certainly true to say that Oskar turns to women as a haven of refuge. He describes himself as wishing to escape from reality into a realm of prenatal

purity and innocence. Born in the sign of Virgo he takes flight like the unicorn into the womb of a woman and is accordingly trapped. This is his experience with all female characters in the novel. The grandmother first offers the tempting apple of escape and of cleanliness. Even Bronski flees from the harshness of reality in his liaison with Oskar's mother. Maria engulfs Oskar in the bourgeois world of National Socialism and in the arms of Lina Greff he is dragged down still further into the mire in an attempt to escape from Maria's influence. Roswitha Raguna offers her immortal body and the romantic sentimentality of the South as a possible escape route. The muse tempts Oskar with art as another variant on the theme of flight from reality. The nurse embodies for Oskar the mirage of purity. Oskar mirrors in his relations with women the tendency to indulge in emotional and by implication political escapism and in so doing to evade responsibility for one's own actions.

Another image which occurs in various forms throughout the novel is that of the roundabout. In a dream Oskar imagines himself seated as a child upon a roundabout which is kept in dizzy, perpetual motion by the figures of Goethe and Rasputin. Such a dream reveals the latent fears of Oskar, the narrator who highlights the intellectual and spiritual climate of his era. At the same

time we are made aware of the indulgent self-pity of Oskar, who imagines the suffering of the children outweighs
and atones for the suffering of the Jews. Nevertheless,
Goethe and Rasputin conjure up the idea of a malevolent
god who has made possible the saturnalian inversion of
all Christian principles. It is being suggested that Oskar as the mirror of his times is subject to the perverted values of Goethe and Rasputin. This gathers a-
round it a complex of associations by being linked non-
discursively with other images and situations. Oskar is
placed upon a revolving platform by the Director of the
Art Academy as the former tries to earn his living as a
model in the immediate post-war years, recalling the
scene when he was celebrated as a Messiah during the
course of a black mass, and emphasising that the roundabout of Goethe and Rasputin has not stopped turning.
The idea of circularity echoes allusively in the course
of Oskar's and Lanke's second visit to the fortifications
on the French coast. The imagery suggesting circularity
forms a mass of correspondences and insinuations, which
are rarely absent for long in the novel. The round shape
of the drum is, for example, frequently emphasised. The
idea of circularity and of futility is especially in evidence in the chapter entitled 'Fortuna Nord' which describes Oskar's reversion to the attitudes of the past in

the altered circumstances of the present and crystallizes
out in the image of 'Umbettung'. The ring-finger also
conjures up the idea of allegiance to the degenerate and
ossified values of the pre-1945 era. It suggests that
the carnival of the past still has an attractive appeal.
One could also point to the fact that the structure of
the novel is circular-- the novel starts in a mental
asylum and finishes in a mental asylum. As in the historical sphere the eternal cycle of recurrence seems inevitable. As we have mentioned earlier in this chapter,
war sweeps across Europe, and especially Danzig, with
horrifying regularity, necessitating in Oskar's native
town a succession of 'Baumeister and Abbruchunternehmer' (p.
475). As Oskar observes in his description of the Polish
landscape, it seems created for the activities of war,
"für die Schlacht, die schon dagewesen, die immer wieder
kommt..." (p. 27). History presents itself, in Oskar's
eyes, as an unbreakable chain of repetitiveness. The
same view of history underlies *Der Butt*, the novel which
was published some eighteen years after *Die Blechtrommel*.
Grass expresses the same idea, in the later novel, in
terms of a fairy-tale, the pattern of which virtually
determines the course of history: "Die Märchen hören
nur zeitweilig auf, oder beginnen nach Schluß aufs Neue.
Das ist die Wahrheit, jedesmal anders erzählt." (p. 692).

The fantasies of Oskar and the fairy-tales in *Der Butt*
all have the quality of a nightmare, of a merry-go-round
from which no escape seems possible. In reviewing the
imagery of head and tail one is quickly aware of the fact
that the imagery of circularity is one which gives shape
to events on the personal plane as well as to events on
the political plane. In fact the one may be regarded as
an oblique reflection of the other. In this context one
is reminded of Manfred Jurgensen's contention: "Das
Grass'sche Sprachbild ist eine Vergegenständlichung der
historischen Erfahrung." (p. 18).[20] Furthermore one is
keenly aware of the fact that much of Grass's thinking
is pictorial, that the image is the starting point for
the novel-- the sight of the boy playing the drum trig-
gered off *Die Blechtrommel*-- and that the imagery of the
novel contributes to its coherence and forms a thematic
framework. And in this sense the imagery militates
against and compensates for the ambiguity and ambivalence
which are an inherent part of the narrative perspective.

The Chronological Framework

The other framework which holds the novel together
is quite obviously the chronological framework. We have
already noted the time scale in accordance with which
Oskar writes his autobiography. Sometimes reference to

historical facts serves merely to fix events at a particular point in time: Oskar's grandfather, for example,
meets his watery death "im Jahre dreizehn, also kurz bevor es los ging." (p. 37); and Mama and Matzerath get
married "im Jahre dreiundzwanzig, da man für den Gegen-
wert einer Streichholzschachtel ein Schlafzimmer tape-
zieren, also mit Nullen mustern konnte..." (p. 44).
There is an off-hand manner even about these two brief
references to the historical background. Frequently historical or political details are introduced into the text
in a much more deprecatory and ironical manner. For example, Jan Bronski is rejected for the army, "was in
Zeiten, da man alles nur einigermaßen gerade Gewachsene
nach Verdun schickte, um es auf Frankreichs Boden in die
ewige Waagrechte zu bringen, allerlei über die Konsti-
tution des Jan Bronski besagte." (p. 41). Matzerath's
acquisition of party membership is couched in equally
ironical terms: Matzerath "trat im Jahre vierunddreißig,
also verhältnismäßig früh die Kräfte der Ordnung erken-
nend, in die Partei ein und brachte es dennoch nur bis
zum Zellenleiter." (p. 131). The irony may be accompanied, as can be seen from these instances, by a satirical element. The blackmarket in postwar Germany, which
is the preparation for the economic miracle is epitomised
in the figure of Kurt Matzerath who shows great skill in

exploiting a source of goods which are in short supply:
"Er hatte eine Quelle, verriet die Quelle aber nie, sagte
jedoch immer wieder, selbst vorm Schlafengehen an Stelle
eines Nachtgebetes: 'Ich habe eine Quelle!'" (p. 521).
Here irony and satire are reinforced by a mildly fantastic element.

Political events are mentioned only cursorily and
this is the case for the main part in the examples we
have quoted so far. Such a technique would seem to accord with the mode of presentation which Grass considers
to be typical of Alfred Döblin: "So setzt Döblin die
Akzente: Sieg, Niederlage, Staatsaktionen, was immer
sich datenfixiert als Dreißigjähriger Krieg niederge-
schlagen hat ist ihm einen Nebensatz, oft nur die be-
wußte Aussparung wert." (p. 13).[14] Thus we have the
strange paradox that in *Die Blechtrommel* which Enzensberger categorizes as "a historical novel", political
happenings are pushed to the periphery of the narrative.
In this Grass follows the example of Döblin, his mentor,
who regards history as an absurd process (p. 8). The
method Grass uses in *Die Blechtrommel* is the procedure
which Döblin employs in *Wallenstein*: "Die verstrickten
Zeremonien listiger Vorbereitung in Wien, oder bei Hof
des Maximilian von Bayern gesponnen, wälzen sich, ver-
zerrt und wie vor Hohlspiegel gestellt, mystisch

gesteigert über Seiten, während das Ergebnis höfischer
Anstrengungen, sei es die Absetzung Wallensteins, sei es
die Weigerung des sächsischen Kurfürsten, Gustav Adolf
und sein Heer durch kursächsisches Land passieren zu
lassen, lediglich mitgeteilt wird, betont achtlos, weil
es nun mal dazu gehört; aber Geschichte, und das heißt
die Vielzahl widersinniger und gleichzeitiger Abläufe,
Geschichte, wie Döblin sie bloßstellen will, ist das
nicht." (p. 13). In *Die Blechtrommel* the defeat of the
German armies in North Africa (p. 379) or at Stalingrad
(p. 379) are treated in the same perfunctory fashion as
the events of the Thirty Years' War in Döblin's *Wallenstein*. The court intrigues and the armies' confused
search for winter quarters in Döblin's novel are replaced
in Grass's novel by the self-centered activities of the
petty bourgeois. Each separate sphere recaptures the
atmosphere of history as a confused mass of absurd and
simultaneous trends. In *Die Blechtrommel* the gulf between the grandiose political events and the happenings
being described is greater than in *Wallenstein*, in that
the social circles which Grass describes are the at least
ostensibly non-political sphere of the lower middle
class. Grass mentions the fact that in Grimmelshausen's
Simplizissimus Wallenstein does not appear; a similar
situation exists in *Die Blechtrommel*, for scant attention

is paid, for example, to Hitler in Grass's narrative--
merely the confrontation between a picture of Beethoven
and one of Hitler takes place on the wall of the Matzerath
sitting room (see p. 132). As in Döblins novel, the
events in *Die Blechtrommel* are presented in a distorted
fashion as though being viewed through a concave mirror.
Grass reinforces his analysis of Döblin's attitude to
history by comparing Döblin's with Schiller's presentation of the Thirty Years' War: "Schiller war bemüht,
uns den Dreißigjährigen Krieg überschaubar gegliedert
darzustellen. Da ergibt sich eines aus dem anderen.
Seine ordnende Hand knüpft Bezüge, will Sinn geben. Das
alles zerschlägt Döblin mehrmals und bewußt zu Scherben,
damit Wirklichkeit entsteht." (p. 14). The ordering
hand which imposes a pattern upon the current of political happenings is absent in both Döblin's and Grass's
novels, for both authors regard history as an absurd
process which is not subject to an all-embracing purpose.
In *Die Blechtrommel* the events during the Nazi regime
and in the post-war era are not interconnected in such a
way that the reader is easily able to survey this period
of history as though from the historian's point of view.
One event-- either in the political or in the personal
sphere-- does not proceed from another. The thread of
causality has been severed. Grass is more concerned to

capture the atmosphere of an era. In doing so he would claim that this is a realistic approach. Grass proceeds in a manner which is similar to Grimmelshausen and Döblin: he leaves 'das große Schlachtgeschehen' aside, and chooses a viewpoint which is akin to "die beschränkte Perspektive des tumben wie schlauen Überlebenden" (p. 14).

The number of chapters in *Die Blechtrommel* which have as their content a major political event is very small: two in particular spring to mind, the 'Kristallnacht' in which Jews were imprisoned or murdered and their businesses and synagogues set on fire, and the defence of the Polish Post Office. Only three other chapters could be represented as dealing primarily with political happenings-- the party rally as related in 'Die Tribüne', the experiences of the Jew in 'Desinfektionsmittel', and the expulsion of the Germans from Danzig in 'Wachstum im Güterwagen'. All these chapters are ahistorical in that the perspective is that of the ingenuous child who can only see what affects him directly. Furthermore satirical and fantastic elements rule out the possibility of a factual account or of demonstrating causal relationships. The chapter entitled 'Glaube Hoffnung Liebe', for example, takes the form of a nightmarish fairy-tale which reaches its climax in the

sentences: "Ein ganzes leichtgläubiges Volk glaubte an
den Weihnachtsmann. Aber der Weihnachtsmann war in Wirklichkeit der Gasmann." (pp. 236-37). The defence of the
Polish Post Office culminates in Jan Bronski building a
delicately balanced house of cards, an image which suggests that Jan is totally divorced from reality, scarcely able to comprehend what is going on around him. The
other initially puzzling fact about *Die Blechtrommel*,
the so-called 'historical novel', is, of course, the
fact that Grass does not deal with those circles in which
political decisions are made, but situates his action
exclusively in the social environment of the lower middle
class. Geno Hartlaub in an interview with Grass quotes
his interviewee as saying that in *Die Blechtrommel* he
has tried to show "wie latent politisch die unpolitischen
kleinbürgerlichen Schichten als Träger einer Weltan-
schauung wie die des NS-Regimes gewesen sind. Besonders
in Deutschland haben die Arbeiter den Hang zum Kleinbürgertum mit seinen Verwaschenheiten, seiner Hybris und
seinen allgemeinen bekannten Eigenschaften, die im pri-
vaten Bereich liebenswert sein können, aber gefährlich
oder grotesk werden, wenn dies Kleinbürgertum die politische Führung ergreift." (p. 212).[24] Günter Grass has
thus made it clear that he consciously restricted the
choice of his material to the world of the petty bour-

geoisie and that this personal sphere is intended to
reflect the national sphere, though it would be wrong, I
think, to equate the personal directly with the national
sphere. The eccentric narrative perspective makes such
a direct equation difficult and leads to an artificial
interpretation. The result is that the reader forces
the novel into an allegorical straitjacket and Grass had
denied that his novel can be understood in terms of an
allegory. As in the case of Döblin, events are reflected
in a distorted fashion, as though 'through a concave mirror'.

Nevertheless events on the personal plane are linked
with events on the political or military plane and thereby the activities in the sphere of politics or war are
belittled and made to look ridiculous. An obvious example can be found in Oskar's affair with Lina Greff:
"Vjazma und Brjansk; dann setzte die Schlammperiode ein.
Auch Oskar begann, Mitte Oktober einundvierzig kräftig
im Schlamm zu wühlen. Man mag mir nachsehen, daß ich
den Schlammerfolgen der Heeresgruppe Mitte meine Erfolge
im unwegsamen und gleichfalls recht schlammigen Gelände
der Frau Lina Greff gegenüberstelle. Ähnlich wie sich
dort, kurz vor Moskau, Panzer und LKW's festfuhren, fuhr
ich mich fest..." (p. 364). Maria's and Oskar's liaison
unfolds, whilst Fritz Truczinski makes a tour of the

Western capitals in 1940 (p. 321). Sherbet becomes the
'objective correlative' for the explosion of national
feeling which led to the German invasion of the countries
of Western Europe in 1940: Maria and Oskar delight in
the effervescence of sherbet in Maria's cupped hand. In
this context the word 'Volk', which for the Nazis had
such an evocative appeal, is introduced nonchalantly
into the narrative, as though it had scarcely any contribution to make to the general meaning of the passage,
and Oskar even includes a negative to accentuate the off-
hand manner: "Da kochte, ich weiß nicht, wessen Volkes
grünliche Wut." (p. 324). Their amorous experiments enter a second phase, in which Oskar pours the sherbet into
Maria's navel and adds his saliva so that an eruption of
volcanic proportions can take place: "und als es in dem
Krater zu kochen anfing, verlor Maria alle für einen
Protest nötigen Argumente: denn der kochend brausende
Bauchnabel hatte der hohlen Hand viel voraus." (p. 331).
Here as in other parts of the novel the grotesque relationships between man and woman are sometimes used to emphasise the extent to which real love is absent from
their lives-- Maria's and Matzerath's love-making would
be an example of this-- but they are also employed as a
means of reducing political and military affairs to the
level of the ridiculous.

The theme of explosiveness seems in the third book
of the novel to satirise the German economic miracle.
The passionate feeling which characterizes Oskar's and
Maria's amorous adventures during the war has its counterpart in the post-war period in the insistent demand
for happiness. Oskar describes his overpowering desire
for happiness as he sits eating his breakfast: "und
verspürte, auf etwas Knorpel im Speck beißend, jäh und
bis in die Ohrenränder ein Bedürfnis nach Glück, gegen
alles bessere Wissen wollte ich Glück, alle Skepsis wog
nicht das Verlangen nach Glück auf, hemmungslos glücklich wollte ich werden..." (p. 530), and later: "Wie
ein Vulkan brach das Glück aus..." (p. 532). Accordingly
Oskar sets out to find happiness. He is employed as a
stone-mason who inscribes tombstones. Like Germany during the war, he deals in death. The personal quest for
happiness finds its image on the economic and national
plane in the power-station which is incessantly engaged
in explosive activity: "Das neue, zischende explodieren
wollende Kraftwerk Fortuna Nord." (p. 547). The power-
station erupts with the same venomous force ('Kraft') as
do Korneff's boils, those 'Verhärtungen' (see p. 536)
which eject their poison at periodic intervals, in this
instance against the background of snippets from the
Lord's Prayer. The power-station rises up into the air

like a phallus and thus one is reminded of the other phallic emblems to which Oskar draws our attention, for example, the ring-finger which he discovers whilst transferring a corpse from one graveyard to another. The nationalism of the pre-1945 period has been succeeded by the materialism of the post-war era. The political and historical framework which is obliquely linked with events on the personal level, the imagery and the associations which are both backward- and forward-looking, obscenity-- and to a lesser extent blasphemy, all combine to serve the overriding purpose of satirical reduction.

Many of the happenings on the personal level can be related to the historical and political framework. The way Matzerath meets his death, for example, comes to symbolize the collapse of Nazi Germany: the shopkeeper and cook from the lower middle class, the attitudes of which assisted Hitler to power, chokes in an attempt to swallow his Nazi party badge and is riddled through with bullets from a Russian machine-gun. Agnes Matzerath's death takes place against the deteriorating relations between Germany and Poland, and signifies more importantly, as we have suggested already, the triumph of unreason over reason. Greff's suicide on the gigantic elaborately constructed drumming machine occurs in October 1942, shortly after the German occupation of Stalingrad (see

p. 370). The nihilistic activities of the dusters ('Die

Stäuber') are being undertaken whilst Paris is being

evacuated and when the Germans have retreated to the

Vistula (Oskar expresses the historical fact in a more

ironical form: "Nach langem Lauf kam die Heeresgruppe

Mitte an der Weichsel zum Stehen." (p. 443)). They in-

dulge in destructiveness for its own sake, are referred

to as 'Halbwüchsige' and swear allegiance on the drum to

a saviour who possesses a miraculous weapon-- a glass-

cutting voice-- in the same way that at the time Hitler

was launching his miraculous weapons-- his V-1s and V-2s

(see p. 447)-- against Britain. They seem to epitomize

the total breakdown of all civilised values and they can

in any case be related to the gangs of youths such as

the 'Edelweißpiraten' who did in fact exist at that time

(see p. 448). Given these facts, it seems doubtful

whether they should be compared with the members of the

July conspiracy against Hitler, as it is suggested by

Georg Just (p. 180).[25] In all such instances the events

of the time are deprived of their grandeur, trivialised

and made to look sordid. Oskar is not a satirist: Grass

employs him as the ironic device for exposing events and

attitudes to ridicule, the principle method being that

of interconnecting elements which are incongruous and

thus producing a comic combined with an alienating effect. Even in the episode entitled 'Die Tribüne' Oskar
does not emerge as a satirist, he is not presented as
an opponent of National Socialism. He is largely in-
different to any form of political belief. Nevertheless
he breaks up the party rally, wittingly or unwittingly,
and is the medium through which this political gathering is made to look ludicrous, in that the participants
all finish up by dancing the Charleston and disappearing, suitably paired, into the nearby woodland (see p.
139). However, there is one occasion when Oskar does
set himself up as a satirist in his own right and that
is in the chapter entitled 'Glaube Hoffnung Liebe'.

The more usual situation is that Grass the satirist
dons the mask of Oskar, the narrator, in order to unmask the others. One has to bear in mind that the dividing line between irony and satire is fluid and that,
as Northrop Frye has said, satire is militant irony.
The cyclic view of history, which is apparent in the
novel, diminishes the satiric impact as does the ambiguity inherent in the narrative perspective. There is
also some truth in Enzensberger's observation-- at least
in this novel-- that Grass lacks the moral instinct of
the true satirist as well as the absurd hope that the
state of the world can be changed.[1] Nevertheless there

are satirical elements in *Die Blechtrommel* and more especially in the third book of the novel. There the satiric thrust is directed against the continuity of the
German development, that those modes of thinking and
feeling which constituted the solid substratum for the
Nazi ideology still exist today, though possibly in a
modified, though not necessarily fundamentally altered
form. We have already noted that the fervour with which
nationalistic ideals were pursued during the Nazi period
is the fervour which gave rise to the German economic
miracle-- one miracle has been replaced by another.
Through the medium of Oskar Grass denounces the inability
of German society to come to terms with the past. Such
lack of orientation can be seen expressed in a number of
ways. The art students, for example, revel in accusation
of such a generalized nature that they overlook the details of history. Their teacher, Professor Kuchen, a
kind of artistic Rasputin, whose only colour seems to be
black, claims that expression is all and maintains that
Oskar "drücke das zerstörte Bild des Menschen anklagend,
herausfordernd, zeitlos und dennoch den Wahnsinn unseres
Jahrhunderts ausdrückend aus." Then he proceeds to issue the instruction: "Zeichnet ihn nicht, den Krüppel,
schlachtet ihn, kreuzigt ihn, nagelt ihn mit Kohle aufs
Papier!" (p. 555). The art students recognize Oskar's

misgrowth, the malformation which took place when, at
the end of the war, he attempted to renounce his drum,
and yet they encourage him in his immaturity. They delight in despair and pessimism and in this sense are as
divorced from reality as those who suppress all knowledge of the past. They force him once again into the
role of Christ-- or Anti-Christ-- which he may or may
not wish to adopt. One of the art students, Raskolni-
koff, who, as one might expect, is somewhat obsessed by
guilt and atonement, forces the drum upon Oskar and thus
resurrects once more the barrier between Oskar and reality (p. 568). A short time later Oskar celebrates the
resurrection of his drum and Klepp and he found a jazz
band.

.Oskar's attitude to art-- which is his name for
beating a drum-- is just as suspect as that of the art
students and art professor or that of Lankes. As we
have noted, Lankes converts his own inhumanity into art.
Oskar claims in the same context that 'his art also
cries out for bread': "es galt, die Erfahrungen des
dreijährigen Blechtrommlers Oskar während der Vorkriegs-
und Kriegszeit mittels der Blechtrommel in das pure,
klingende Gold der Nachkriegszeit zu verwandeln." (p.
664). Oskar intends to cling to the childish viewpoint
and this is to be the source of inspiration for his art.

In keeping with his creed, he reduces the customers in
Schmuh's Onion Cellar to the level of children: he suffers the little children to come unto him. He has them
behave like children: "Alte Wege trommelte ich hin und
zurück, machte die Welt aus dem Blickwinkel der Dreijährigen deutlich, nahm die zur wahren Orgie unfähige
Nachkriegsgesellschaft zuerst an die Leine, was heißen
soll, ich führte sie in den Posadowskiweg, in Tante
Kauers Kindergarten, hatte sie schon soweit, daß sie die
Unterkiefer hängenließen, sich bei den Händchen nahmen,
die Fußspitzen einwärts schoben, mich, ihren Rattenfänger
erwarteten." (pp. 643-44). In this chapter-- 'Im Zwiebelkeller'-- the post-war German society is revealed as
a society which is characterized by immaturity and by
'the inability to mourn', to use the title of Mitscher-
lich's book. Oskar allows himself to be employed by a
concert agency which is organized by Meister Bebra. He
sets out on tours of West Germany and entertains large
audiences with solo performances on his drum. The publicity campaign builds him up as a magician, a faith-
healer (a word which was used originally in conjunction
with Rasputin) and as a Messiah. Once again Oskar enters
into the role of the Messiah, suggesting that he is re-
verting to the habits of the pre-1945 period. The audiences react in the manner of three-year olds when

Oskar relates episodes from the life of the miraculous
Rasputin on his drum (p. 670). The merry-go-round set
in motion by Goethe and Rasputin keeps on turning; circularity still holds sway. Infantilism is still presented as the disease of German society and as a sign that
the members of the Federal Republic are inclined to suppress the uncomfortable facts connected with National
Socialism. In light of Oskar's activity as a drummer in
post-war Germany it is easy to understand Hanspeter
Brode's assessment of *Die Blechtrommel* as a protest
against the wide-spread tendency to suppress the Nazi
period.

Grass also attacks the continuity of German political thinking in the chapter entitled 'Die letzte Straßen-
bahn oder Anbetung eines Weckglases'. Oskar describes
how two men have arrested Viktor Weluhn, who was involved
in the defence of the Polish Post Office but managed to
escape, and how they try to shoot him in accordance with
an order of execution issued in 1939. Only the fantastic
intervention of Oskar saves 'poor Victor' from death and
perhaps introduces a mildly optimistic note in the course
of this condemnation of the German attitude towards Poland. This is obviously not the first time in the book
that Grass attacks the German treatment of Poland. On
one occasion, for example, Oskar makes an ironic comment

on the Great Powers' tendency to divide up Poland (p.
476). The massive military onslaught on the Polish Post
Office contains an implied criticism of the German behaviour to Poland. Hanspeter Brode has drawn attention
to a statement which Grass has made about Poland and in
which he explains, "daß mich die deutsche, an Polen be-
gangene Schuld bei meiner Arbeit als Schriftsteller ent-
scheidend bestimmt hat." (p. 99).[26]

The Theme of Guilt

In an interview with Heinz Ludwig Arnold Günter
Grass has stated the four main points of comparison between the three works which comprise the Danzig Trilogy.[7]
The first similarity which he singles out is the theme
of guilt: "Alle drei Ich-Erzähler in allen drei Büch-
ern schreiben aus Schuld heraus: aus verdrängter Schuld,
aus ironisierter Schuld, im Fall Matern aus pathetischem
Schuldverlangen, einem Schuldbedürfnis-- das ist das
erste Gemeinsame." (p. 11). Elsewhere (see page 6 in
this chapter) Grass speaks of Oskar's 'fingierte Schuld'
and 'seine wirklichen Verschuldungen'.

It is not difficult to locate Oskar's simulated
guilt. The narrator, an inveterate impostor, claims on
one occasion to have murdered his mother and his uncle.
He starts off his confession by producing the preposterous

claim that his drum committed the murders, and then replaces this pretence by an ostensibly more honest, but
in reality just as fantastic a statement: "... meine
Trommel, nein, ich selbst, der Trommler Oskar, brachte
zuerst meine arme Mama, dann den Jan Bronski, meinen On-
kel und Vater ins Grab." (p. 291). Oskar even makes this
pair of murders into a list by adding on the names of
Roswitha Raguna and Matzerath. He produces this confession in the presence of Meister Bebra who has set himself up as a judge and who, according to Oskar, plays
his role excellently (p. 668). Oskar presumably does not
want to spoil this fine piece of theatre and plays his
part equally well, for he confesses all.

The theme of guilt once again figures largely in the
final chapter of the novel. However, Oskar's feelings of
guilt do not relate to a specific aspect of reality. On
the one hand Oskar admits that he is pretending to be
afraid-- he speaks of "das mühsame Aufrechterhalten der
Furcht." (p. 704)-- and on the other hand his behaviour
is that of a child-- he is afraid of a kind of bogeyman,
the so-called 'Schwarze Köchin'-- and in addition the
children's game in which this witch occurs, involves a
child being singled out, even though the child concerned,
as A. Leslie Willson points out, is "superficially innocent while paradoxically revealed in a state of terrible

guilt." (p. 132).[27]   Oskar, the confidence trickster, is
bound to conceal the nature of his guilt. As is the case
in assessing any ironical statement, it is up to the
reader to assess where the truth lies. The situation in
Hundejahre is much less ambivalent, in that it is quite
clear that Matern is trying to disguise the fact that he
assaulted his Jewish friend: he cannot accept the reality
of his own past. In *Katz und Maus* it could also be maintained that the narrator has no adequate understanding
of what National Socialism entailed. Both suffer from a
kind of moral blindness, a huge incapacity to recall any
embarrassing or uncomfortable facts from their own past
or from the past of the nation to which they belong.
Few verifiable facts are known about the character of
Oskar. Only one thing stands out as absolutely incon-
testible: he retreats behind the mask of a child at the
age of three and persists in this attitude even when he
has reached the age of thirty, when one might expect the
adult outlook to predominate. It is both interesting
and significant that in his game with Meister Bebra Oskar
purchases the forgiveness of his father-confessor by
signing a document. According to the contract concerned
he is obliged to undertake a series of concerts which
will consist of solo performances on his drum. He explains the arrangements in the following terms: "Manch

einer mag nun glauben, daß jener Vertrag in doppelter
Ausfertigung, den ich zweimal unterschrieb, meine Seele
erkaufte oder Oskar zu schrecklichen Missetaten verpflichtete. Nichts davon! Als ich mit Hilfe des Dr.
Dösch im Vorzimmer den Vertrag studierte, verstand ich
schnell und mühelos, daß Oskars Aufgabe darin bestand,
alleine mit seiner Blechtrommel vor dem Publikum aufzu-
treten, daß ich so trommeln mußte, wie ich es als Drei-
jähriger getan hatte und später noch einmal in Schmuhs
Zwiebelkeller. Die Konzertagentur verpflichtete sich,
meine Tourneen vorzubereiten, erst einmal auf die Werbe-
trommel zu schlagen, bevor "Oskar der Trommler" mit
seinem Blech auftrat." (p. 669). The signing of the
document marks the dividing line between the world of
fantasy, i.e. the game of make-believe in which Dösch as
father-confessor and judge and Oskar as penitent sinner
indulge and the world of reality, at least in terms of
Oskar. Whether the contract can be legitimately be compared with a pact with the devil-- and Oskar carefully
denies that this is so-- is debatable, the agreement the
two of them draw up, however, is quite specific. We know
that Oskar can carry out the contract, that is, he can
beat his drum as a three-year old, and we also know that
the effect is that he reduces nominal adults to level of
children, and we shall also find out shortly that he does

abide by the agreement. By referring to the surrender
of his soul and the terrible misdeeds, Oskar tries to
belittle what he does achieve and direct attention from
it. The contract accurately describes Oskar's situation:
he is to encourage members of the public to remain infantile in their emotional reactions and in their behaviour, whilst the agency prepares the audiences for his
appearances. Publicity would have him regarded as a magician and Messiah and thus an image is imposed upon him.
Oskar moulds society and society moulds him. He encourages the public in its immaturity and its escapism. As
in the pre-1945 period Oskar places the drum between himself and reality. In the same way the drum becomes a
barrier between the individuals who constitute society
and reality, whether this be of the present or of the
past. Oskar effectively prevents society from understanding its past and coming to terms with it. He enjoys being mindless, is encouraged to be so and infects
society with the same degree of irresponsibility. This
is his guilt-- he flees from reality and persuades others
to follow his example. They persist in the "Unwissen-
heit..., die damals in Mode kam und noch heute manchem
als flottes Hütchen zu Gesicht steht." (p. 292).

Conclusion

As can be seen, it may be said that Grass sets up
Oskar as the ingenuous narrator in *Die Blechtrommel* and
then withdraws completely, ostensibly leaving the narrator in sole charge. He tells his story from an assumed,
an ironical point of view, pretending to be either a
child or a madman or both simultaneously. Our author
never interferes directly in the story-telling but he
does allow Oskar to unmask himself. Sometimes the imagery serves to break through the narrator's barrier of
pretence and deceit. Of course, there are occasions when
the reader is not sure whether Grass himself might not
be undermining his narrator by allowing discrepancies to
appear of which his narrator is unaware. In other words,
the reader is frequently unsure whether an utterance or
a word is intentionally ironical or unconsciously ironical. Sometimes Oskar takes the reader into his confidence and openly states that he is lying or exaggerating.
On other occasions Oskar's statements are contradictory.
Frequently, however, the narrator playfully ironises himself or is ironised by some form of exaggeration, a
flight of fancy, an innuendo, ambiguity or other stylistic
warning signal. So systematically is doubt cultivated
in the mind of the reader that ultimately the reader is
more or less unable to take any of Oskar's statements at

their face value, even where stylistic warning signals
seem to be absent. However, even though the reader has
no sure grip on empirical reality, at least two elements
constitute stabilising factors within the novel, the imagery and the chronological framework of political
events.

Wayne C. Booth draws attention to the fact that
people are uncertain whether Joyce was ironising the
hero in *The Portrait of the Artist as a Young Man.*[9] There
is a similar element of uncertainty in *Die Blechtrommel.*
Oskar hides behind his mask, refusing to allow any real
insight into his character, and preferring concealment
and dissembling to the adult obligation for accepting
moral and political responsibility. The question about
which one is to some extent unsure is whether it is the
author's intention to expose to ridicule Oskar's flight
from reality, believing that this has a generalised application to twentieth-century Germany, or whether Oskar's escapism is a necessary but incidental factor in
the kind of narrative perspective which Grass has chosen
to employ. It would appear, however, that Oskar's pose
is motivated by his desire for psychological facelessness and moral and political irresponsibility. He wishes
in effect to cover up his own sense of guilt by refusing
to reveal his own character and by blaming individuals

and circumstances for his own shortcomings. In this
sense one could legitimately claim that Oskar has a representative function to fulfil, even though he is an
oblique and ironic expression of the trends of the time.
In other words, Oskar's story is not 'a tale told by an
idiot full of sound and fury, signifying nothing'.

Oskar's undermining of the truth with the accom-
panying atmosphere of doubt and ambivalence is not an
isolated feature within the novel, for Oskar's plunge
into the 'darkest abyss of romance' is coupled with the
destruction of reason, a process which reaches its cul-
mination in National Socialist Germany, as described in
Die Blechtrommel. All characters pay homage to the cult
of unreason which is allusively configured by the associations connected with Rasputin and the imagery of head
and tail. The imagery serves to throw into relief the
corruption of truth, morality and Christianity which is the
decisive characteristic of the society to which Oskar belongs. There are no positive values within the novel and
accordingly the characters are not motivated by ethical
considerations. The relationships between men and women
in the novel are sordid: the love-play of all the characters is ludicrous and grotesque. The characters' irrational behaviour, their allegiance to unbridled emotion,
finds its counterpart in an amorality of situation, and

also in the circularity of the plot. In the world that
Oskar describes decisions are no longer determined by
moral considerations. He depicts a world in which choice
is no longer meaningful, in which alternatives are equally abhorrent, equally amoral, equally inhuman in their
effects. This fact is reflected in the basic absurdity
and abnormality of the human situations which are depicted in the novel. The complete lack of moral, religious
or philosophical principles within the novel and the absence of truth as an ideal to which men aspire, are conditioned to a large extent by the narrative perspective.
Oskar, the narrator, views, or pretends to view, Nazism
and the post-war period through the eyes of a child, in
other words, he sees an immoral age through amoral eyes.
In this process all values are fantastically inverted.
Oskar indulges in a carnival of amorality and infantilism
which is paralleled by the grim saturnalian eruption of
National Socialism and in the hedonism of the post-war
economic miracle. The narrator describes what Grass has
elsewhere chosen to call "die blinde amoralische Realität
mit ihren elementaren Interessen."[28] He mirrors the
psychological, moral and political atmosphere of his time
in grotesque and distorted fashion. Kurt Lothar Tank
maintains in his book "daß in ... Oskar der Geist und
Ungeist einer Epoche beschworen ist." (p. 6).[5] Oskar

gives shape to the amorality of the age through which he
lives. He reflects 'as through a glass darkly' the extent to which truth, morality and religion have been
eroded and devitalised under the impact of bourgeois attitudes and politics.

The introduction of the egocentric, amoral and highly imaginative narrator allows that degree of alienation
and detachment which is the basic precondition for Grass's
ironical-- and sometimes satirical-- survey of the German development. Oskar, the flawed reflector of reality,
permits the reader to view the world from an unusual
angle and hence sharpens his perception of the real
world. The ironist-- using Oskar as his narrator-- does
not describe the realities of the world in objective
terms but produces rather a travesty of the situation.
The ironic viewpoint and the world of fantasy which Oskar describes direct our attention to actuality and
prompt us to decode the irony and to draw comparisons
between the fantastic and the real world. There is constant interplay between these two worlds in the mind of
the reader and from this interaction the critical attitude is fostered. The fantasy and the naive attitude of
the childish narrator serve as a means to abstract the
characters from their usual setting and thus expose them
to our critical gaze. The ironical and the fantastic

sharpen our critical awareness.

Oskar epitomises the German outlook, whilst Danzig is the microcosm of Germany. In this sense then *Die Blechtrommel* is a historical novel, yet one in which political events are mentioned in a casual, take-it-or-leave-it manner. As in the case of the film the novel emerges as a lament, the sorrowful admission of the grievous wrongs perpetrated against the Poles and the Jews and the sense of deprivation which proceeds from the expulsion of the Germans from Danzig. At the same time *Die Blechtrommel* constitutes a critique of the German development, on occasions a bitter satirical attack on the continuity of German political attitudes and actions.

Notes

1. Hans Magnus Enzensberger, "Wilhelm Meister, auf Blech getrommelt," in *Einzelheiten* (Frankfurt: Suhrkamp, 1962). Also in Loschütz, see note 12 and in Schlöndorff, see note 2.

2. Volker Schlöndorff, Die Blechtrommel, *Tagebuch einer Verfilmung* (Darmstadt and Neuwied: Luchterhand, 1979).

3. Page numbering of *Die Blechtrommel* refers to the Luchterhand edition, Neuwied and Berlin, 1966.

4. Günter Grass, "Rückblick auf *Die Blechtrommel* oder der Autor als fragwürdiger Zeuge," in Volker Schlöndorff's book; also in Rolf Geißler, ed., *Günter Grass, Materialienbuch* (Darmstadt and Neuwied: Luchterhand, 1980); and in Günter Grass, *Aufsätze zur Literatur* (Darmstadt and Neuwied: Luchterhand, 1980).

5. Kurt Lothar Tank, *Günter Grass* (Berlin: Colloquium, 1965).

6. Idris Parry, "Aspects of Günter Grass's Narrative Technique," *Forum for Modern Language Studies*, Vol. III, No. 2 (1967), 99-114.

7. Heinz Ludwig Arnold, *Günter Grass, Text und Kritik*, 1/1a, 1978.

8. D. C. Muecke, *Irony*, Methuen, 1970, p. 26.

9. Wayne C. Booth, "The Artist as Satirist," in *The*

Rhetoric of Fiction (Chicago and London, 1961).

10. Henry Hatfield, "The Artist as Satirist," in *The Contemporary Novel in German*, ed. Robert R. Heitner (Austin and London, 1967), pp. 117-34.

11. Georg Just, "Die Appellstruktur der *Blechtrommel*," in *Grass Kritik - Thesen - Analysen*, ed. Manfred Jurgensen (Berne and Munich: Franke, 1973).

12. Manfred Bourrée, "Das Okular des Günter Grass," in *Von Buch zu Buch-- Günter Grass in der Kritik*, ed. Gert Loschütz (Berlin and Neuwied: Luchterhand, 1968).

13. Henri Plard, "Über *Die Blechtrommel*," in *Text und Kritik* as under note 7.

14. Günter Grass, *Über meinen Lehrer Döblin und andere Vorträge* (Berlin: Literarisches Colloquium, 1968); also in Günter Grass, *Aufsätze zur Literatur* (as under note 4).

15. Ezra Pound as quoted in René Wellek and Austin Warren, *Theory of Literature*, 1949, p. 187.

16. William York Tindall, *The Literary Symbol* (Bloomington and London: Indiana University Press, 1955), p. 117.

17. Burton Pike, "Objects vs. People in the Recent German Novel," *Wisconsin Studies in Contemporary Literature*, Vol. III, No. 3 (Autumn 1966).

18. Jochen Rohlfs, "Erzählen aus unzuverlässiger Sicht.

Zur Erzählstruktur bei Günter Grass," in *Text und Kritik* as under note 7.

19. See Alan Bullock, *Hitler, a Study in Tyranny*, 1952, p. 117.

20. Manfred Jurgensen, *Über Günter Grass, Untersuchungen zur sprachbildlichen Rollenfunktion* (Berne and Munich: Francke, 1974).

21. See Wellek and Warren as under note 15.

22. David Roberts, "Aspects of Psychology and Mythology in *Die Blechtrommel*. A study of the Symbolic Function of the 'hero' Osker," in *Grass, Kritik - Thesen - Analysen*, ed. Manfred Jurgensen, as under note 11.

23. William L. Scharfman, *The Organization of Experience in The Tin Drum*, Minnesota Review, Vol. 6, 1966, pp. 63-64.

24. Geno Hartlaub, "Wir, die wir übriggeblieben sind...," in *Von Buch zu Buch-- Günter Grass in der Kritik*, ed. Gert Loschütz, as under note 12.

25. Georg Just, *Darstellung und Appell in der* Blechtrommel *von Günter Grass* (Frankfurt/M: Athenäum, 1972).

26. Hanspeter Brode, "Die Zeitgeschichte in der *Blechtrommel* von Günter Grass. Entwurf eines textinternen Kommunikationsmodells," in *Günter Grass, Materialienbuch*, ed. Rolf Geißler, as under note 4.

27. A. Leslie Willson, "The Grotesque Everyman in Günter

Grass's *Die Blechtrommel*," *Monatshefte*, Vol. LVIII, No. 2 (1966).

28. Günter Grass, *Über das Selbstverständliche* (Neuwied, 1968), p. 175.

CHAPTER II

Katz und Maus: *guilt and exploitation*

The dust-cover of *Katz und Maus* provides--
apart from the name of the author and the publisher-- at
least three items of information. Firstly, we are told
that Grass's book is a 'novella'; secondly, we learn
the title of the book; and thirdly, we are presented
with a picture of a black and white cat which has around
its neck a red and white ribbon from which dangles the
Knight's Cross. No mouse can be seen on the picture.
The figure of the cat is partially enclosed by an uneven
band of green. Let us examine the significance of these
three pieces of information. Firstly then, the reader
will find that the description of the book as a 'novella'
is entirely correct. Grass's 'novella' does conform to
all the rules to which this genre is expected to conform.
Indeed at one stage in the narration a headmaster produces
the Goethean statement suggesting that at least one of
the main requirements of a 'novella' has been fulfilled:
"Unerhörtes habe sich zugetragen." (p. 107).[1] As a 'novella' it exhibits all the features of compactness and

novella

conciseness which one associates with the 'novellas' of
the nineteenth century; it concentrates upon a specific
aspect of a person's life or development, hence avoiding
the broad narrative sweep expected of the novel and like
many of its antecedents this 'novella' incorporates into
the narrative objects of symbolical value which not only
serve to draw the strands of the plot together but also
highlight significant episodes and motifs in the story.
A 'novella' may base its narrative upon trivial and com-
monplace details-- though it is not really the case in
Katz und Maus-- and may seek at the same time to 'detriv-
ialize' the contents of the narrative, in other words,
emphasise the universal nature of the problem involved
by the mode of presentation and to some extent by the use
of symbolism. The second piece of information is contained in the title itself. We assume from the title
that the event or events described in the 'novella' will
be adequately summarised by the relationship of cat and
mouse. The cat, we all know, enjoys chasing the mouse,
not necessarily because it is in need of food but because
it derives a sadistic pleasure from hunting down its victim and tantalizingly playing with it, until the death of
the mouse puts an end to the game. The reader will not
be disappointed: the title of the book provides the central imagery which becomes the framework of the 'novella'

and dominates the mode of thinking and of feeling of the
two main characters: the narrator, Heini Pilenz, a thirty-two year old social worker living in West Germany, and
Joachim Mahlke, who met his death or disappeared in June
1944. Indeed the whole action of the story proceeds from
a boyish prank which the narrator played upon Mahlke in
the summer of 1940 (see p. 6). Pilenz admits reluctantly,
though not initially, that it was he who set a cat onto
Mahlke's Adam's apple, the mouse-like, abnormally large
protuberance in his throat. The cat's attack signals the
starting point for the story, in that it makes Mahlke
aware of his physical inadequacy and it is this awareness
which serves to motivate his actions. The feelings of
guilt from which Pilenz subsequently suffers force him to
become a narrator: "Ich aber, der ich Deine Maus einer
und allen Katzen in den Blick brachte, muß nun schreiben."
(p. 6). The cat's attack thus has a twofold significance.

At least initially it is clear that the mouse of the
title is the 'mouse' in Joachim Mahlke's throat, for his
huge larynx is frequently referred to as a 'mouse'. However, the fact that Pilenz sets a cat onto Mahlke's throat
does not allow one to equate Pilenz with the cat. Commentators have differed in their attempts to identify the
cat. John Reddick automatically assumes that Pilenz is
the cat, which he describes as an amalgam of Cain and

Judas, the betrayer who tantalizingly hunts down his victim, to whom Reddick ascribes the role of Abel and of
Christ.[2] Johanna E. Behrendt puts forward the opposite
view that the cat is not outside but within Mahlke himself.[3] Hans Magnus Enzensberger sees the cat as representing society.[4] Hermann Pongs regards it as fate;[5]
while another commentator draws parallels between the cat
and the Virgin Mary, who seems on occasions to merge almost indistinguishably into Eve, the eternal temptress.[6]
Pilenz's agonized question as to whether there are such
things as stories which have an ending (p. 133) suggests
that stories have a constant, haunting element but does
not exclude the possibility that they may continue in a
slightly modified form and in this instance it even allows the cat to have a shifting identity. Only a close
examination will allow the reader to fathom the cat's
mysterious identity.

The third piece of information on the dust-cover,
the drawing, is yet more ambiguous and ambivalent. Obviously the picture begins to acquire significance only
after the reader has completed the book. Ultimately the
green background of the picture will allow the reader to
recall that the schoolboy's prank takes place in the
grass of a sportsfield, that Mahlke's military prowess
was demonstrated in the countryside of Russia, and that

the hero of the story finally disappears into the hold of
a partially submerged minesweeper which is itself surrounded by the grass-green water of the Baltic. Eventually the reader will be inclined to explain the mystery of
the dust-cover by recollecting that Mahlke intended to
hide in the radio cabin of the ship which he had furnished
as though it were a chapel dedicated to the Virgin Mary.
At this point the reader may produce a number of statements, which are, however, largely conjectural: Mahlke
plunges, as it were, into the amniotic sea and, inverting
the process of birth, re-enters the womb from which he
proceeded; the would-be Christ is re-enveloped by the
womb. Cat-like, he haunts the mind of one of the war's
survivors; and from beyond his watery grave he dictates
in Christ-like fashion the thoughts and feelings of the
spellbound narrator. Only detailed analysis of the text
can prove or disprove the validity of such statements.
What is known is that Grass himself designed the dust-
jacket-- so much is stated at the back of the book. Cat-
like, the author plays his little game with the unsuspec-
ting reader. In order to probe the enigma of this drawing let us examine the various aspects of the 'novella',
firstly, the character of Mahlke, secondly, the character
of Pilenz and, thirdly, the relationship between protagonist and narrator. In the process we shall investigate

the imagery of cat and mouse and this will contribute to
an understanding of the 'novella' as a whole.

Joachim Mahlke is described as being 14 years old
shortly after the beginning of the Second World War. The
reader is then presented with the story of Mahlke between
the years of 1939 and 1944, when he disappears into the
hold of the minesweeper at the age of eighteen. His story
is told against the background of the events of the Second World War. Such events take place, however, on the
periphery of his consciousness though preoccupation with
his own particular problems may be considered normal for
a person of his age. Pilenz even allows him his own time-
reckoning: "Vor dem Freischwimmen, nach dem Freischwimmen." (p. 33). If one had to locate his ego, then one
might be tempted to situate it in his Adam's apple, for
this becomes the focal point of his existence, that pivot
around which everything else revolves. Not that his larynx had always played such a dominant role in his life,
for, before he learnt to swim, he was a nothing-- at
least according to Pilenz-- a something that nobody no-
ticed (see p. 32). He hears of miraculous things about
the submerged minesweeper and this goads him on to gain
his swimming certificate. Once he has attained this, he
starts to perform the 'miracles' on ship. He out-swims
and out-dives his classmates and salvages all manner of

strange objects from the hold of the ship. He finds down below, for example, a fire-extinguisher, hoists it to the surface and proceeds to spray the sea with foam. By his feats of exhibitionism he soon establishes, according to Pilenz, a legendary reputation for himself. We are told that he wears a variety of articles around his neck ranging from a screwdriver to a tin-opener, and a pendant depicting the Virgin Mary. The narrator maintains that the articles and Mahlke's feats of daring are intended to divert attention from Mahlke's goitre-like Adam's apple. Pilenz draws together what he considers to be the main elements in his hero's character in a section which has been referred to as the core of the 'novella':[7] "Eigentlich mögen später Gerüchte und Handfestes dagegen gesprochen haben-- gab es für Mahlke, wenn schon Frau, nur die katolische Jungfrau Maria. Nur ihretwegen hat er alles, was sich am Hals tragen und zeigen ließ, in die Marienkapelle geschleppt. Alles, vom Tauchen bis zu den späteren, mehr militärischen Leistungen, hat er für sie getan oder aber-- schon muß ich mir widersprechen-- um von seinem Adamsapfel abzulenken. Schließlich kann noch, ohne daß Jungfrau und Maus überfällig werden, ein drittes Motiv genannt werden: Unser Gymnasium, dieser muffige, nicht zu lüftende Kasten, und besonders die Aula, bedeuteten Joachim Mahlke viel, und zwangen Dich später, letzte

Anstrengungen zu machen." (p. 43). Here Pilenz seems to
make it quite clear what the three decisive elements were
in Mahlke's life-- though there is some sense of improvi-
sation in the way Pilenz lists these elements: firstly
the Virgin Mary, secondly, his Adam's apple, and, thirdly,
his old school. A second quotation which may help to in-
dicate the possible political implications of the 'novella' occurs in Grass's collection of political essays entitled *Über das Selbstverständliche* (1968):   "Das Ritter-
kreuz belohnte militärische Leistungen, deren Ziele ein
verbrecherisches System gesteckt hatte." (p. 182).

　　Let us look first at the quotation from the 'novella'
itself. Pilenz claims that the only woman to whom Mahlke
devotes himself is the Virgin Mary. All his actions,
whether at school or later in the army, are undertaken
with her in mind. Along with the school and his Adam's
apple she is one of the principal motive forces within
his life. One should not imagine, however, that his ado-
ration of the Virgin Mary stems from a conventional attitude to Catholicism. Shortly before his disappearance,
Pilenz has Mahlke explain the nature of his beliefs, emphasising in particular that he does not believe in God
(p. 156). Gusewski, the priest, maintains that Mahlke's
worship of the Virgin Mary borders on pagan idolatry.
This is particularly apparent in the narrator's description

of Mahlke stretching out his hands towards Mary, "jene
überlebensgroße Gipsfigur" with her flat chest and glass
eyes (see p. 115). What he is idolizing seems, to judge
by Pilenz's statements, something which is hollow, sterile
and lifeless, something which is valueless in its remote-
ness from life. Despite these less endearing qualities
Mahlke seems attracted to her almost on a sexual level.
Hence Mahlke can state that he does not intend to get married. Like Oskar and many of the characters in *Die Blechtrommel*, Mahlke surrenders himself to things, rather than
to people.

How does his devotion to the Virgin Mary manifest
itself? Pilenz's statement-- the so-called 'novella-
core'-- suggests that Mahlke's feats as a boy were inspired by the Virgin Mary. The narrator describes Mahlke's
feats on the minesweeper. His constant companions in his
sallies into this underworld are a screw-driver and a pendant, depicting the Virgin Mary. She, unlike the screw-
driver, is allowed to take part in Mahlke's activities in
the gymnasium. She has to accompany him in all his most
daring exercises, whilst the screwdriver remains in the
changing-room. Gymnastics appears to fulfil the same
function in Mahlke's life as diving. Both present him
with opportunities to explore the heights and depths of
his existence and also to impress his fellows. It is also

worth remembering that in *Die Blechtrommel* Christ is described as a gymnast who displays great athletic prowess
in hanging on the cross. Hence one is not surprised to
find later that the Chapel of the Virgin Mary was originally a gymnasium or that the school's gym itself appears
very much like the inside of a church. Though Mahlke
shows great ability both as a swimmer and a gymnast, the
impression is created that he is not able to cope with
ordinary terrestrial reality. The spheres of operation
of Mahlke as a boy have their counterpart later on in the
two fields of war associated with the aeroplane and the
submarine. The idea that Mahlke is the equivalent mentally and emotionally of a fish out of water is suggested
later in the 'novella' when the narrator describes how
Mahlke prays at the altar to the Virgin Mary: "Auf den
Strand geworfene Fische schnappen so regelmäßig nach
Luft." (p. 58). Land is not Mahlke's natural habitat.
He is a terrestrial misfit.

The two pendants are intended to serve the same purpose for Mahlke wears them ostensibly in order to divert
attention from his Adam's apple. In doing so he may, wittingly or otherwise, achieve the opposite effect. The
Adam's apple is, however, something more than just a physical deformity which is the source of embarrassment. On
the symbolic level it is an indication of the feeling that

he is different from his fellows and a sign of his own inadequacy. If one ponders upon the religious associations
of 'Adam's apple', then Mahlke's over-sized larynx is the
external manifestation of his own alienation, a reminder
of his own sinfulness. He shares in a sense of original
sin, which stems not from an act of doing, but rather from
a state of being. Both Mahlke and Oskar are victims of a
physical deformity which is the externalization of a state
of psychological unbalance.

Mahlke also uses other objects to conceal his Adam's
apple. After the war has broken out, Mahlke introduces
pompons amongst his school-fellows. Once they have become too popular amongst his friends, Mahlke replaces them
by a huge safety pin which is intended to keep a woollen
shawl in position under his chin. He makes a final and
decisive break with pompons on the occasion of a fighter-
pilot's visit to the school. The airman with the much-
coveted decoration round his neck relates his war exploits
to the pupils in the hall of the school. During the
course of the address Mahlke finally removes the pompons
from his neck and it is clear from this episode onwards
that all his efforts will be concentrated on gaining such
a decoration, for only the possession of such a 'Bonbon'
can compensate completely for his feeling of inferiority
and assuage his sense of discontent. The next time a war-

hero, in this instance a U-boat commander, comes to the
school, Mahlke steals the hero's medal from the gym changing room, unbeknown to his teacher and his class-mates.
Pilenz's suspicions, however, are confirmed when he swims
out to the minesweeper. Here he finds Mahlke sitting naked on the deck with the war medal dangling by its ribbon
from his neck. For the first time Mahlke has found something which can adequately dispel his feelings of inferiority, which can bring his Adam's apple to rest (p. 103).

In *Die Blechtrommel* Oskar, the dwarf, likens himself
to Christ. In *Katz und Maus* the narrator compares Joachim
Mahlke with the person of the redeemer. This comparison
does not occur often but it is of sufficient frequency to
be of significance. In describing some of the treasured
objects in Mahlke's room in the 'Osterzeile' the narrator
refers to the stuffed owl in the following terms: "Auch
die Schnee-Eule hatte den ernsten Mittelscheitel und
zeigte, gleich Mahlke, diese leidende und sanft entschlos-
sene, wie von inwendigem Zahnschmerz durchtobte Erlöser-
miene." (p. 25). When Pilenz visits Mahlke on the minesweeper, the latter is described as having the redeemer's
countenance (p. 102). On a later occasion when the narrator observes his hero in church in front of the altar
to the Virgin Mary, he notes his similarity to Jesus (p.
114 and p. 88). Mahlke appears, to judge by the narrator,

to be adapting aspects of Catholic thinking and feeling
to his own needs. He bears the stigma of Christ's passion and in so doing preserves some of the outward trap-
pings of Christianity. The trimmings he has retained
are those which serve to satisfy, if not to glorify, his
own ego. In associating himself with Christ, he accen-
tuates the awareness of his own suffering and throws his
own image of himself out of balance. His striving to
emulate Christ is the result of his inability to accept
his own human limitations and imperfections. Mahlke perhaps suggests that he cherishes this image of himself as
the redeemer when he almost physically assaults one of
his class-mates for having drawn on the board a picture
of him complete with halo and a Christlike expression of
suffering (p. 45)-- though it may be that he also objects
to the blasphemous nature of the drawing.

There is a special significance in the fact that
Mahlke does not believe, so the narrator claims, in God.
Joachim Mahlke comes to an awareness of himself and his
special physical peculiarities as he enters puberty. He
leaves the years of unknowing and innocence behind. He
frenetically searches for an appropriate fig-leaf to cover his physical-- and psychological-- nakedness. It is
not coincidence that when Pilenz visits him on the minesweeper he finds him sitting naked on the deck dangling

the stolen Knight's Cross from his neck-- and Mahlke even
tries to dangle it in front of his genitals (p. 104). For
Mahlke the military decoration is the ultimate fig-leaf,
the one which allows his fragmented mind to recover its
original harmony. A number of references to harmony and
symmetry occur throughout the text (see p. 41, p. 103,
p. 128, p. 147). One particular reference is especially
telling: the Knight's Cross is described as "proclaiming
symmetry as a creed." (p. 103). Whilst his schoolmates
sun themselves on the deck of the minesweeper, Mahlke in
his role of Adam and would-be Christ labours to atone for
his sense of disproportion: "Mahlke machte es sich nicht
leicht: wenn wir auf dem Kahn dösten, arbeitete er unter
Wasser." (p. 14). His feats are miracles of over-achievement: he feels compelled to over-compensate for his phys-
ical-- and psychological-- inadequacies. The first Adam
wishes to become a second Adam. He wishes to attain salvation, to achieve wholeness. He wishes to bring redemption to the world, but the only world of which he is aware
is the inner world of Mahlke. His quest for redemption
is an act of spiritual self-abuse because it is turned in
upon itself. Nevertheless he still pursues the goal of
purity, the aim of liberating himself from all inconsis-
tencies and paradoxes. He still wishes to redeem himself.
Accordingly, he views himself as the son and lover of the

Virgin Mary and hence cannot believe in Christ or for that matter in God, for both of them cannot be allowed to exist in his world since they would be rivals for the Virgin's favour.

The acts in which Mahlke indulges are for the most part senseless-- though this would not be unexpected from a person whose behaviour is still that of an adolescent. Spraying the sea with foam from a fire-extinguisher is a particularly good example of an action which, though entertaining and impressive, fulfils no purpose (p. 10), and which has incidentally sexual overtones. Playing a gramophone, which he has recovered from the hold of the ship, without a record is equally pointless (p. 27). His masturbatory feat has the same air of futility. This is emphasised most trenchantly by the fact that the seagulls devour his seed. Only they benefit from his act of giving. Mahlke is part of an unproductive cycle. The gulls eat his life-giving sperm in the same way that they snap up the boys' sputum which consists of the masticated remains of the birds' droppings. All this takes place on the wreck of a ship which is gradually rotting away and whose superstructure is covered with rust and the gulls' excreta. The childrens' cycle of infertility has its counterpart in the nominally adult cycle of death and destruction: the fighter-pilot engages in the Battle of

Britain-- a battle which is lost-- and shoots down enemy
planes only to be shot down himself over the Ruhr in 1943
(p. 62). Mahlke's orgy of killing on the Russian front
is ultimately followed by his own non-resurfacing-- or
non-resurrection-- from the hold of the ship. This roundabout of death and destruction is reinforced in particular
by the stench of corpses which pervades the whole of Germany during the war years (p. 119). This is not to maintain that Mahlke is incapable of altruism-- he does rescue
one of the schoolboys from drowning (p. 68) and his removal of the contraceptive from the door handle of the
classroom may also belong to the category of acts which
proceed from a consideration of others, though Mahlke does
enjoy the approbation which he thereby receives (p. 28).
However, destructiveness and sterility assume a more dominant role in the 'novella' and during the years in which
the action takes place than positive features of human behaviour.

The senseless peculiarity of his actions above all
provoke the admiration of his classmates and their approv-
al stimulates him still further. This is particularly
true on the occasion of his transferring the contents of
his attic room to his underwater radio cabin which he
dedicates in effect to the Virgin Mary (p. 74). Mahlke's
exploits on the minesweeper prepare him for the amoral

deeds in the arena of war. The visits of the fighter-
pilot and U-boat commander also prepare the knight for the
gladiatorial deeds which will earn him the award of the
cross. The two talks achieve a twofold effect: they
make him aware of the supremacy of the Knight's Cross over
all other much-prized fig-leaves and divert his mind from
the reality of war on the one hand by the description of
war as a sport and on the other hand by clothing war in
romantic terminology. Mahlke has reacted to a schoolboy's
prank in a humourless, egocentric manner and sets forth
for the field of battle, not, however, having outstepped
the confines of the childish perspective. In another
sense, however, Mahlke reduces the conflict to what it is,
a senseless game. The schoolboy in uniform (see p. 150)
cannot accept the inconstancies of his own inner world,
wishes to attain wholeness and be released from suffering
and imagines that this can be achieved by acts of unwholesome destruction. Mahlke, the Saviour, suffers from the
delusion that he may gain redemption without his having
any meaningful relationship with others, for the only
'people' who have any relevance for his life are the flat-
chested, glass-eyed Virgin Mary and his dead father. Ultimately, because his own internal world is out of joint,
he turns mindlessly to the destruction of the external
world. Only because his mind remains diverted from

reality, is he capable of going to war, almost unaware of
the implications of his actions. The letters he sends to
his mother and aunt highlight the nature of his puerile
behaviour. He sends them drawings of Russian tanks,
which with childish precision are marked with a cross as
a sign that he has 'bagged' them (pp. 131-33). On a later
occasion Pilenz speaks of the Knight's Cross as "jener
eiserne Artikel, der das kindliche Kritzeln und Durch-
kreuzen so vieler russischer Panzer zu belohnen hatte..."
(p. 160).

The hero recounts his over-achievement in war to Pilenz, the narrator, as the latter rows him across to his
underwater chapel. He claims that the Virgin Mary appeared to him in battle. She was accompanied not by the
Christchild but bore instead the picture of his father
and the fireman in front of their locomotive just before
they died attempting to save the lives of others (pp.
169-70 and p. 131). She placed the photo over her stomach.
Mahlke had only to direct his fire at the picture to ensure a direct hit on the tank. Not only was he destroying
the tank-- and presumably the occupants-- but he was also
ejaculating a stream of deadly shells at the Virgin whilst
at the same time symbolically killing his father. He is
a superman of war; he performs the ultimate in over-
achievement, killing enemy, Virgin Mary and father

simultaneously. In attempting to reintegrate himself, to attain a state of purity, he annihilates all that he claims to value most. Now the Christchild, who has impregnated the Mother of God with his deadly sperm, demands the acclamation which is his due. However, he is refused admittance to the school-hall, that paradise which has been the goal of all his endeavours and where he hoped to demonstrate his prowess as a military superman.

Having reached the threshold of salvation he is thrust back into a world which is bereft of all meaning. Denied the delights of paradise and denied release from suffering, the hero reacts yet again in a self-centred manner to the blow which he has received. So rigid is his obsession with self-healing that he is trapped in the thorny labyrinth of his own mind: "Aber der Große Mahlke befand sich in einer Allee, ähnlich jener tunnelartig zugewachsenen, dornenreichen und vogellosen Allee im Schloßpark Oliva, die keine Nebenwege hatte und dennoch ein Labyrinth war." (p. 154). The military superman yet again turns superchild. The pseudo-Christ finds that he cannot save himself. He turns his back on a reality which he has in any case never understood. His experiences have not led him to self-knowledge. His final trick as a clown (see p. 23) is to dive on a Friday, bearing the Knight's Cross before him, into the hold of the minesweeper,

thereby rejoining the Virgin Mary whom he has destroyed
in battle. Since that Friday there has been no Monday on
which Mahlke has resurfaced, though the narrator does not
appear to exclude this possibility of resurrection.

If one views the 'novella' solely in terms of the
character Mahlke, then the reader might readily accept
Johanna E. Behrendt's thesis that the cat which traps
Mahlke is within Mahlke himself. His desire to outstrip
his schoolmates and to outshoot his rivals, whether they
be his father or the Virgin Mary, this godless behaviour
stems from an innate sense of inadequacy. His yearning
to emulate Christ leads to his superhuman achievements.
Schiller's dictum "In deiner Brust sind deines Schicksals
Sterne" could easily apply to Mahlke. However, if one
judges Mahlke's story in the light of the narrator's remarks, then another version of 'truth' may begin to
emerge. Indeed many commentators would wish to qualify
Schiller's words and regard Pilenz, the narrator, as the
person who is the guilty one and who helped to drive
Mahlke to death. In other words they would shift the emphasis and claim that Pilenz makes Mahlke aware of his inadequacy and goads Mahlke on to over-achievement in life--
and in death, in the sense that Mahlke continues to dominate Pilenz's mind even after his disappearance.

One fact about Pilenz, the narrator, emerges at an

early stage in the 'novella'. Pilenz is not the most reliable of narrators. Even with regard to the central
event in Mahlke's life, Pilenz is reluctant to state quite
unambiguously what did in fact happen. When he first mentions this incident, he supplies three possible versions
of the truth: "So jung war die Katze, so beweglich Mahlkes Artikel-- jedenfalls sprang sie Mahlke an die Gurgel;
oder einer von uns griff die Katze und setzte sie Mahlke
an den Hals; oder ich, mit wie ohne Zahnschmerz, packte
die Katze, zeigte ihr Mahlkes Maus: und Joachim Mahlke
schrie, trug aber nur unbedeutende Kratzer davon." (p. 6).
In the next line he accepts responsibility for having
placed the cat on Mahlke's neck, but does so in such a
grandiose manner that one almost has the impression that
he is attaching too much significance to this action-- and
for that matter to himself. Pilenz prevaricates not only
about the cat's attack on Mahlke. There are many other
instances of the narrator's equivocation. He suffers or
pretends to suffer from lapses of memory: he is unsure,
for instance, about the facial appearance of Mahlke (p.
44). There is uncertainty as to whether Mahlke introduced pompons to his part of Germany or whether they were
his invention (p. 47). He sometimes describes imaginary
conversations as though they did take place (p. 110). He
is unsure, so he maintains, of whether he is restructuring

the past in the light of the present (see p. 82, p. 27).
Statements are made only to be followed by a correction,
which does not enhance the narrator's credibility (p.
151). There are other occasions when the narrator makes
statements the validity of which he destroys by the subsequent introduction of a subjunctive (p. 157).

However, he also tells untruths, sometimes of a fundamental nature; this is especially so in the hours before the hero's disappearance. For example, he lies
about the length of time he has hired the boat (p. 171).
After obtaining some food Pilenz returns to Mahlke and
maintains that the authorities have been asking about him
on two occasions-- though this is clearly in conflict
with a previous statement. Then he goes on to claim that
Mahlke's mother has already been arrested (p. 167). Such
lies allow Pilenz to enjoy a feeling of superiority. For
one brief, but decisive, moment in his life he can take
pleasure in the fact that he is now on top: now he can
kick physically (p. 168)-- and psychologically-- the person on whom he has lavished so much love-- and-- on oc-
casions-- so much hate.

The distortions of the truth and the falsehoods which
Pilenz produces achieve a twofold effect: they make the
reader adversely disposed towards the statements the narrator makes and in a perverse sense they draw attention

to the personality and motives of the narrator. Perhaps
they even incline the reader to think that such an untrustworthy biographer is unlikely to have come to a prop-
er understanding of the person he feels impelled to write
about. Pilenz is at pains to emphasise that the story he
is telling is about Mahlke and not about himself (p. 25).
The over-insistent desire on the part of the narrator to
remain in the background makes the wary reader suspicious
and inclines him to question Pilenz's motives.

Pilenz is obviously full of admiration for Mahlke,
though his admiration degenerates into horror and disgust
from time to time (p. 77). He becomes a zealous altar-
boy at communion so that he can peer down Mahlke's collar
and see the various objects dangling from his neck (p.
30); he picks up Mahlke from his home so that he can accompany him to school (p. 101); and it is Pilenz who
coins the title "Der Große Mahlke" in order to describe
the admiration he feels for him (p. 97). Pilenz's admiration for Mahlke borders on idolatry almost in the
same way that Mahlke idolises the Virgin Mary (p. 115).
He is certainly obsessed by him, not only during the war
years, but after his death as well. Many examples can be
found of how Pilenz cannot rid his mind of thoughts of
his hero. For instance, he describes how when he sets
out to visit friends or acquaintances in post-war Germany,

he is "immer noch auf dem Weg zu Mahlkes Mutter und Mahlkes Tante, zu Dir, zum Großen Mahlke." (p. 118; see also
p. 65, p. 102, p. 156, and p. 168). Pilenz's feelings
for Mahlke seem to be of a near claustrophobic intensity.
Possibly they stem originally from the fact that Pilenz
is attracted to his hero simply because the object of his
veneration is so decisive. Occasionally the reader is
aware that Pilenz's hero-worship is tinged with homosex-
uality. Perhaps it is no coincidence that Pilenz maintains that he and his former classmates cannot remember
the appearance of Mahlke's upper lip and think that they
might be confusing Tulla Pokriefke with Joachim Mahlke
(p. 44). Perhaps there is significance in the fact that
the narrator tries to oust thoughts of Mahlke by thoughts
of Tulla who ironically is in any case a somewhat masculine girl: "Während ich schwamm und während ich schreibe,
versuchte und versuche ich an Tulla Pokriefke zu denken,
denn ich wollte und will nicht immer an Mahlke denken."
(p. 99). Pilenz's worship of his hero also extends to
Mahlke's sexual organ which he describes as being "viel
erwachsener gefährlicher anbetungswürdiger..." (p. 40).
It is certainly true to say that Pilenz, by his own admission, does not make any headway with the ladies. To suggest that Pilenz's hero-worship is tinged with a homosex-
ual element does make much of the narrator's behaviour

comprehensible.

What is nevertheless clear is that Pilenz suffers
from a guilt complex. Initially, however, it is not clear
exactly what the nature of his guilt complex is. He explains to us that he feels himself to be under a compul-
sion to write. He tells us that 'the fellow who invented
us' forces him, for professional reasons, to act as narrator (p. 6). Pater Alban takes over the role of father-
confessor and Pilenz relates to him the story of Mahlke,
of cat and mouse and what he describes as 'mea culpa' (p.
101). On another occasion he refers to his guilt and says
that he would not have felt the need to write if Mahlke
had hidden the medal below the deck of the minesweeper,
or if he and Mahlke had not been friends (p. 104). It is
Pater Alban who suggests that Pilenz should get the whole
thing off his chest by writing (p. 125). In giving this
advice the priest uses the term 'sich freischreiben' which
suggests the idea of 'writing one's way to inner freedom'.
A similar though more common term-- 'sich freischwimmen'--
is employed to describe Mahlke's efforts to pass his swimming test and at the same time to swim his way to freedom.
Such an expression conveys the idea of getting away from
parental or similar supervision and of finding one's feet,
presumably in the adult sphere. Both Mahlke and Pilenz,
it could be claimed, suffer from a feeling of alienation,

from a sense of inadequacy. Both lack the capacity to
maintain their minds in a state of equilibrium, they have
difficulty keeping matters in perspective, neither of them
has managed to tread the road of freedom from adolescent
preoccupation with self to the establishment of a meaningful relationship with others and with the outside world
in general.

Let us return to our original problem. What is the
specific basis for Pilenz's guilt complex? Pilenz does
commit at least four acts which would be sufficient to
justify, retrospectively, a troubled conscience. Firstly,
it is he who suggests amongst other things that Mahlke
could hide on the minesweeper (p. 162); secondly, though
he reminds Mahlke to take the tin-opener with him before
the latter dives into the hold, it emerges afterwards
that Pilenz had put his foot on it and had finally thrown
it away (p. 174 and p. 175); and thirdly, Pilenz does
not return to the boat on the evening of the same day (p.
176). Above all else, of course, Pilenz places the cat
on Mahlke's neck, and thereby sets in motion the chain of
events which leads eventually to Mahlke's disappearance.
He also indulges in symbolical actions which imply that
he is not loath to be rid of Mahlke which reveal at least
an aspect of Pilenz's attitude to his so-called friend:
for example, Pilenz wipes the drawing of Mahlke as a

redeemer off the blackboard (p. 45); he removes the hero's name and favourite sequence contained in the 'Stabat
mater' from the wooden partition of the latrine (p. 138);
the altar boy, Pilenz celebrates the Last Supper with his
saviour (p. 159); and finally-- a symbolical act like
the throwing away of the tin-opener-- he packs the photo-
graph of Mahlke's father and the locomotive at the bottom
of his bag which he ultimately loses in fighting near
Cottbus (p. 177).

The narrator's actions and his lies certainly reveal
him at least as a traitor in attitude. He takes revenge
in emotional terms on a person who at least ostensibly is
the epitome of masculinity, who has been an object of
veneration for him, but who disregards his admiration.
It is almost as though he kills the thing he loves. Perhaps he can brook no rivals, perhaps he is jealous of the
Virgin Mary, of Mahlke's father and of Tulla Pokriefke.

Pilenz contributes to Mahlke's downfall in two ways:
firstly, he aggravates his hero's innate hypersensitivity
and feeling of inadequacy by placing the cat on Mahlke's
throat and thus helps to condition his response to the
shock of not being allowed to speak in his schoolhall;
and, secondly, he inclines Mahlke to think of suicide by
telling him lies about the arrest of his mother and the
arrival of the men who are looking for him. He is guilty

persecution
N.S.   *Desire to hunt people.*

of creating an atmosphere of mind which plays upon Mahlke's weaknesses. In this sense Mahlke is a relatively
blameless though rather mindless victim, whilst Pilenz
justifiably suffers from a troubled conscience. It is
clear, however, that in his obsessive sense of guilt Pilenz is concerned primarily about his own self and the
state of his own mind. He is not really concerned about
the person or fate of Joachim Mahlke. His objective is
to purify his own mind. He seeks peace of mind with the
same degree of intensity with which Mahlke attempted to
cleanse his mind from imperfection. Both pursue aims
which are in essence amoral and egocentric.

It could also be maintained paradoxically that Pilenz
appears to revel in his constant breast-beating. His
guilt complex becomes the main motivation within his life.
He tells us, for example, that he has taken up a poorly
paid job as a social worker, more or less in order to assuage his restless conscience (p. 138). Remove Pilenz's
guilt complex and his character would soon lost its focus,
much in the same way that Mahlke's mouse and his attempts
to satisfy it form the substance of his being. Mahlke
conforms to the climate of his time by playing the hero
and hence unwittingly supports a criminal regime, in the
same way that Pilenz feels it his duty to suffer from a
guilt complex because of his involvement in Mahlke's

downfall.

The guilt complex to which Pilenz is so fervently attached has indeed many strange aspects. He fails to come to terms with the past and hence cannot establish a healthy relationship with the present. This inability stems in essence from the fact that his preoccupation with his own self blocks his avenue of approach to reality. Behind shuttered windows both Mahlke and Pilenz engage in emotional self-abuse. Mahlke, the superchild sets out for the playground of war in Russia and is but dimly aware that war involves killing. His war game expresses itself in childishly drawing tanks and crossing them out. Pilenz is also bilssfully unaware of the destruction of human life which is caused by Mahlke's quest for wholeness and Mahlke's preoccupation with his own ego. The narrator dismisses the invasion of France as the "Rummel in Frankreich" (p. 19) which is the equivalent of saying the "toings and froings in France;" and he is equally offhand about the German occupation of the Crimea and Rommel's activities in North Africa (p. 99). Pilenz, the narrator writing after 1959 (see p. 177), has not outgrown his original childish attitude. Like his hero he is concerned not about the killing that was war, but about the 'superman's downfall', and more particularly about whether he, the narrator, may be justified in viewing

himself as blameless. Like Mahlke, he is a do-it-your-
self redeemer who operates exclusively on his own home
territory. He is sorry for himself but not for others.
He has made self-pity into the supreme law within his own
walled city. He is a victim of moral blindness.

In the closing paragraphs of the 'novella' Pilenz
describes how what began with cat and mouse still torments
him to-day. We have no reason to doubt his word. The
narrator is haunted by the vision of Mahlke's disappearance, of what in German could be referred to as 'Untergang' which has the double meaning of going down (i.e.
diving) and of downfall. Mahlke haunts him from beyond
his watery grave. This first Adam conditions the narrator's attitudes and responses in the present. Unlike
the second Adam he offers no respite to his suffering, he
cannot heal his tormented soul. Pilenz may have acted
the betrayer in Mahlke's life, he may have played the cat
to Mahlke's mouse. However, in Mahlke's after-life Pilenz is certainly no longer the cat. He cannot even
switch roles. Only if Mahlke were to resurface, would
Pilenz gain release from his torment, for such a resurrection would provide proof that Pilenz did not bring
about Mahlke's downfall. This is a vain hope and it is a
sign of Pilenz's lack of realism that he attends meetings
of those survivors who gained a Knight's Cross during the

war and imagines that he could see Mahlke there (pp.
177-78).

Pilenz may be regarded as the cat in Mahlke's life
particularly if we view him as a representative of the
group attitude towards Mahlke. On the other hand it must
be admitted that Mahlke would not have proved susceptible
to the schoolboy's prank and fallen victim to the all-
enveloping atmosphere of National Socialism, had he not
some innate weakness. In any case, if Mahlke's larynx
is equated with the mouse, in other words if the mouse
sticks in his throat, then this would suggest that Mahlke
can indeed be considered to be the cat. Be that as it
may, Pilenz is not the cat in Mahlke's after-life. Over
fifteen years after the disappearance of Mahlke, it is
Mahlke who stalks Pilenz. The narrator is pursued also
in a slightly different way. He is trapped on the one
hand by the person of Grass as author within the 'novella'
into telling Mahlke's story and he is compelled on the
other hand by his own 'guilty' conscience to write the
biography of a person who during his life might have been
Pilenz's victim. The picture of the black cat as drawn
on the dust-cover of the 'novella' looks down from the
wall of Pilenz's mind and plays its game with the mouse
below. During the 'novella' the cat and the mouse have had
no fixed abode, they have had a shifting identity.

However, at the close of the story, Pilenz has lost all claims to the title of the cat.

In conclusion, it may be stated that the relationship of Mahlke and Pilenz has a more general significance. Günter Grass has stated this is one of his letters.[8] The story of Mahlke, he claims, exposes church, school, heroism and indeed the whole of society. The reader will readily see the applicability of this statement to the 'novella'.

Even though Pilenz proves to be an unreliable narrator and even though all his statements about Mahlke are qualified by this realisation, they both emerge as individuals who have only a partial understanding of their own situations. Both of them view their own lives and problems in purely personal terms. Private considerations overrule public considerations. Mahlke engages in war in order to compensate for what he considers to be his own deficiencies. He is not inspired by any sense of allegiance to the ideology of the political movement and the state which he is serving. Nor is there indication that he has any understanding of the political realities of the time. In his mindlessness he is exploited and corrupted by a criminal regime which awards the Knight's Cross to those who achieve military distinction in the pursuit of its aims (see quotation from *Über das*

Selbstverständliche). The fact that his humanity is de-
graded in this way is an indictment of the educational
system, institutionalised religion and the community to
which he belongs. In the last resort it could be claimed
that even he cannot be absolved from blame. In his defence it must be stated that he is still an adolescent at
the time of his death. Pilenz, on the other hand is viewing the events of youth from a distance of 15 years. The
passage of time should allow a balanced perspective. However, this is not the case. Pilenz still regards the
past in exclusively subjective terms. His viewpoint is
still characterised, so it appears, by the immaturity of
the adolescent. His mind is blinkered by the insistent
desire to rid himself of his feelings of guilt. His preoccupation with his own personal problems ensures that he
is unable to establish a relationship between the private
and the public spheres. Like Mahlke, he is amoral and
apolitical. He is incapable even of benefiting from hindsight. He fails in his attempt to cleanse his mind of
guilt and he fails to come to terms with the past. Guilt
in itself does not guarantee a realistic assessment of the
past. If Mahlke's behaviour implies criticism of "church,
school, heroism and indeed the whole of society," then
Pilenz's attitudes are obliquely condemnatory of the post-
war German reality.

Notes

1. Page numbering in *Katz und Maus* refers to the Luchterhand edition, Neuwied and Berlin, 1961.

2. John Reddick, *The 'Danzig Trilogy' of Günter Grass*
   (London: Secker and Warburg, 1975), p. 90.

3. Johanna E. Behrendt, "Die Ausweglosigkeit der mensch-
   lichen Natur. Eine Interpretation von Günter Grass'
   Katz und Maus," *Zeitschrift für deutsche Philologie*,
   Vol. 87 (1968), 546-62.

4. Hans Magnus Enzensberger, *Einzelheiten* (Suhrkamp,
   1962), p. 228.

5. Hermann Pongs, *Dichtung im gespalteten Deutschland*
   (Stuttgart, 1966), p. 36.

6. N. L. Thomas, "An analysis of Günter Grass' *Katz und
   Maus* with particular reference to the religious
   themes," *German Life and Letters*, Vol. XXVI (April,
   1973), 227-38.

7. Karl Korn, "Epitaph für Mahlke," *Frankfurter Allgemeine
   Zeitung*, 7.10.1961; also in Gert Loschütz, *Günter
   Grass in der Kritik* (Luchterhand, 1968), p. 31.

8. John Reddick, p. 23.

CHAPTER III

Hundejahre: The German and the Jew

Hundejahre more than the other two books of the Danzig Trilogy has incurred the disapproval of the critics,
particularly of Walter Jens in his article entitled significantly, "Das Pandämonium des Günter Grass."[1] Jens
objects especially to the triple perspective, the lack of
a central figure and the treatment of Heidegger. He produces the following conclusion: "die *Hundejahre* sind das
schlecht komponierte, aus einigen grandiosen, manchen
wackerroutinierten und zahlreichen sehr schwachen Episoden
bestehende, insgesamt viel zu lange und anfangs über Ge-
bühr verschlüsselte Buch eines bedeutenden, auf kleinem
Felde großen Autors und Selbstimitators, der sich diesmal
übernommen hat." (p. 88).

Though *Hundejahre* may be regarded as the least satisfying book of the Danzig Trilogy, much of the criticism of
it stems from a series of misconceptions, some fundamental, some less so. One obstacle to the appreciation of
the novel-- and this has been the case with nearly all
Grass's works since 1959-- has been the fact that almost

inevitably *Hundejahre* has been compared, and usually un-

favorably, with *Die Blechtrommel*. What needs to be em-

phasised here is that *Hundejahre* is part of a larger unity,

i.e. the Danzig Trilogy, and makes a contribution to the

whole which is different from the one which *Die Blech-*

trommel makes. In answer to Jens' criticism, Frank Richter

has produced the following defence: "Vielmehr sucht

Günter Grass nach der Abrechnung in der *Blechtrommel*, nach

den Fragen in *Katz und Maus*, in den *Hundejahren* nach einer

Antwort. Die *Hundejahre* sind die konsequente Weiterent-

wicklung der beiden vorausgegangenen Werke."[2] Further-

more, the triple perspective can to a large extent be

justified in that it accords with the underlying concept

of the book and in that the three narrators complement

each other in their attitude to the past and, wittingly

or unwittingly, produce the answer to which Frank Richter

refers. For those who accuse Grass of lack of control,[3]

it should be observed that the episodes are embedded in

a tightly structured system of interrelationships and as-

sociations which suggest quite the opposite of formless-

ness or lack of discipline. In attempting to counter

some of this criticism and to come to an understanding of

Hundejahre, let us look at the three principal aspects of

the novel, firstly, the narrative perspective, secondly,

the two main characters, and thirdly, the imagery. In

conclusion, we shall need to consider whether *Hundejahre*
may legitimately be considered as an extension of *Die*
Blechtrommel and *Katz und Maus*.

Narrative Perspective

As has already been mentioned, the reader has to
contend with three narrators in *Hundejahre*. The division
of the novel into three books is not surprising-- the
reader is accustomed to this form from *Die Blechtrommel*--
but the allocation of three different narrators to each
of the three books is, at least initially, somewhat bewildering, particularly since, as Kurt Batt observes,
there do not seem to be any differences in attitude between the three narrators.[4] The first book, 'Frühschichten', is related by Brauxel and covers the period from
1917 to the birth of Tulla in 1927; the second book,
'Liebesbriefe' is narrated by Harry Liebenau and deals
with the years from 1927 to 1945; and the third book,
entitled 'Materniaden', has as its narrator Walter Matern,
whose task it is to handle the post-war years. Brauxel,
who does not immediately reveal his identicality with
Amsel (and Haseloff and Goldmäulchen) supervises the other
two authors. He describes his role in the following
terms: "... er steht dem Bergwerk und dem Autorenkollek-
tiv vor, er zahlt die Vorschüsse, bestimmt die Termine

und wird die Korrekturen lesen." (p. 132).[5] The fact
that Brauxel employs his two colleagues is emphasised on
a number of occasions and his hold on the financial reins
is his means of exercising control over the two of them.
He is determined to exert pressure on his employees, and
is prepared, if need be, to write a conclusion which
would follow immediately on what he chooses to call "des
Schauspielers Bekenntnisse." (p. 132). Harry Liebenau
acknowledges his financial dependence on Brauxel (see p.
356) and provides us with an example of how the editor
intervenes and determines the content of the book: "Und
mit dem Schlußmärchen muß ich beginnen, denn Brauxel
telegrafiert dringlich: "wassermannkonjunktion rückt
näher stop knochenberg türmen stop fehlgeburt einleiten
stop hund laufen lassen und schluß machen rechtzeitig.'"
(p. 356). The last three items refer to vital elements
in Brauxel's and Grass's denunciation of the German treatment of the Jews, of the philosophy of Heidegger and of
National Socialism in general. Brauxel also dictates to
Matern how he should deal with his confessions and the
latter acknowledges his subservience to his employer,
though he does so in a partially rebellious and indelicate
manner: "Was will Brauxel? Er löchert Matern. Nicht
genug, daß er sich für ein paar Kröten Vorschuß seiten-
lang auskotzen muß; jetzt hat er ihm wöchentlich Rapport

zu geben: 'Wieviele Seiten heute? Wieviele morgen? Wird
die Episode mit Sawatzki und Frau Nachwirkungen zeigen?...
In welcher Buhne der Männertoilette Köln-Hauptbahnhof
fand sich der Marschbefehl in den Schwarzwald? Geschrieben oder gestochen?'" (p. 473). The editor in chief, the
Jewish businessman, reasserts his intellectual superiority over Matern, who once assaulted him physically: he
takes intellectual revenge on a person who comprehends
the post-war world more or less exclusively in terms of
physical revenge.

There are occasions when the reader might suspect
that the editor is indeed correcting the text of his co-
authors or even making additions. In the ninety-first
'Materniade' which is also described as being 'einsich-
tig' we read the following: "Blase die Rache ab, Matern!
Locke den Hund Pluto nie mehr hinter dem Ofen hervor.
Genug entnazifiziert! Mache deinen Frieden mit dieser
Welt; oder verbinde die Pflicht, auf Herz, Milz und
Nieren zu hören, mit der Sicherheit monatlicher Ein-
künfte." (p. 546). The reader is accustomed to have the
narrator address himself in the third person-- this occurs in both *Die Blechtrommel* and *Hundejahre*-- but this
advice seems-- in realistic terms-- to be conveyed by the
voice of the editor-in-chief, and not by Matern himself.
The same voice intones a cry of despair when mention is

made of the near hopelessness of persuading Matern to
change his ways and give up his odyssey of revenge:
"Welcher Hammerschlag muß ihn treffen, damit er abläßt
von Leuten, die ihn hinter sich hören, den Knirscher."
(p. 547). The reader has no means of determining whether
this is indeed a rare moment of disembodied insight on
the part of Matern or whether it is an editorial intervention.

Brauxel alias Amsel does give us a clear-cut indication of what his objective is in supervising the compi-
lation of this diary. He quotes ironically from Wein-
berger's book entitled *Geschlecht und Charakter* and thereby explains in pompous terms what his aim is as an editor:
"und es ist, vorläufig gesprochen, vielleicht die welt-
historische Bedeutung und das ungeheure Verdienst des Ju-
dentums kein anderes, als den Arier immerfort zum Bewußtsein seiner Selbst zu bringen, ihn an sich ('an sich'
festgedrückt) zu mahnen." (p. 220). Amsel, the Jew and
artist, relentlessly pursues the objective, that of mobil-
ising Matern's awareness of himself and that of his fellow-countrymen. It is Amsel's task to remind Matern of
the act of brutality he committed against his blood brother and to remind the Germans of the crimes which were
perpetrated against the Jews. However, Matern is resis-
tant to the truth and is reluctant to dredge the

embarrassing facts of his own past to the surface. He
admits-- or pretends to admit-- that he has no memory:
"Er besitzt einen Löffel, aber kein Gedächtnis. Alle wollen ihm zu einem verhelfen: der zentrale Hund; die mit
Luft gefüllte Konservendose; der englische Fragebogen;
und jetzt schickt Brauxel Vorschüsse und setzt Termine,
die von den Auftritten und Abgängen gewisser Planeten bestimmt werden: Matern soll von damals quasseln." (p. 431).
In fact the three narrators can be differentiated one
from another in terms of the quality of their memory.
Brauxel says of himself that he still takes pleasure in
recollecting the past accurately (p. 19) and then goes on
to explain how Matern's ancestors, and especially the
grandmother, were subject to theatricality and violent
responses (see p. 28). He regards the recollection of
the past as an act of narration. He says of himself:
"nichts erzählt sich Brauxel lieber als Märchen." (p. 29).
Thus his mission is to persuade Matern to relate his
life's story. Narration is for him a form of confession,
a coming to terms with the past. Amsel endeavours to prod
Matern's memory into activity, for this is the only road
by which Matern can be saved from damnation. It is in
this sense that Goldmäulchen's exhortation in the inferno
of Jenny's bar should be understood: "'denn solange wir
noch Geschichten erzählen, leben wir. Solange uns etwas

einfällt,...solange uns Geschichten noch zu unterhalten
vermögen, vermag keine Hölle uns unterhaltsam sein. Du
bist dran, Walter! Erzähle, solang Dir Dein Leben lieb
ist!'" (p. 641).

Amsel's memory is active and accurate; Matern's
memory is sluggish and recalcitrant, whilst Harry Liebenau is described as having a "Schubkästchengedächtnis."
(p. 568). Admittedly, this label is produced by Walter
Matern in a fit of ill-humour. Nevertheless, closer investigation will reveal the validity of this observation.
Matern proceeds to substantiate his statement by giving
details of how Harry's mind works: "Ordnet, wo er geht
steht sitzt, enggeschriebene Zettelchen. Kein Thema, zu
dem ihm nicht Fakten einfallen..." (p. 568). Brauxel has
a similar impression of him when he interviews him in
connection with his application for the post of author of
the second book. Liebenau has accumulated a mass of facts
about Danzig and Brauxel has to admit that his own knowledge is increased during the course of the interrogation
(see p. 133). Liebenau also produces evidence against
himself: "der... eignete sich nur zum Zugucken und Nach-
plappern." (p. 360) is what he says of himself; on another occasion he produces the confession: "Das war
schon immer meine Stärke: hinterdreinzockeln, neugierig
sein, zuhören." (p. 286). Though Liebenau's memory is

retentive, and in many spheres comprehensive, he is capable of distorting and suppressing facts, especially in
instances in which his conscience is troubled. In one
case he denies that any members of his school class were
involved in denouncing Oswald Brunies, his German teacher
and father of Jenny Brunies, though in the next sentence
he concedes that they did mention the fact that he had
been eating sweets (see p. 334). He hides behind the
collective 'we' and tries to shuffle off any responsibility. In the same section he produces another denial
which does not carry conviction: "Ich glaube nicht, daß
ich es war, der am Ende sagte: 'Gewiss hat Studienrat
Brunies drei- oder höchstens viermal von den Cebiontablet-
ten gekostet.'" (p. 336). Finally, after producing an
apology for himself, he concedes that he did level a dam-
aging political accusation against his teacher, the fact
that Brunies did not display a flag on the Führer's
birthday. His memory is obviously at fault when he adopts
a self-righteous attitude towards Matern, dissociates
himself from him by claiming that he would be subject to
the same incriminations if he were a few years younger
(p. 568). His behaviour towards Jenny is hypocritical
and borders on treachery. For example, he refuses to see
her when she comes to take her final leave of him. The
door-bell rings and the Liebenau family will not open the

door. Harry is aware of the falseness of his behaviour
and he is left with a troubled conscience (see pp. 344-45).
Liebenau's prevarications and his treachery remind the
reader of another narrator who adopts similar attitudes,
but also possesses a similar disposition i.e. Heini Pilenz in *Katz und Maus*. Both are passive, both like to
think of themselves as objective witnesses, they suffer
from a feeling of malcontent and yet even after the passage of a decade or so, they are still unable to view the
Nazi period in perspective. They both write out of a dim
sense of guilt, but this does not stem from any real understanding of the past.

Like Matern, Harry addresses himself in the third
person and enjoys rare moments of insight-- or are these
yet again examples of editorial intervention? He describes himself as "ein Vielwisser, der Bücher mit his-
torischem und philosophischem Inhalt durcheinander las..."
(p. 375) and as "ein Phantast, der viel log, leise sprach,
rot wurde wenn, dies und das glaubte und den andauernden
Krieg als Ergänzung des Schulunterrichtes betrachtete."
(p. 375). Though-- irony of ironies-- he intends to become a historian (p. 346), he is incapable of establishing a meaningful relationship between facts. His facts
are divorced from reality. Accordingly he indulges in
wrong-thinking. His haphazard reading of various authors

whom he reveres from time to time so colours his thinking
that it forms a mental blockage, a barrier between him
and the outside world: "Mit Hilfe dieser Vorbilder ge-
lang es ihm, einen tatsächlichen, aus menschlichen Knochen
erstellten Berg mit mittelalterlichen Allegorien zuzu-
schütten. Er erwähnte den Knochenberg, der in Wirklichkeit zwischen dem Troyl und dem Kaiserhaufen gen Himmel
schrie, in seinem Tagebuch als Opferstätte, errichtet,
damit das Reine sich im Lichten ereigne, indem es das
Reine umlichte und so das Licht stifte." (pp. 375-76).

He explains his failure to break through to reality
and his inadequate powers of reasoning in terms of his
attachment to Tulla, who is represented in the novel as
the embodiment of evil and maliciousness: "Auch war ich
von Anfang an verseucht. Selbt als Oberschülerin, in
einigermaßen reinlichen Kleidern blieb ihr der Knochenleimgeruch; und ich haftete und wehrte mich kaum." (p.
330). The image of bones interlinks Tulla, the concentration camp of Stutthof, the bone-glue which is used in
Liebenau's woodyard and the soap, which, made out of
bones, is the means of ensuring cleanliness and purity.
Elsewhere, Harry Liebenau employs the same set of associations to suggest that Tulla has benumbed his senses
and holds him in her thrall: "Immer schon war ich hinter
meiner Cousine her, genauer gesagt: zwei Schritte hinter

Dir und Deinem Knochenleimgeruch versuchte ich Dir zu folgen." (p. 147). Poisoned by her bitterness and violence,
he carries out her every bidding, seeing little reason
retrospectively-- with the 'historical' detachment of
more than sixteen years-- to reproach himself for having
done so. His blind submission to Tulla and his lack of
critical awareness after the passage of time are emblematic, on the one hand, of his desire to shrug off responsibility and to present himself as the helpless victim of
the atmosphere prevailing at the time, and on the other
hand, of his intellectual and emotional inability to face
up to the realities of the past and present.

It is clear then that the three narrators incorporate,
each in his own way, a different attitude to the past:
Amsel sees and understands, Harry Liebenau sees but does
not understand and Walter Matern neither sees nor understands. Both Liebenau and Matern suffer from a defective
vision, both stand in need of 'miraculous spectacles'.
If one regards the three narrators as victim, witness and
man of action as does Volker Neuhaus,[6] then one could accept such a statement only if one were to add the qualification that the author of the love-letters, whose very
name suggests a garden of love, is in reality, quite the
opposite of an apostle of love and is by no means to be
considered as an unbiassed witness. A further qualifica-

tion might point to the fact that the victim and man of action begin to change roles in the third book of the novel-- this is something we shall need to discuss later.

Harry is presented as an apolitical individual, a person who lacks any political maturity. It can be claimed-- and will be claimed-- that Amsel tries to enlighten his blood brother, Walter Matern. One of his purposes in having the diary written is to subject Matern to a process of education. Amsel, educator and artist, appears to be making no such attempt with Liebenau. If Amsel pursues an educative aim in the case of Liebenau, it is rather that Liebenau is offered up as a demonstration lesson of how not to behave. Liebenau makes a revealing statement at the beginning of the 'Love Letters', one of which throws light on Harry's attitude to himself of on the editor's attitude to his colleague or perhaps even on both: "man rät mir, Dich (i.e. Tulla) und Deinen Rufnamen an den Anfang zu setzen, Dich, da Du überall Stoff warst, bist und sein wirst, formlos anzusprechen, als beginne ein Brief. Dabei erzähle ich mir, nur und unheilbar mir..." The word 'unheilbar'-- and its emphatic position-- suggest an attempt on the part of Liebenau to defend himself by claiming that he is a prisoner of his own character and, coupled with references to Tulla's insidious influence, to present himself as the helpless

victim of his own personality and of the climate of his
times.   Equally well, the idea of Liebenau's incurability
may remind us of the fact that the editor-in-chief does
not try to alter his colleague's mode of thinking, preferring to concentrate his attention on Matern, the more aggressive and violent of the two co-authors.

The narrators may be compared-- and their characters
analysed-- in terms of the quality of their memory.   At
the same time the three of them assume a representative
function, for Liebenau and Matern are a reflection of the
German population at large.   These are the arguments which
need to be produced if one wishes to counter Jens' criti-
cisms which were mentioned in the opening paragraphs of
this chapter.   Harry Liebenau describes how at the end of
the war the Germans wished to indulge in a collective act
of amnesia: "Vergessen wollen alle die Knochenberge und
Massengräber, die Fahnenhalter und Parteibücher, die
Schulden und die Schuld." (p. 427).   Both Liebenau and
Matern share this general tendency, the desire to make a
fresh start, to make the year 1945 the year zero, as
though the past had never existed.   Like the dog, the two
co-authors seek a new master in the West (see p. 427).
The dog finds Matern, whilst the two narrators are engaged
by Amsel.   Both are impenitent and yet in their sub-con-
science an uneasy conscience makes itself dimly felt.

They are emblematic in their forgetfulness of the German attitude to the past. Amsel also refers-- in ironic manner-- to the Germans' mindlessness, their inclination to erase the past from their memories: "Ach, wie sind sie geheimnisvoll und erfüllt von gottwohlgefälliger Vergeßlichkeit! So kochen sie ihr Erbsensüppchen auf blauen Gasflammen und denken sich nichts dabei." (p. 646). This remark, coupled with Amsel's reference to the German nation's potentiality for producing the original scarecrow ('die Urvogelscheuche') does not fail to hit the mark in the subterranean passages of Matern's mind, for it provokes him into throwing the pen-knife away yet again.

The narrative perspective in the three books of *Hundejahre* is largely determined by the differing attitude of the three co-authors to the past. Both Liebenau and Matern, like the narrators in the other two books of the Danzig Trilogy, write out of a sense of guilt, "im Fall Matern aus pathetischem Schuldverlangen." (see p. 71, Chapter I). Like Pilenz, Liebenau and Matern have something to hide. Furthermore, Amsel confesses the indebtedness of the three narrators to Oskar Matzerath and thereby suggests similarities in the mode of narration of the two respective novels: "Frühschichten Liebesbriefe Materniaden: Brauxel und seine Mitautoren gingen bei jemandem in die Schule, der zeit seines Lebens fleißig war, auf

lackiertem Blech." (p. 117). Accordingly, the three narrators employ a style of detachment which varies little
in fact from book to book and achieves the same alienating
effect as in *Die Blechtrommel*. However, their attitudes
differ, as we have already suggested, in that their characters and motivation are dissimilar. Amsel assumes a
humoristic, ironical approach and is in any case dealing
with that period of time during which the friendship of
the two schoolboys had not been subjected to any undue
strain. For example, it is not Amsel who describes the
assault which Matern and his comrades launched against
him. Liebenau adopts an air of spurious objectivity,
since he wishes to play the role of the innocent, non-
involved spectator. Matern makes every effort to conceal
his participation in the attack on Amsel and thus his
narration is a continuous act of dissimulation. Even
though both Liebenau and Matern are in the last resort
untrustworthy as narrators, the reader has a surer grip
on reality in *Hundejahre* than is the case in *Die Blechtrommel*. His orientation is much more secure, because
Amsel, the editor-in-chief, provides him with a set of
criteria in accordance with which he may assess the re-
liability of Liebenau's and Matern's statements. In addition, the imagery and the episodes also reinforce the
didactic objectives which Brauxel pursues. As in *Die*

Blechtrommel there is a discrepancy between the assumed
point of view of the narrator and the messages conveyed
in coded form by the imagery and the episodes. The objective correlatives, for example, the dog, and the individual stories liberate themselves from the narrator,
acquire an independent status and undermine the statements of the narrator, as it were behind his back. For
instance, the episode in which Harry Liebenau and his
father are invited to see the Führer and manage to see
only the dog Prinz, achieves a satirical effect without
Liebenau, the narrator, intending that it should do so.
The same point could be made in connection with Liebenau's
description of the final stages of the war in Berlin in
terms of a military search for the Führer's dog. It can
be maintained with justification that there is little or
no difference in style in the language employed by each
narrator. However, it could be claimed that episode, imagery, the not implausible relationship between the editor
and his colleagues and their motivation divert attention
from the basic similarity of style in the three books.

The Two Main Characters

Having considered the narrative perspective, our next
task is to look at the central theme of the novel, that
is, the relationship between Eddi Amsel and Walter Matern,

Jew and Gentile, artist and man of action. On at least

two occasions, Amsel makes a clear-cut, more or less self-

evident statement about the substance of the novel. For

example, he describes *Hundejahre*, though the possibility

exists that Brauxel may be referring merely to the first

book, as "diese Schrift, die von Walter Matern, der Hündin

Senta, der Weichsel, Eduard Amsel und seinen Vogelscheuchen

handelt..." (p. 95). The arrangement of the items in

this clause is particularly interesting in that Matern and

the dog form a pair as do Amsel and his scarecrows, whilst

they are separated by the name of the river, which, as

Michael Hollington observes, is invoked as an image of the

course of history. One might legitimately regard the

diary to which Grass has given the name *Hundejahre* as an

artistic attempt-- on the part of Amsel and of Grass--

to build a bridge across the river and thus bring the Jew

and the German closer together. The other quotation also

places emphasis on the friendship of Matern and Amsel as

the main content of the novel and justifies the book's

length in terms of the trials to which this friendship is

subjected: "Freundschaften, die während oder nach Prügel-

eien geschlossen wurden, müssen sich, das wissen wir alle

aus atemberaubenden Filmen, noch oft und atemberaubend

bewähren. Auch der Freundschaft Amsel-Matern werden in

diesem Buch-- allein deswegen wird es sich in die Länge

ziehen-- noch viele Proben auferlegt werden müssen." (p.
43). This quotation establishes once again the relationship between Amsel and Matern as the central theme of the
novel and also provides an example of Amsel's humorous
and ironical attitude to the events of his own life. His
non-serious treatment of the subject in hand achieves a
distancing and alienating effect, thus encouraging a critical response in the mind of the reader. Ambiguity also
places the reader on his guard: he is unable to determine whether the word 'friendship' is to be understood
ironically as virtually the opposite of what friendship
should be or whether it should be regarded as an optimistic reference to what their relationship should or might
become.

From the outset, Amsel presents himself as having a
lively, highly imaginative mind which is constantly ob-
serving the people and events around him. He speaks of
his "wacher Sinn für die vielgestaltete Realität." (p. 40),
maintains that this is the basis of his art, that of
building scarecrows, and even in the process of being tormented by his persecutors, "wollten seine in Fett ver-
packten grüngrauen Äugelchen das Beobachten, Abschätzen,
das sachliche Wahrnehmen typischer Bewegungen nicht auf-
geben." (p. 42). His sense of humour is constantly in
evidence and he is not disinclined to play tricks on the

reader. At one stage, for example, he describes himself--
quite accurately-- as "der beweglichste Held," adding to
this statement the words, "Brauxel ausgenommen" at a time
when the reader has not had the chance to discover that
Amsel, Brauxel, Haseloff and Goldmäulchen are one and the
same person (p. 32). There are many occasions when Amsel
embarrasses the reader, by leaving him in a state of uncertainty. On one occasion, Amsel claims in conversation
with August Pokriefke, Tulla's father, that he has never
heard of Adolf Hitler (p. 197). One critic certainly
takes this statement at its face value and interprets it
as an example of Amsel's naive ignorance of political affairs, this ignoring the possibility of it being an instance of Amsel's ironic playfulness. He tells us that
his profession consisted from the outset in the invention
of scarecrows (p. 32). He tries to maintain that, unlike
the normal run of scarecrows his products can cause panic
amongst the birds, even though they are "zwecklos und gegen nichts gebaut." (p. 40). He produces a similar claim
at a later stage even though he does add a qualification
which seems at least partially to be at variance with the
initial statement: "Dennoch baute Eddi Amsel keine Vogelscheuchen gegen die ihm vertrauten Spatzen und Atzeln;
gegen niemanden baute er, aus formalen Gründen. Allen-
falls hatte er vor, einer gefährlich produktiven Umwelt

seinerseits Produktivität zu beweisen." (p. 218). What
he would be unable to deny is that his scarecrows, the
products of his art, do have an effect on human beings,
in particular, on Walter Matern. On the first occasion
on which Matern sees his own counterfeit in the figure of
a scarecrow, he changes from being Amsel's assailant to
being his protector (p. 42); on the second occasion,
Matern grinds his teeth as a sign of displeasure and as
an indication that the joke has gone too far (p. 237)--
not long afterwards, Amsel is attacked by nine hooded figures, of whom one is his friend Matern, and loses his
thirty-two teeth; and on the third occasion when Matern
sees the scarecrows exhibited in Brauxel's mine, he is
disturbed, but still unable to accept the past as a reality. On the basis of these three examples, it is clear
that Amsel's scarecrows do influence human behaviour,
though the most desirable effect is not necessarily always
achieved. When Amsel produces scarecrows of the SA men
and has them raise their arms in party salute, he once
again tries to maintain that he is not intending any criticism: "keinerlei Kritik wolle er äußern, sondern Pfunds-
kerle wie Schweinehunde, gemischt und gewürfelt, wie nun
mal das Leben spiele, mit künstlerischen Mitteln produ-
zieren." (p. 237). It is not clear whether the reader is
to accept such a statement at its face-value or whether

Amsel is merely feigning innocence. The impact Amsel's
artistic products make on Matern is such that the SA men,
headed by Matern, resolve to teach the artist a lesson,
to judge by Sawatzki's statement after the war (see p.
450).

Amsel is certainly an enigmatic character and is by
no means flawless. He persuades Matern, for example, to
join the SA, because this is his only way of obtaining
party uniforms for his scarecrows-- "halb aus Jux und
halb aus Neugierde, besonders aber damit Amsel zu jenen
extrem braunen Uniformstücken kam, nach denen er die Ge-
rüste zukünftiger Scheuchen verlangten, gab Walter Matern
Schrittchen um Schrittchen nach." (p. 225). Amsel thus
precipitates indirectly what is referred to elsewhere as
"Amsels Leiden" (p. 115). Matern changes uniform and, in
keeping with the time-honoured principle that 'Kleider
machen Leute', he changes his attitude to his blood brother. Presumably, Amsel is able to exert influence over
his friend during that period of time in which they wear
each other's clothes (see p. 87-- "Dieser Kleiderwechsel,
das sei vorweggenommen, war während Jahren ein Bestand-
teil, wenn nicht Bindeglied der Freundschaft zwischen
Walter Matern und Eduard Amsel."). Amsel's decision to
persuade Matern to join the SA could be taken as evidence
that he is capable of pursuing art for its own sake as is

the case with Jenny Brunies, the ballet dancer, who in
some ways may be regarded as his female counterpart.   In
the post-war period Amsel remains a contradictory character in that he himself is in his own fashion making a
profit from the West German economic miracle;   he regards
himself as "ein nüchterner Mann der freien Marktwirtschaft," (p. 28) having also been a person of some influence when the black market was still flourishing (see
p. 428).   In short, Amsel is a paradoxical individual who
is subject to conflicting interests and impulses: he is
not 'astrein' in the political sense (see p. 518 and elsewhere), but also in terms of his own personality.   He ac-
cepts-- and embodies-- the contradictions of life and
tries to convince Matern that life by its very nature is
impure.   This is Amsel's educative objective in the years
after the military defeat of National Socialism.   It is
quite clear that after 1945 Amsel intends that his art
should have a didactic effect.   Art and artist mature, so
it would be claimed, under the impact of National Socialism.

What must be obvious by now is that Amsel can scarcely be discussed in isolation.   Almost inevitably one is
forced to discuss him in relationship to Matern, for the
two of them in tandem constitute, as we have already observed, the essential substance of this novel.   It could

be maintained that the two of them are interdependent, relying on each other for their very existence. They belong together, an inseparatable pair of blood brothers, like God and the Devil (see p. 73), or Cain and Abel (see p. 285). They complement each other in many ways: chief narrator and co-narrator as well as object of the narration, observer and observed, artist and man of action, would-be rather confessor and reluctant confessor, Jew and German, master and man, then victim and persecutor and finally, a reversal of roles, mentor and recalcitrant pupil. Two events are decisive elements in their relationship: the one occurs in the first few pages of the novel-- Matern's act of throwing the knife into the river-- and is repeated in the closing stages of the book, immediately before the visit down the mine (see p. 647); the other is the assault which Matern and his comrades launch against Amsel with their fists (pp. 252-56). The knife which Matern throws into the Vistula is emblematic of the friendship of the two boys, for it was a present which Amsel gave to his friend (p. 13) and was used to draw the blood with which their blood brothership was sealed (p. 16). By throwing the knife away, Matern commits a symbolic act of violence and tries to repudiate the friendship. He severs a bond which links the two of them. The fall of the knife into the river marks allusively Matern's fall from grace. Brauxel describes the episode with the knife as Matern's attempt to break away from his dependence on his blood brother: (Matern) "geriet in Abhängigkeit. Amsel machte ihn zum Paslack. In kurzatmigen Revolten versuchte er auszubrechen. Die Geschichte mit dem Taschenmesser war solch ein ohnmächtiger Versuch; denn Amsel blieb ihm, so kurzbeinig dicklich er durch die Welt kugelte, immer voraus." (p. 72). After having watched his friend cast the knife into the river, Amsel bets that Matern will accept a knife from him, if he presents him with one (p. 18). In the penultimate chapter of the novel, Amsel wins his bet (p. 632)-- Matern does accept a knife from him, in fact the selfsame knife, for Amsel has had the mouth of the Vistula dredged (p. 634). Shortly afterwards, however, Matern rebels once more against the person who has established himself as his intellectual and spiritual superior (p. 647). Amsel views this merely as a temporary defeat, remains undaunted and vows that the knife will be returned to his blood brother (p. 647). Matern remains impenitent and mindless, whilst Amsel intends to keep on prodding his memory into activity and awakening his powers of conscience. The episode with the knife spans the whole novel and constitutes a cohesive factor within the work as a whole.

Whilst Amsel's mode of expression is artistic, Matern's mode of expression is violent. Whilst Amsel thinks
with his head, Matern thinks with his fist. When Matern
starts to defend Amsel against the tormenting of the local children, this is not a fundamental transformation on
the part of Matern, but rather that he has decided to
change the object on which he wishes to vent his violence.
When he switches allegiance again, it is Amsel who bears
the full brund of his physical assault. Violence and
treachery are constant characteristics of his behaviour.
His biographer traces Matern's irrational impulses back
to his ancestors, whom he describes as "entsetzliche Auf-
rührer" (p. 281)-- the episode with the knife is labelled
significantly as an act of rebellion. Matern is proud
of belonging to this long line of robbers and arsonists,
chief amongst whom was the medieval 'Räuber Materna' (see
p. 10, p. 54, p. 62, and p. 94). Matern reverts to the
behaviour of his ancestors in the same way as the dog degenerates into a wolf. Like his forefathers, he has an
innate propensity for theatricality and "große, ja opern-
hafte Auftritte." (p. 28). This being so, it is not surprising that as an actor he is naturally inclined to trag-
ic rather than comic roles-- "Matern meinte, das Tragische
sei bei ihm ohnehin mitgegeben, und nur in Komischen
hapere es noch bei ihm." (p. 219). Unlike Amsel, Matern

suffers from a defective sense of the ridiculous which is accompanied almost inevitably with an inability to laugh at himself, a lack of self-criticism and self-awareness, and an incapacity for keeping things in perspective. His stunted sense of humour requires the nourishment which only Amsel, "Gottes Eintänzer" (see p. 625), can provide.

When Matern takes over as autobiographer in the third book of the novel and starts to depict the post-war period, he is concerned to polish up his image. He maintains that he has no memory, or pretends he has no memory. He tries to exclude himself from the group of SA men who attacked Amsel (see p. 435). Ostensibly, he is unable to recall his 'Frühschichten', to establish contact with the lower layers of his mind. Characteristically for post-war Germany, he attempts to regrade himself in the course of an interrogation conducted by an allied officer, Brooks by name (presumably another alias for Brauxel). For example, he gives an aura of respectibility to his robber ancestors by reclassifying them as 'Freiheitshelden' (see p. 435, p. 460, p. 475). On other occasions he emphasises that his forefathers have always defended the weak (p. 465) and that Simon Materna in particular would have set the world aflame in order to feed the hungry and succour those in bondage (p. 643). The greatest deficiencies in his memory emerge in connection

with the assault on his blood brother. In this sphere he
does not content himself with merely restructuring the
past but produces rather the big lie which is startling--
and almost amusing-- in its gigantic departure from the
truth: "Ja, ich habe ihn geliebt. Und sie haben ihn mir
genommen... Aber die anderen waren stärker, und ich konnte
nur ohnmächtig zusehen, wie Terror diese Stimme zerbrach.
Eddi, mein Eddi!" (p. 465). In the course of the radio
discussion he claims that in an emergency he would risk
his own life in the defence of a Jew and that his friend
was beaten up "ohne daß ich ihm helfen konnte." (p. 609).
Only the intervention of the 'Erkenntnisbrille' reveals
the truth which Matern is in any case still loath to accept.

Though Matern is keen to gloss over or blot out the
unsavoury aspects of his own career, he is quite prepared
to act out the role of judge in post-war Germany, i.e.
try to come to terms with the past by judging others rather than himself. He appears to be unaware of the paradoxical nature of his behaviour. This is, however, per-
fectly in keeping with the fact that he prefers to avoid
analysing his own situation and tends to operate within a
framework of predetermined roles or images. Thus, bliss-
fully unaware of his own vulnerability, he launches himself into a campaign of vengeance upon those who in his

blinkered opinion did him wrong during the Third Reich.
In the process he frequently metes out vengeance, not on
those who perpetrated the original act of injustice, but
on people or things associated with them. Under the ban-
ner of "unbewältigte Vergangenheit" he kills a canary
(p. 462), throws a stamp collection into the stove (p.
463) and in a fit of frustration wreaks retribution on
Heidegger by taking his gate off its hinges (p. 477). In
his journeyings through West Germany Matern wields his
penis like a sword of vengeance and the extremes to which
he resorts are in themselves a condemnation of the would-
be judge himself. In a scene which is especially typical
of his perverted thinking and behaviour, he rapes Inge,
the wife of Jochen Sawatzki, who expelled him from the SA,
in a confession box, whilst she must confess her sins to
the dog who acts as the priest (pp. 486-87). In all seriousness he can claim that he has come "zu richten mit
schwarzem Hund und einer Liste Namen in Herz, Milz und
Nieren geschnitten." (p. 449). The mere mention of the
dog reminds the reader of the bestiality of the Nazi period and the reference to "Herz, Milz und Nieren" recalls
that Tulla and the dog were fed on offal whilst they lived
together in the kennel (p. 172). He even manages to intone a general denunciation of the Germans en masse,
thereby ignoring the beam in his own eye: "Aber das ist

wieder mal typisch: von einem Extrem ins andere und immer
den Teufel mit Beelzebub. Dabei ehrliche Makler, aber mit
wenig Witz und viel zuviel Behagen. Außerdem lernen sie
nie aus ihrer Geschichte: meinen immer, die anderen. Wollen partout die Kirche im Dorf und niemals gegen Wind-
mühlen. Soweit ihre Zunge klingt: Wesen und Welt genese.
Salome des Nichts. Gehn über Leichen nach Wolkenkuckucks-
heim. Haben immer den Beruf verfehlt." (p. 522). Even
in these sweeping generalisations, some of which do apply,
ironically, to Matern, he is reciting a series of clichés,
as it were, leitmotifs, which, as he constantly reminds
us, can easily develop into 'Mordmotive' (eg. p. 543 and
p. 647 and elsewhere). There is also one occasion when
he pontificates about "unsere immer noch unbewältigte
Vergangenheit." (p. 536). His pronouncements and his behaviour suggest mindlessness, his inability or reluctance
to use his 'Kopf'. The roles which are allotted to him
when he works for the radio company are probably correct
indications of his psychological state and of the fact
that the basic features of his character have not under-
gone any change: "Matern, die dröhnende Funkpädagogik,
spricht grollt röhrt als permanenter Räuber, Wolf, Auf-
rührer und Judas." (p. 567).

Though Matern remains impenitent, reluctant to admit
his complicity in the assault on Amsel-- in fact rebelling

in the likeness of his ancestors against this allegation--
there are some dim, muffled intimations from his subconscious, almost from a subterranean level, that a realisation of his wrongdoing may be possible. Admittedly he
flees to the East in reacting against the findings of the
radio discussion and admittedly he hurls the knife back
into the water, yet he is oppressed by a sense of unease:
he states for example that he has something between his
teeth that will not come out (p. 449). He is haunted by
the picture of climbing over the barrier which separates
civilised from uncivilised behaviour: "Seit Hundejahren
tagtäglich über den gleichen Zaun." (p. 524). Though his
mind still revolves round the idea of venting his wrath
on others, he is horrified by the sight of the pudding
depicting thirty-two human teeth: he retreats to the
toilet and "erbricht sich gründlich und jahrelang." (p.
525). The torture of his own inner hell has begun even
before Amsel takes him below ground to view the scarecrows, portraying in extreme form the modes of behaviour
of which Matern has been guilty. The constant repetition
of the words, "der liebe Gott schaut zu." (eg. p. 444 and
elsewhere) is an oblique indication of the possibility
of divine retribution. Matern is aware of his own de-
pravity, but then promptly transfers his sense of guilt
to others, who are then made into the scapegoat for his

own wrongdoings. It is significant that he describes
himself as a human scarecrow even before he visits the
underground scarecrow factory. He has disintegrated into
a series of roles, before he inspects the exhibition of
scarecrows depicting dehumanised activities: "Schaut
mich an: glatzköpfig auch innen. Ein leerer Schrank
voller Uniformen jeder Gesinnung. Ich war rot, trug
braun, ging in Schwarz, verfärbte mich: rot. Spuckt mich
an: Allwetterkleidung, verstellbare Hosenträger, Steh-
aufmännchen läuft auf Bleisolen, oben kahl, innen hohl,
außen mit Stoffresten behängt, roten braunen schwarzen--
anspucken! Aber Brauxel spuckt nicht, sondern schickt
Vorschüsse... während ich knirsche: Ein Glatzkopf will
Gerechtigkeit. Es geht hier um Zähne, zweiunddreißig."
(p. 514). This passage demonstrates most clearly how,
in quite literal terms, he punishes himself through the
medium of others, in other words, tortures himself in his
odyssey of revenge, thereby producing a sense of dislocation and a loss of identity. It is Amsel's mission in
life to reintegrate his friend, to make him whole.

Imagery

As usual Grass introduces us to the central symbol of
the novel on the dust-cover of the book and as usual a
statement can be found inside the book to the effect that

the author designed the dust-cover. The picture of the
dog's head conjures up at least five sets of associations:
firstly, it is a reminder of the period of time during
which Germany went to the dogs (see p. 185) and until
Brauxel takes possession of the dog, there is no suggestion that the 'dog-days' or 'dog-years' came to an end
with the demise of National Socialism; secondly, the dog
is black, a colour emblematic of evil and mourning;
thirdly, the dog's head and neck are made up of the bones
of the arm and hand and the fingers are positioned in the
way a child-- or an adult-- would place them in order to
cast a shadow upon the wall-- the red tongue is a symbolical extra; fourthly, the arm is outstretched at the correct level for the Nazi party salute; and fifthly, the
bones coupled with the associations already mentioned call
to mind one of the end results of the Third Reich, that
is, the extermination of the Jews, as examplified in the
novel by the 'Knochenberg' at the concentration camp of
Stutthof near Danzig. It could be mentioned additionally
that the fingers so arranged in the shape of a dog's head
could easily be converted into a fist and thus recall the
episode in which "Arbeiter der Stirn und Faust" aimed a
series of blows at the head of a Jew.

Even if one disregards the dust-cover, it is clear
that the dog is a central image within the novel. At the

beginning of the first 'Materniade' the autobiographer
tells us that this is so-- and in fact with references to
this post-war period, rather than to the pre-45 era. ("Der
Hund steht zentral" is the first sentence of his book--
p. 431). A parallel is constantly being drawn between
the dog and the Hitler regime. Events in the life of the
dog are being placed side by side with events which are
connected directly or indirectly with Hitler. It is perhaps not irrelevant and certainly interesting to note
that Winifred Wagner did address Hitler as Wolf. Grass
has made the following illuminating statement: "Es hat
mich gereizt, dem Stammbaum zu folgen und die Menschen um
diese Hunde herum jeweils sekundär zu sehen."[7]

Many examples could be quoted to demonstrate the
significance of Grass's pronouncement and to show the
satirical relationship between the dog and Hitler. For
instance, when Harry Liebenau and his father are invited
to meet the Führer, it is not Hitler they see but the Alsatian Prinz (pp. 298-305). The deteriorating political
situation and the increasing bestiality of the regime are
suggested in terms of the dog: we learn that Senta, Harras's mother, is descended from a Lithuanian she-wolf
(p. 45) and has to be shot because she reverts to type
(p. 84); the police lieutenant warns Liebenau, Harry's
father, that Harras might suddenly degenerate (p. 166).

The treacherous malice and evil of Tulla are conveyed
through the medium of the dog's behaviour: like the
wolves that escape from the zoo and attack a child (p.
239), Harras attacks the pianist Felsner-Imbs on three
occasions, twice egged on by Tulla (p. 213 and p. 227)
and once of its own accord (p. 241).   In such instances,
human and animal virtually become interchangeable.   One
particularly devastating illustration of how Tulla is
represented as having the habits of a dog can be seen in
the episode in which she goes and lives with the dog,
crawling on all fours, barking like a dog, eating the
dog's food and resisting all attempts of her parents to
persuade her to return home (pp. 168-80).   Not only Tulla
but her brothers and Harry eat the dog's meat at one stage
or another and as though it were some nauseating communion,
the act of eating becomes a sign of their spiritual bondage (p. 170).   The allusive link between the Alsatian and
Hitler is constantly in evidence in Liebenau's 'Liebesbriefe':   Hitler is afraid of being poisoned and often
has to vomit (p. 184), whilst Harras is in fact poisoned
(p. 294);   the master and his dog-- Prinz having been a
present by the people of Danzig to the Führer-- are shown
on the cinema screen (p. 377);   and Harras's kennel is
described as being a place of historical interest (p. 390).
Even the attempt on Hitler's life has its symbolical

counterpart in the microcosm of Danzig: Harry's father,
full of despair and disillusionment, smashes the now emp-
ty kennel to pieces on Hitler's birthday, 1944 (p. 392).
In the section that follows Harry Liebenau refers to
Stauffenberg's unsuccessful attempt on the life of Hitler
in the Wolfsschanze, the Führer's kennel in East Prussia.
Liebenau, the ostensibly objective witness, continues,
presumably unwittingly, the parallelism between Hitler
and the Alsatian, dwelling more insistently on the associations of the wolf: he depicts the 'Götterdämmerung'
of Hitler's regime in the form of a systematic military
search for Prinz, whilst employing the terminology of
Heidegger's philosophy (pp. 414-27);   the operation itself is nicknamed 'Wolfsgrube' (see p. 415 et seq.), which
is taking place whilst the Russians are attempting to
track down the human counterpart of the wolf in Berlin;
in his final will and testament Hitler bequeathes the
dog, Prinz, to the German people (p. 423);   meanwhile, according to Liebenau, the dog has interpreted events cor-
rectly and decamped to the West, hence setting an example
which everybody attempts to follow (p. 427);   and from
that time onwards, Matern attempts to take up the story
and tells us how it accompanies him on his journeys through
Germany, as a constant reminder of the past ("ein alters-
schwaches und dennoch herumlaufendes Stück Vergangenheit

auf vier Beinen."-- p. 557) and as a sign that the German
mentality has not yet changed. Many of the events in connection with the dog are related by Harry Liebenau, who
likes to think of himself as the innocent, virtually helpless victim of Tulla and by implication of the climate of
his times. One could scarcely consider him to be a critic
of the age through which he lives. Nevertheless, the
episodes and the imagery with which his narrative is shot
through constitute an allusive condemnation of the mode
of thinking and behaviour which was characteristic of the
Third Reich. In other words there is a discrepancy between the ostensible objectivity of the narrator and the
suggestively transparent nature of the narrative. Episode and imagery coupled with only partially concealed
signs of a guilty conscience unmask and denounce the observer and the period which he observes.

It will be obvious from previous remarks, particularly those relating to the character of Eddi Amsel, that
scarecrows may be regarded as standing in opposition to
the symbol of the dog. Amsel builds scarecrows initially
out of playfulness, but soon realises that the products
of his art are able to affect the behaviour of man: "Es
hätte also ein Künstler zum erstenmal begreifen müssen,
daß seine Werke, wenn sie nur intensiv genug der Natur
entnommen waren, nicht nur Macht über die Vögel unter dem

Himmel hatten, sondern auch Pferden und Kühen, desgleich
dem armen Lorchen, also dem Menschen, die ländlich ruhige
Gangart stören konnten." (p. 60). In keeping with this
realisation they become the means by which aspects of human behaviour may be isolated, distorted and-- hopefully--
banished. Volker Neuhaus refers to this process as 'ver-
scheuchen'.[8] As has already been suggested, Matern has
disintegrated into a series of scarecrow-like characteristics. In the visit down the scarecrow mine Amsel hopes
to bring Matern to an awareness of his lack of wholeness
by showing how some of the features of his personality
have virtually acquired an independence of their own and
have thus 'undermined' his humanity. The scarecrows are
for Amsel a means of artistic expression. Many of them,
taken from 'Preußens nutzbar gemachte Historie' (p. 61),
are intended to help Matern break away from the insidious
influences of his own ancestry and temperament.

Another set of images also appears in *Hundejahre*,
though not in a dominant position. The imagery concerned
is of particular interest in that it recalls the imagery
of head and tail which is so much in evidence in *Die
Blechtrommel*. In the opening chapters of the book Günter
Grass, through his narrator, is at pains to emphasise the
continuity of history and repetitive nature of man's behaviour patterns. He achieves this by reference to the

constantly flowing Vistula, Matern's ancestry and the
dog's pedigree. The same effect is also produced by men-
tioning the story of the "kopflose Ritter und kopflose
Nonnen." (p. 10). Matern's grandmother is especially
keen on this story and often loses her way in "die fin-
steren Gänge und Verliese der endlosen, weil heute noch
nicht abgeschlossenen Geschichte von den zwölf kopflosen
Nonnen und den zwölf Rittern mit Kopf und Helm unterm
Arm..." (pp. 73-74). The knights and the nuns decapitate
each other, collect the blood from each beheading, exchange heads and haunt inns and mills. They even appear
at the scene of battles, "terrifying Poles, Hussites and
Swedes." (p. 80). Their activities reach a climax from
the Materns' point of view when the wind-mill is set on
fire. The prospect of their chaotic violence coming to
an end seems slim: "Zwölf und zwölf hatten vor, solange
ruhelos zu bleiben, bis ihnen Erlösung zuteil wurde und
jeder sein Haupt oder jeder Rumpf jedes Haupt tragen
konnte." (p. 80). The circularity and the senseless violence of history, the futility and the irrationality of
men's actions, seem to be encapsulated in this image and
it recalls the capitulation of reason in the face of the
forces of chaos and passion as adumbrated in the imagery
of head and tail in *Die Blechtrommel*. The destructive
forces at work within nature and by implication within

society are allusively suggested in the first instance in
the image of the eels-- as in *Die Blechtrommel*. In *Hundejahre* Amsel witnesses how eels slither through the morning dew to the udders of cows and drain them dry of their
milk (p. 54). The sight of this unnatural happening
prompts Amsel to produce a scarecrow made up of a pig's
bladder to represent the udder, and the skins of real
eels with the result "daß die Aale sich, dicken Haaren
gleich, in der Luft strängelten, kopfstanden auf dem
Euter. So wurde das Medusenhaupt von zwei gegabelten
Stangen über Karweises Weizen gehoben." (p. 55). In this
way, a clear similarity is established between this scene
and the episode in *Die Blechtrommel* in which eels devour
a horse's head. The head of Medusa reigns ominously, a
Niobe-like figure, over the field of wheat, metaphorically
turning those who gaze on her to stone.

The sexual symbol of the eel recurs in modified form
in the third book of the novel, but with basically similar associations. Matern's father, the miller foretells
the future by listening to the meal-worms in a sack of
flour (p. 495), in keeping with a talent which he had already possessed before his flight to the West (p. 63).
So skilful is he in his prophecies, that the industrial
and political leaders of the Federal Republic come to rely on him. Thus the corruption of the West German miracle

is conjured up by the metaphorical use of the word 'worm':
"Von Anfang an war im Vater des Wirtschaftswunders der
Wurm drinnen, wundersam wunderwirkend. 'Hört nicht auf
den Wurm, im Wurm ist der Wurm.'" (p. 501). The complementary image of the head suggestively haunts the novel:
the dust-cover presents us with the head of a dog, Matern
is constantly presented as being mindless, as though,
like one of the knights, he had lost his head; accordingly, what he does during and after the Third Reich are actions which stem from mindlessness or wrongheadedness;
and those who do not conform to the political atmosphere
have their heads punched in, as was the case with Amsel
or one treated in such a way that all that remains of
them is a skull and bones (Tulla is the one who characteristically returns to the army camp with a skull-- see
p. 372). Matern is "ein Arbeiter der Stirn und Faust"
whose fist and whose phallus dominate his mind.

Even later novels suggest a preoccupation with a
similar kind of imagery-- the dust-cover of *Aus dem Tagebuch einer Schnecke* offers us the picture of a head over
which the more kindly figure of the snail can be seen
crawling; the dust-cover of *Der Butt* shows a fish-- yet
another sexual symbol-- whispering into an ear; and
Grass's most recent prose work has as its title *Kopfgeburten oder Die Deutschen sterben aus*.

By now it will not be difficult for us to agree with
Günter Grass when he says in an interview with Heinz Ludwig Arnold that four common elements link the books of
the Danzig Trilogy together: firstly, the narrators'
feeling of guilt; secondly, the place and time; thirdly,
what Grass chooses to call "die Erweiterung des Wirklich-
keitsverständnisses: das Einbeziehen der Phantasie, der
Einbildungskraft, des Wechsels zwischen Sichtbarem und
Erfindbarem"; and fourthly, the fact that each book is
an attempt "ein Stück endgültig verlorene Heimat aus politischen geschichtlichen Gründen verlorene Heimat, fest-
zuhalten."[9]

Episode and imagery both contribute to the extension
of the reader's understanding of reality, and the basis
for both components of *Hundejahre* as well as the other
two narrative works is the narrative gusto and the tre-
mendous vigour of the imagination. The attempt to view
events as being embedded in the continuity of the German
mentality and German history also achieves the same effect. What is particularly stimulating-- and at times
perplexing-- is the discrepancy between the statements
the narrator makes and the often opposing message conveyed
in veiled terms by episode and imagery. The reader's grip
on reality is sometimes made very insecure by the irony
and understatement which are so typical of the various

narrators' styles and by the basic unreliability of the
narrators themselves as a result of their sense of guilt.
Grass's attempt to extend the reader's emotional and intellectual horizon by the interweaving of fantasy and
reality is accompanied almost inevitably by bewilderment
and unsureness on the part of the reader. Episode and
imagery may assist orientation, presupposing, of course,
that the reader is prepared to unravel their meaning. It
is certainly true that the imagery used in all three
works is, as one might expect, pictorial in origin and
hence conveys its meaning by associations and not by ra-
tional interconnections. It is also interesting, in passing, and in some ways helpful to realise that certain basic images-- the ones connected with head and tail are the
ones we have isolated-- are common in modified form to all
three works. However, any attempt to establish causal
relationships between events in any systematic manner or
to view character exclusively in psychological terms is
doomed to failure.

One particularly important difference between *Hundejahre* and its companions is the fact that for the first
time a character emerges, i.e. Amsel who introduces into
the narrative a set of positive criteria and seeks to put
his values into practice. Amsel sets himself up as the
positive counterpart to Matern. Amsel is the only

character in the Danzig Trilogy-- apart from the author--
who tries to convert into reality the objective Grass
stated in an interview with Berlin students: "er wolle
die Vergangenheit lebendig erhalten, damit sie nicht historisch abgelegt werde."[10] In other words, Amsel endeavours to rescue the past from the would-be historian Harry
Liebenau who tries to dissociate himself from the past and
belittle its significance- This is not to say that Amsel
is a paragon is virtue, he is not goodness in its purest
form. Purity is a concept which was far too contaminated
by the Nazi racial laws. The world which Grass considers
to be the only acceptable one is the one which consists,
not of black and white, but of murky greys, of intermediate shades and tones. Amsel's mission in life is to get
Matern to accommodate himself to the ambiguities and un-
certainties of life. Amsel's objective reflects Günter
Grass's description of *Hundejahre*: "Nicht der Roman der
edlen schönen Jüdin und des tierischen Nationalsozialisten,
nicht des stubenreinen Demokraten und stubenunreinen Kom-
munisten, sondern ein Roman der angeschlagenen Vorstel-
lungen und der angeschlagenen Figuren, für die die Am-
bivalenz, die Doppeldeutigkeit unserer Zeit, die Vorlage
gibt."[11] Amsel acts as his brother's keeper and wishes
to detach him from this tabloid thinking for which absolute values provide the basis. His task is to wean him

away from the rigidity of all the ideologies with which Matern has experimented at one stage or another, whether this be communism, National Socialism or Catholicism.

The second significant difference between *Hundejahre* and the two previous works is that in comparison with *Die Blechtrommel* and *Katz und Maus* it ends on a mildly optimistic note. In all three works the three 'main' characters take flight from reality: Oskar retreats into a lunatic asylum, having ascended from the Paris underground; Mahlke drives into the submerged hulk of the submarine and the last words in the 'Novelle' are: "Aber Du wolltest nicht auftauchen;" and Matern tries to escape from West Germany, one of the reasons being that he is annoyed by the findings of the public discussion (p. 613). His route to utopia, the heaven, of the German Democratic Republic is blocked by Goldmäulchen who, mindful of Matern's sin, conducts him to the raging inferno of Jenny's snack bar and, after presenting him with his former knife, escorts him through the thirty-two chambers of the underground scarecrow hell. The scarecrows are intended to jolt Matern out of his complacency and reflect in distorted form his own shortcomings and transgressions. After having thrown away the knife it is as though Matern surrenders to his blood brother: the words "Mach mit mir, was Du willst!" (p. 648) seem to be a sign of capitulation.

Matern is also terrified and exhausted by the hell which
he sees around him in Brauxel's subterranean factory (p.
668). At this moment, Amsel, true to his mission, reminds
him of the hell into which Matern has just plunged himself by throwing away the knife. Amsel is in the process
of emerging as victor; the two roles into which Amsel
and Matern have been cast, have now been reversed; and,
as was once the case, Amsel has re-emerged as Matern's
superior in intellectual and spiritual terms. The possibility of Matern coming to terms with his errors also exists, as Frank Richter states: "Zwar bleibt der Dialog
zwischen Eddi Amsel und Walter Matern fruchtlos, doch verglichen mit der totalen Negativität der *Blechtrommel* deu-
tet sich in den *Hundejahren* die Möglichkeit eines Lern-
prozesses an, der die Negativität der *Blechtrommel* über-
winden könnte."[12] The final scene which returns to the
associations connected with immersion-- as in *Katz und
Maus*, though in a potentially positive sense-- also allows
the possibility of reconciliation. The two men have ascended to the surface, they cleanse their bodies, as
though an act of baptism were taking place, mass having
been sung previously (p. 644): "Das Wasser laugt uns ab.
Eddi pfeift etwas Unbestimmtes. Ich versuche ähnliches
zu pfeifen. Doch das ist schwer. Beide sind wir nackt.
Jeder badet für sich." Eddi still plays the tune and

Matern follows his example; and yet what is whistled is
not the clear-cut tones of an unambiguous melody. Eddi
whistles the intermediate tones-- he is endeavouring to
familiarise his friend with a world in which nothing is
pure, in which everything is indefinite and ambivalent
and yet a world in which each person has to find his own
salvation.[13] The last words in this novel allow for Matern being able to recognise the world as it is, and per-
mit the possibility of his obtaining redemption.

Not only has self-awareness become feasible in *Hunde-*
jahre, but the circumstances in which this self-appraisal
might take place are also more favourable than is the case
in *Die Blechtrommel* or *Katz und Maus*. Matern is constantly accompanied by his blood brother who is concerned to
acquaint him with the error of his ways and the nature of
reality. Amsel remains undaunted though his task is for-
midable. Many of the external influences to which Matern
and Liebenau were subject either no longer exist or have
been neutralised: Tulla is no longer to be found in the
post-war world; furthermore, she suffered a miscarriage
during the war (p. 385) so that the child she was to have
born cannot take up her legacy; and the dog which initially escorts Matern on his journeys of vengeance and is
the symbol of Nazi bestiality is claimed and brought under control by Amsel (p. 681). The latter who is

described by Liebenau as "der Künstler und Hundebezwing-
er" (p. 196) banishes the dog in contrast to the situation
at the end of *Die Blechtrommel* where 'die schwarze Köchin'
continues to haunt and terrify Oskar with visions from the
past. The objects which lie in the path towards self-
realisation are internal and are the result of Matern's
mentality. In short, it is conceivable in *Hundejahre*
that the circularity of history and the repetitive nature
of man's behaviour may be modified-- the vicious circle
may be broken. The artist may achieve his objectives.
In this sense then *Hundejahre* is an extension of the other
two works and introduces a note of optimism which is entirely absent in *Die Blechtrommel* and *Katz und Maus*.

Notes

1. Gert Loschütz, *Von Buch zu Buch-- Günter Grass in der Kritik* (Neuwied and Berlin: Luchterhand, 1968), pp. 85-92.

2. Frank Richter, *Die zerschlagene Wirklichkeit* (Bonn: Bouvier, 1977), p. 37.

3. Paul Konrad Kurz, "*Hundejahre*-- Beobachtungen zu einem zeitkritischen Roman," *Stimmen der Zeit*, Vol. 80, No.1 (1963-64), 117; see also Heinz Klunker, "Günter Grass und seine Kritiker," *Europäische Begegnung*, Vol. 12, No. 7 (1964), 467.

4. Kurt Batt, "Groteske und Parabel-- Anmerkungen zu *Hundejahre* von Günter Grass und *Herr Meister* von Walter Jens," *Neue Deutsche Literatur*, Vol. 12, No. 7 (1964), 65.

5. Pagination in *Hundejahre* refers to the edition published by Luchterhand, Neuwied and Berlin, October 1963.

6. Volker Neuhaus, *Günter Grass* (Stuttgart: Metzler, 1979), p. 86.

7. F. v. Ingen and G. Labroisse, editors, "Gespräch mit Günter Grass," *Deutsche Bücher 1976* (Amsterdam, 1976), p. 253.

8. Volker Neuhaus (as under note 6), p. 90.

9. Heinz Ludwig Arnold, editor, *Günter Grass, Text und*

Kritik (1978), pp. 10-11.

10. Manfred and Barbara Grunert, editors, *Wie stehen Sie dazu? Jugend fragt Prominente* (Munich and Berne, 1967), p. 84.

11. Hugo Loetscher, "Günter Grass" in Loschütz (as under note 1), p. 196.

12. Frank Richter (as under note 2), p. 36.

13. Jürgen Rothenberg, *Günter Grass. Das Chaos in verbesserter Ausführung* (Heidelberg: Carl Winter, 1976), pp. 111-12.

CHAPTER IV

Davor *and* örtlich betäubt: *Evolution or Revolution*

If Johann Sebastian Bach's music may be referred to
as 'polyphonic', then Grass's work may be described as
'polythematic'. This is particularly the case with the
novel *örtlich betäubt* which appeared in 1969. Various
elements-- themes, images and strands represented by characters and actions-- are interwoven-- polyphonically-- to
form a satisfying and stimulating whole. For those whose
ears are not attuned to the simultaneous presence of a
number of interacting components, Grass has produced a
monothematic version in the form of the play *Davor* which
had its first performance in 1969. It immediately aroused
the ire of left-wing writers. One of such critics sum-
marily dismissed it as "a work of integration by a completely integrated and corrupted author."[1] Ignoring the
abuse, we may grasp the play as a God-given-- or Grass-
given-- opportunity to come to an understanding of the
more complex work *örtlich betäubt*, for the play may be
viewed as a foretaste of the novel to come. The two
works are so closely interlinked that the same characters

appear in both (though the number is reduced in the play),
the central themes in both works are identical, the plots
are indistinguishable-- that is, if one compares the play
with part II of the novel-- and what the characters in
the play actually say can frequently be traced back ver-
batim to the novel. When we read-- or, better still, attend a performance of-- the play, we are in effect dealing
with a simplified version of the novel.

The play revolves round the efforts of a teacher to
discourage a seventeen-year old pupil from setting his dog
alight in front of a café in Berlin as a means of protest
against the war in Vietnam and in particular against the
use of nepalm. Various methods are used to divert the
pupil, Philipp Scherbaum, from his plan: Starusch, the
teacher, shows Philipp illustrations of how human beings
have been burned in the course of history (p. 48);[2] he
suggests Bonn rather than Berlin as the place where the
dog could be sacrificed (p. 52); he threatens to report
him to the police because of his planned irrational act
(p. 66); he even tries to confuse him by proposing that
he will buy his own dog and set it alight (p. 67); Starusch advises Philipp to start writing poetry again as an
alternative means of drawing the attention of the public
to the inhumanity of war (p. 91); a dentist with whom the
teacher is undergoing a course of treatment suggests that

Starusch and his pupil should visit the spot where the dog is to be burnt (p. 97); the dentist then recommends his patient to bring the boy to see him and he shows him his equipment, pointing out the advances that dental surgery has made (p. 109); and finally the dentist goes so far as to encourage the pupil in his plan of action (p. 126). Eventually the would-be rebel and idealist gives up his plan (p. 141). As can be seen, there is little action in the play, and in fact the declared aim of both the teacher and the dentist is to prevent any action taking place, for one of the dentist's principles is that discussion prevents action ("Gespräche verhindern Taten"-- p. 59 in the play and p. 103 in the novel).[3]

The play consists of a dialogue between teacher and pupil. At no point is there any danger that the exchange of ideas might come to an abrupt end. In this sense it would be wrong to think of the play as presenting a confrontation between rightwing and leftwing ideas, or between the establishment and a revolutionary, iconoclastic opposition. Philipp Scherbaum has in any case not the make-up of the out-and-out extremist. He is in essence far too good-humoured for that. The dialogue is maintained because the pupil is even-tempered and well-balanced. He is too tolerant to be a fanatic. Teacher and pupil never treat each other as enemies, scarcely even as

opponents but rather as partners engaged in a conversation. Starusch approvingly describes his pupil in the
following terms: "Keiner, der führen will und Anhänger
sucht. Er kann nicht fanatisch gucken. Nicht mal unhöf-
lich ist er. Seine Stimme verkündet nicht. Er ist kein
Messias. Er bringt keine Botschaft." (p. 129 in *Davor*,
pp. 145-46 in *Örtlich betäubt*). By nature hs is tempera-
mentally preconditioned to accept compromise as a means
of making progress. He has no doctrine of salvation to
offer. The model which supplies him with his guiding principles is not Che Guevara who is his girl friend's pin-up,
but Helmut Hübener who circulated pamphlets against National Socialism during the war and was executed in the
Berlin prison of Plötzensee (pp 131-32 in *Davor*, pp. 150-
51 in *Örtlich betäubt*). Scherbaum is appalled by the inhumanity of men and feels the injustices of the world as
though he were experiencing them directly himself. Starusch provides the following insight into his pupil's
character: "Scherbaum leidet an der Welt. Das fernste
trifft ihn. Er glaubt, mit dem Krieg in Vietnam Tür an
Tür zu leben. Keinen Ausweg sieht er-- oder nur den einen:
er will seinen Hund öffentlich verbrennen und so der Welt
ein Zeichen geben." (p. 57 *Davor*, p. 102 *Örtlich betäubt*).
Burning his dog is Philipp's response to the incomprehen-
sibility of the world, it is an attempt to shake people

our of their complacency and so alter the social and political conditions which allow injustuce to take place.

Starusch, Scherbaum's partner in the dialogue, is in a
sense a much less consistent and much more contradictory
character than his pupil. Starusch first made his début
in the literary world under the nickname of Störtebeker
in *Die Blechtrommel*. On frequent occasions in conversation with Phillip Scherbaum and Philipp's girl-friend,
Vero Lewand, and others he reminds them of his youthful
exploits as the leader of a group of hooligans, so-called
'dusters', during the war-years. Then he and his followers, as the forty-year old schoolteacher explains retrospectively, were against everything and everyone (p. 98
Davor, p. 125 *Örtlich betäubt*). Starusch's rebellion was
a purely egoistic revolt against everything that was re-
motely connected with authority. It was anarchistic, and
sought to destroy rather than remedy. Scherbaum's youthful rebellion, however, has a considered moral basis. His
object is to educate people and initiate a process of reform; the burning of the dog is a means to this end. Because of his youthful experiences Starusch is sympathetically disposed towards Philipp's plan to offer up the sacrificial dog. Accordingly he admits that if he were like
Phillip he would tell him to carry out his plan (p. 98
Davor, p. 125 *Örtlich betäubt*, though in a more qualified

form). Starusch admits to his dentist that he feels the
fascination of the revolutionary impulse: "Als wenn ich
keine Lust hätte. Dreinschlagen. Abräumen. Zehntausend
Bulldozer, die den gesamten Konsumramsch... klare Verhältnisse. Der revolutionäre Urtrieb kurz nach dem Zähne-
putzen, kurz vor dem Frühstücken." (p. 52 *Davor*, p. 100
Örtlich betäubt). Nevertheless Starusch remains opposed
to absolute standards, utopias, paradise and similar
dreams of perfection. He makes this quite clear to Irmgard Seifert, his colleague and girl-friend: "Erlösung,
und zwar zu Lebzeiten? Gibt es nicht. Nur Arantil gibt
es, das Spezialanalgetikum gegen Zahn- und Kieferschmer-
zen." (p. 37 in *Davor*).

Starusch has been taught to dispense with the heroic,
ideals have for him only limited applicability. He illus-
trates in effect the problems of growing old-- to phrase
it in a negative manner. Glamorous objectives become
tarnished-- he is keen on quoting from the Lamentations
of Jeremiah ("How is the gold become dim!"). He needs to
shield his nerve ends against the cold draughts from the
outside world. His teeth decay. He has learnt to adapt
himself and to view compromise as a means of moving forward. He struggles almost pathetically to remain aware
of and respond sensitively to wrongs perpetrated by man.
This finds ironic expression in a conversation between

him and his pupil. Scherbaum asks him how he reacts to the events in Vietnam and whether such news does not make him feel indignant. His middle-aged answer is as follows: "Oft versuche ich traurig zu sein," and in the same vein: "Ich gebe mir jedes Mal Mühe, empört zu sein." (p. 38 *Davor* pp. 10-11 *Örtlich betäubt*). He describes the acquisition of experience and wisdom, the long trek from puberty to middle-aged maturity, in the following, somewhat pugnacious manner: "Wir haben gelernt, uns durchzuboxen. Die Lage sondieren. Ellenbogen einsetzen. Notfalls anpassen. Praktiker, die das Mögliche anstreben und-- falls sich nicht unerwartet Widerstände ergeben-- sogar erreichen." (p. 39 *Davor*, p. 96 *Örtlich betäubt* with some additions). He even produces the negative credo: "Und ich hasse Bekenntnisse. Ich hasse Opfer." (p. 127 *Davor*, p. 155 *Örtlich betäubt*). In the novel his statement of belief is more complete in that he extends his objections to include dogmas, eternal truths and the unambiguous. One is reminded of the similar views expressed by Enzensberger in reply to attacks by Peter Weiss: "I'm no idealist. I prefer arguments to confessions, doubts to emotions. I hate revolutionary chatter, and I don't need ideologies free of contradictions. In cases of doubt reality is what decides."[4]

Eventually Starusch-- with the assistance of the

dentist-- does dissuade his pupil from carrying out his sacrificial act though Scherbaum's reasons for giving up his plan are perhaps not as flattering to his teacher as the latter might have wished them to be: he says that he wants to throw in the sponge because he does not want to become like his teacher (p. 148 *Davor*, p. 165 *Örtlich betäubt* in a slightly different form). Just before Scherbaum revokes, the two of them, teacher and pupil, intone a Bach-like duet which almost takes the form of a lament:

Starusch: Aber die Jahre schafften mich.

Scherbaum: Sie verlieren schon genug Zeit mit mir...

Starusch: Ich paßte mich an.

Scherbaum: ... weil ich mich nicht entschließen
 kann...

Starusch: Ich suchte den permanenten Ausgleich.

Scherbaum: ... und ein Versager bin.

(pp. 138-139 *Davor*, p. 156 and p. 159 *Örtlich betäubt*, though the last line occurs only in the play).

In a sense it would be true to say that three of the characters in the play indulge in a communal act of renunciation in the closing scenes: the pupil capitulates, Irmgard Seifert, who had always claimed she would confess her misdeeds during the Nazi period to her class in school, also renounces her intention of doing so (p. 148 *Davor*, p. 166 *Örtlich betäubt*) and Starusch decides--

temporarily or otherwise-- to opt out. He is too much
aware of the repetitive nature and paradoxes of life, he
knows in advance how his own thought processes-- and
those of others-- operate even before a sentence is completed. As he puts it, "Vorgeschmack überlappt den Nach-
geschmack." (p. 142 *Davor*, p. 164 *Örtlich betäubt*). The
dentist echoes the same idea a short time later when he
states, "Schon im Davor beginnt das Danach." (p. 146
Davor, p. 169 *Örtlich betäubt*). Thus the dentist provides the play with its title, emphasising thereby the
idea that characters and events are influenced by what
has taken place before. He suggests by his statements
and by his example that continuity is a precondition of
progress and the future-- and the present-- are dependent
upon the past. This last quotation, stemming from the
dentist in the play, though from the narrator in the novel, is not necessarily to be interpreted in a positive
sense. Men and the society to which they belong may be
fashioned in either a positive or negative manner or for
that matter the good and the bad may coexist. In an interview with a Munich newspaper Grass made the following
comment on *Davor*: "Meiner Meinung nach gibt die Tat, als
Ergebnis, nicht soviel her, wie die Zeit, die davor liegt
... Fast alles, was mich interessiert, passiert in der
Spanne, die davor liegt."[5] This view of events and of

history profoundly affects the attitudes of the characters
in the play and in the novel but also conditions the atmosphere of both works. The dentist may legitimately regard the history of dentistry as a series of discoveries
and inventions which have helped to ameliorate the suf-
ferings of mankind. He can act out his professional life
in the confidence that progress, albeit gradual, is a
practical possibility. Eberhard Starusch as the teacher
of history is much less sanguine in his approach. He is
much more acutely aware of the snail-like pace of progress
and all too conscious of the fact that continuity is not
a good in itself and that men may be cast into a right or
wrong historical mould. He recognizes this fact, not
only by reference to social and political developments
but also by reference to his own inner turmoil. He mentions the fact that Hitler was rejected by the Academy of
Art in Vienna and goes on to make the following generalisation: "... Denn unser Volk verträgt das nicht: Abge-
wiesene Zukurzgekommene Versager. Überall hocken sie und
lauern auf Rache. Sie erfinden sich Feinde und Geschichten, in denen ihre erfundenen Feinde tatsächlich vorkommen
und liquidiert werden. Schnurgerade denken sie mit dem
Maschinengewehr. Sie variieren den Tod immer des gleichen
Widersachers." (p. 53 *Örtlich betäubt*). In making such
observations Starusch, another of Grass's unreliable

narrators, is commenting, not only upon Hitler, but also,
presumably unwittingly, upon himself, for in the novel
the story-teller provides himself imaginatively, with a
fiancée and, for good measure, a job as engineer and then
commits all manner of violence against her. In the play
the history-teacher is a much more colourless, more one-
sided and less contradictory individual than in the novel.
What applies to Eberhard also applies to the other characters in the play. As Paul Konrad Kurz suggests, all the
characters in the play are types who are meant to represent present-day modes of speech, behaviour and thinking.[6]
In short, the monothematic nature of the play severely reduces its appeal. It is a dialogue piece and according
to Paul Konrad Kurz it would be at home in the classroom
situation, not as a literary but as a political text.
Grass's attitude to history also minimises its theatrical
impact, for Grass's preoccupation with the period of time
preceding an action rather than with the event itself and
its subsequent consequences likewise reduces the play's
dramatic quality. For the view of history which informs
both play and novel-- and it is a view of history which
is common to all Grass's narrative works-- has adverse
effects on the play, whilst being completely compatible
with the broad panoramic sweep of the novel which is such
an attractive and stimulating feature of *Die Blechtrommel*

and *Hundejahre* and also, as we shall see later, of novels
such as *Der Butt* and *Das Treffen in Telgte*.

As has been said, the teacher is a victim of contradictory impulses and characteristics. It is the dentist
who stands out as the consistent advocate of progress and
moderation. The teacher turns to him for guidance and
encouragement, when his attempts at dissuading his pupil
do not appear to be meeting with success. He acts as
second for Starusch in his conversational duel with Philipp Scherbaum, whilst the pupil is seconded by Vero Lewand, his girl-friend. The duel centres round what Grass
has referred to as the classical question: reform or revolution?[7] The dentist supplies Eberhard Starusch with an
intellectual basis, whilst Vero Lewand tries to give Philipp her personal ideological support. The dentist has
recourse to the principles of science-- and in particular
of dentistry-- in encouraging his patient, whilst Vero--
whose name ironically suggests that she is an advocate,
presumably, of the one and only truth-- falls back on the
language of revolutionary communism. In his first conversation with Phillip the dentist for whom Grass does
not provide any name refers to the advances made by dentistry as a proof that progress exists (p. 113 *Davor*, p.
134 *Örtlich betäubt*). He recommends prophylaxis rather
than revolution: decay should be prevented and hence

revolution made unnecessary (see p. 59 *Davor*, p. 103 *Örtlich betäubt*). He views caries as a disease of civilisation (p. 113 *Davor*) and amusingly filches communist terminology in describing the role of preventive medicine:
"Die globale Krankenfürsorge ist, abseits jeder Ideologie,
Basis und Überbau unserer menschlichen Gesellschaft."
(p. 18 *Davor*, p. 60 *Örtlich betäubt*).

In effect he transfers the language of dentistry to
the sphere of society and politics and allusively suggests
thereby the possible solution of social and political maladies. He refers to tartar ('Zahnstein') as ossified
hatred (p. 23 *Örtlich betäubt*) and states that the removal
of tartar is automatically part and parcel of all dental
treatment (p. 146 *Davor*). Dental irregularities become
the symbolical externalisation of an inner state of mal-
aise which may be the motivation behind certain types of
behaviour. In this connection we may recall Mahlke's
oversized Adam's apple and Oskar Matzerath's arrested
growth and subsequent malformation as the outward manifestation of an inner derangement. The fact that Starusch
requires dental treatment is indirectly a sign of his
mental conflict and the fact that Scherbaum ultimately
agrees to dental treatment conjures up the idea that he
is aware of his own deficiencies and accepts the need for
curative measures. More importantly, however, it is an

indication that Scherbaum is prepared to see his ideals
tarnished, and he is willing to subject himself to the
norms of society. Like Jeremiah he might intone-- and
with him the reader-- the lamentation: "Wie ist das Gold
so gar verdunkelt." (*The Lamentations of Jeremiah*, Chapter
IV, Verse 1). The dentist can reassure Scherbaum, however, that in comparison with the protrusion of his teacher's lower jaw his overbite can still be corrected even
now (p. 146 *Davor*, p. 166 *Örtlich betäubt*).

In the process of transferring the language of dentistry to the psychological and political plane the dentist contrasts arantil, the pain-killer he prescribes for
his patients, with wisdom which also helps to dull sensitivity in the face of pain-- and of adversity. He goes
on to compare himself virtually with Seneca, a representative of the Stoic philosophy: he, the dentist, prescribes arantil, whilst Seneca prescribes wisdom-- which
Epicurus would have us equate with apathy-- in order to
dull the pain associated in one way or another with human
existence (p. 143 *Davor*, p. 164 *Örtlich betäubt*). In
keeping with his scientific education the dentist advocates a step by step progression based upon patience, hard
work, empirical evidence and logical thought and accordingly condemns the man of action who in a fit of impa-
tience metaphorically smashes the windows of the green-

house (p. 64 *Davor*, p. 103 *Örtlich betäubt*). It is not
surprising, therefore, that the dentist should be called
upon to comment upon Scherbaum's final revocation. Once
the pupil has given up the plan, his teacher observes
that he has become an adult (p. 150 *Davor*, p. 165 *Örtlich
betäubt*), providing the additional explanation in the
novel that he is in other words broken (p. 165). One
could interpret such a remark variously: it could be explained in terms of maturity, in terms of the acceptance
of his own personal limitations or in terms of the progression of the individual from the state of innocence
to the state of experience, from idealism to disillusionment. The play and more especially the novel convey a
feeling of sadness that the attainment of wisdom involves
the partial or total sacrifice of ideals and the dulling
of sensitivity. Society's response to Scherbaum's deep-
felt distress at the injustice of the world is to reach
out for the pain-killer and deaden the nerve-ends: "Auch
Scherbaum wird zu einem stehenden Gewässer. Da ihn die
Welt schmerzt, geben wir uns Mühe, ihn örtlich zu betäu-
ben." (p. 158). The same sentiment is conveyed in a conversation between the dentist and the teacher on the occasion of one of Starusch's many visits to the surgery.
Starusch expresses concern at the pain he may have to
suffer:

Starusch: Und all mein Schmerz?

Zahnarzt: Wird örtlich betäubt.

Starusch: Muß das denn sein? (p.14 *Örtlich betäubt*).
At this early stage in the novel its reader might not yet
be aware of the metaphorical significance of the language
of dentistry, though the title of the novel might be regarded as sufficient warning signal. The political overtones of the dental imagery are even suggested on the occasion, when the dentist describes his patient's chin as
a "Duce-Kinn" (p. 170). Günter Grass himself has pointed
quite clearly to the social relevance of the novel: *Örtlich betäubt* meint gleichzeitig und über den zahnmedizin-
ischen Anlaß hinaus den Gesellschaftszustand. Ersatzerlebnisse verdrängen reale Erlebnisse oder verformen reale
Erlebnisse, indem sich Ersatzerlebnisse von realen Erleb-
nissen speisen. Im Kopf des Erzählers sowie auf dem Bild-
schirm in der Praxis des Zahnarztes mischen sich Realität
und Fiktion; die Übergänge vom äußeren zum inneren Dialog bleiben fließend, einzigen Halt bietet der Erzählort:
der Zahnarztstuhl, in dem der passive Patient seine Fiktionen wie Erfahrungen freisetzt."[8] The focal point of
the narrative is the dentist's chair which may be likened
almost to a psychiatrist's couch. Given the central role
of the dentist's chair it may be safe to assume that the
associations connected with dentistry will spread out

their tentacles throughout the novel and thus establish
a link with the sphere of society and politics.

As has been indicated, the dentist and the teacher
advocate evolution, whilst Vero Lewand represents the
principle of revolution. Her boy-friend remains open-
minded in his attitude to new ideas and suggestions,
whilst she tends to be much more inflexible, her mode of
thought being circumscribed by communist ideology. (Even
her surname, with its emphasis on the German word for
'wall', suggests perhaps the ossified-- or petrified--
nature of her attitudes). She refers, for example, to
liberalism as the deadly enemy of the revolution (p. 68
Davor), accuses Starusch of being a reactionary (p. 137
Davor, p. 155 *Örtlich betäubt*); tries to embarrass Starusch sexually and thereby hopes to stop him influencing
his pupil any further (pp. 135-40 *Davor*, pp. 154-57 *Örtlich betäubt*); she quotes him from Mao Tse-tung, stating
that no sacrifice should be shunned and all difficulties
overcome in order to attain victory, and adding that society is on the threshhold of a third revolution (p. 78
Davor, p. 110 *Örtlich betäubt*); after Scherbaum has tak-
en over the editorship of the pupils' newspaper, she refuses to be involved, preferring to hand out instead her
own pamphlets, which dispense with the liberal's 'on the
one hand' and 'on the other hand' (pp. 150-51 *Davor*,

compare p. 154 *Örtlich betäubt*). In short, she suffers
from what the dentist refers to in another context as a
limited perspective ("verengte Optik", p. 107 *Davor*, p.
130 *Örtlich betäubt*). It is she rather than her boy
friend who merits this description.

It is clear on the basis of what has been said so
far that in the play Grass makes his case quite plain
against the methods and objectives of any revolutionary
ideology. He wishes to put forward moderation, reason
(or perhaps 'common sense' might be an English equivalent), and tolerance and readiness to compromise as the
guiding principles which should influence our social and
political behaviour. The attitude of the teacher and particularly of the dentist correspond in essence to Grass's
own political views. This becomes abundantly evident if
one reads the statements which Grass has made in recent
years and of which some have been published in his book
of speeches, essays and commentaries entitled *Der Bürger
und seine Stimme*. In a speech given originally in 1969
in Belgrade he produced the following political confession: "Ich bin ein Gegner der Revolution. Ich scheue
Opfer, die jeweils in ihrem Namen gebracht werden müssen.
Ich scheue ihre übermenschlichen Zielsetzungen, ihre absoluten Ansprüche, ihre inhumane Intoleranz. Ich fürchte
den Mechanismus der Revolution, die sich als Elixier für

ihre Anstrengungen die permanente Konterrevolution erfinden mußte... Revolutionen ersetzen Abhängigkeit, lösten
den Zwang durch den Zwang ab." (p. 67). In an address in
Osnabrück in the same year he echoes a remark made by the
dentist in *Davor*: "Doch Politik ist, wenn sie Verhältnisse verändern will, immer schon langfristige, von Niederlagen gezeichnete Arbeit gewesen."[9]

In view of the unambiguous liberal viewpoint in *Davor*
is is hardly surprising that Grass should have been sharp-
ly criticised by left-wing intellectuals. In discussing
Grass's play it is worth recalling that it was first per-
formed one year after the students' protest movement had
also left its mark on literature itself, for militant students and intellectuals had increasingly demanded that
literature should be subordinated to political objectives.
Literature was to be the hand-maiden in the process of a
changing society. It has been maintained that writers,
at the beginning of the sixties, were never particularly
political but they were much more likely to be moralists.[10]
To a certain extent this is true of Günter Grass: in his
first three prose works, *Die Blechtrommel* (1959), *Katz und
Maus* (1961) and *Hundejahre* (1963) he is the moralist deep-
ly shocked by what has been perpetrated in the name of
the German people. He is horrified by the massive physical and human destruction which Germany has wreaked on

the world. He is a social and political critic because
of an acute sense of moral awareness. The satirical momentum in *Die Blechtrommel* and in *Hundejahre* is fuelled
by a feeling of outraged shame. By the end of the sixties
the political climate in Germany has changed. The youth
of the day, the privileged members of an affluent society,
who were not even alive during the Nazi period, had come
to their own conclusions about the failures of the past
and some were turning to radical left-wing ideas as a
means of avoiding the mistakes of their fathers. Their
absolute demands reminded authors like Grass of other absolute demands which had been made in Germany whilst he
was young. He could recall that German politics has always foundered on maximum demands.[11] The play *Davor* and
the novel *Örtlich betäubt* are Grass's reaction to the
more extreme forms of irrationality which characterised
the student rebellion and they are in a narrower sense
his response to the students' clamour for the 'politici-
sation of literature'. His reply is to claim, as he does
in the speech held in Osnabrück in September 1969, that
moderation, and not absolute standards, should determine
political judgement.[12] His reaction to the revolutionary
ideas of the students is in essence still the reaction of
a moralist with the difference, however-- in comparison
with the works of the early sixties-- that the negative

criticism of the German development is accompanied by a
positive political orientation.

The play *Davor* deals with those issues which might be
said to be typical of the social and political atmosphere
of the late sixties. In the novel Grass attempts to place
the confrontation between evolution and revolution against
a broader background. In the play there are references
to individuals and specific episodes-- imagined or otherwise: resistance to Nazism on the part of citizens, the
career of Kiesinger and the exploits and experiences of
Eberhard Starusch and Irmgard Seifert during the Nazi
period. Such allusions to the past are, however, relatively few: they do not assume a dominant position in
the play. In *Örtlich betäubt* Grass establishes and emphasises the constant link between the political reality
of the past and that of the present. His aim is to point
out more insistently how the attitudes of the sixties are
reflected in the attitudes of earlier decades. He wishes
to show those elements of continuity which affect social
and political thinking in Germany. Grass achieves this
by the addition of three main-- largely imaginary-- main
characters. Sieglinde Krings (Starusch's former fiancée),
her father, General Ferdinand Krings, and an electrical
engineer by the name of Heinz Schlottau-- and also by the
introduction of new images, e.g. television, "Sandkasten-

spiel" and deep-freezer, and by reinforcing images which
are already present in the play, e.g. teeth, fish, bulldozer, cakes. Furthermore the themes of failure and defeat, as well as that of violence, acquire added significance. The novel consists of three parts-- Grass once
again makes use of the tripartite division which is already in evidence in his other two major novels, *Die
Blechtrommel* and *Hundejahre*. It is true to say-- though
at the risk of oversimplification-- that the second part
(pp. 90-160) deals principally with the events with which
we are already familiar from the play (Scherbaum's
statement that he intends to burn his dog occurs at the
beginning of part II); that the first part (pp. 5-90)
introduces the new characters and contains few statements
which are present also in the play; and the third part
(pp. 169-92)-- apart from the first page-- has nothing
which can be linked directly with the play.

The main distinction between the play and the novel
is the fact that whilst in the play the characters-- colourless though they may be-- present themselves and their
ideas directly to the audience, in the novel attitudes,
events and non-events are conveyed to us through the medium of a narrator, the history-teacher Eberhard Starusch.
Like many of his predecessors, Oskar Matzerath, Heini
Pilenz and Walter Matern, he describes a 'reality' which

is fractured and fragmented by his own way of viewing the
world, so much so that the dividing line between the real
and the imagined is blurred and often not immediately apparent. The narrator feels the need to create experiences
as a means of compensating himself for his own inadequacies and his missed opportunities. As Günter Grass has
indicated, such pseudo-experiences displace or distort
real experiences.[8] The picture with which Eberhard Starusch presents us is so flawed by his own complexes and
hang-ups that he is far from being a trustworthy narrator.
Starusch may well have given up his leadership of the an-
archist group, the 'Stäuberbände' to which Oskar Matzerath
introduced us in *Die Blechtrommel*, but he has not yet
come to terms with the anarchistic confusion in his own
mind. The reader is in danger of being kicked round Starusch's narrative gymnasium with little or no respect
being paid to the reader's innate inclination to regard
truthfulness as a worthwhile qualification for a narrator.
Nevertheless the narrative technique is a redeeming feature of the novel and allows Starusch to appear as a much
more differentiated individual than in the play and converts the novel into a multifaceted and much more stimulating work of art than its dramatic counterpart.

We are given sone indication of the complexity of
the narrative technique in the opening lines of the novel:

"Das erzählte ich meinem Zahnarzt. Maulgesperrt und der
Mattscheibe gegenüber, die tonlos wie ich, Werbung erzählte: Haarspray, Wüstenrot Weißeralweiß... Ach, und
die Tiefkühltruhe, in der zwischen Kalbsnieren und Milch
meine Verlobte lagerte, Sprechblasen steigen ließ: 'Halt
du dich da raus. Halt du dich da raus...'"

   "(Heilige Apollonia, bitte für mich!) Zu meinen
Schülerinnen und Schülern sagte ich: "Versucht, nach-
sichtig zu sein. Ich muß zum Zahnklempner. Das kann
sich hinziehen. Also Schonfrist." (p. 5).

   It is clear that the narrator, Eberhard Starusch, is
the only source of information. He provides us with his
version of conversations he has had with a variety of individuals, in this instance with the dentist and then
with his own pupils in the school. In the dentist's surgery, however, there is a television set and onto its
screen the patient projects a series of memories, associations and fantasies. The television apparatus obviously
does not provide any objectivisation of events. In fact
quite the contrary is true: Starusch's capacity for un-
leashing his imaginative extravaganzas is enhanced by the
television rather than diminished. The above quotation
provides a good example of this: the narrator-- as television producer-- has his fiancée packed away in a deep
freezer, gurgling captions as though in a series of

newspaper cartoons (at this stage the innocent reader is
not to know that the fiancée herself is merely a figment
of the television producer's fevered imagination). Starusch mixes his associations, memories and fantasies and
goes in for advertisement-- self-advertisement-- in the
same way as any good commercial television company. His
publicity stunts have the same link with truth as a commercial advertisement. On other occasions Starusch projects his adventures into the framework of a newspaper
report and thus slips into the guise of a third person
(see pp. 37-40, pp. 44-45, pp. 53-55). Another fact
which emerges from the first few lines is one which Grass
has mentioned elsewhere: the dentist's chair is the location for the narrative.[8] From it, as though from a
psychiatrist's couch the patient unburdens himself,
launching fictions and experiences in the direction of
the dentist, who, true to his mission as alleviator of
pain, attempts to cure, or at least minimise, both dental
and psychological maladies. One other final point is apparent in the opening paragraphs of the novel: a number
of narrative strands are being interwoven at the same
time and past, present and future appear to co-exist almost simultaneously. In one of his imaginary conversations with his pupil, the narrator refers to this aspect
of story-telling: "Denn schauen sie, Scherbaum, die

Gleichzeitigkeit einer Vielzahl von Tätigkeiten will be-
schrieben werden..." (p. 13).   Irène Leonard in her book
on Günter Grass has referred to this as "the artistic
principle underlying both this novel and its successor,
Aus dem Tagebuch einer Schnecke."[13] Certainly the free
association of ideas and images and the stream of consciousness constitute the structural coherence to which
the dentist's chair as the focal point of the narrative
also contributes.   In passing it may be observed that the
first few lines of the novel also announce one of the central themes of *Örtlich betäubt*:   that of involvement or
non-involvement.   From her resting place Starusch's so-
called fiancée tries to sell the delights of opting out.

The novel's narrative technique allows the narrator
cum protagonist to emerge as a much more paradoxical character than his counterpart in the play.   In the novel Starusch is characterised as the advocate of non-violence
even though his imagination revels in the possibilities
of violence.   The dentist points out Starusch's predisposition to violence.   Before treatment begins, the dentist
informs his patient that his overbite ('Hackbiß') and his
protruding jaw suggest innate brutality (p. 13).   Starusch
reports the contents of a conversation to Irmgard Seifert
in which the dentist summarises his patient's condition:
"das alles-- die Summe aus Zahnbild und Psyche-- verrät

Sie: eingelagerte Gewalttätigkeiten, Mordanschläge auf
Vorrat." (p. 23). The dentist completes the analysis by
stating that his patient's hatred of self and others can
be traced back to his failures both in his sexual and his
professional life (p. 50). Starusch's mental condition
is described as not being untypical of other-- some imaginary, some known-- members of German society from past to
present: Starusch would have us believe that he was rejected by his fiancée (see p. 79), whilst Hitler was
turned down by the Viennese Academy of Fine Arts (p. 53),
and Field-Marshal Krings, who is the father of Sieglinde
and is modelled on the Nazi General Ferdinand Schörner,
was defeated in battle during the Second World War. The
wounds of defeat keep on festering, the infection undermines physical and mental health, and the diseased out-
burst of violence may affect the body politic.

Accordingly Starusch relates a series of anecdotes
which are purely products of his own imagination and which
stem from his own sense of inadequacy and self-derision.
Such fanciful experiments with violence are in themselves
a kind of pain-killer and serve, in Starusch's mind, to
anaesthetize him against the pain of failure. In one of
his stories he describes how a man murders his fiancée
with a bicycle chain, and manages to escape capture for
nine years until he is forced to surrender himself to the

police because of acute toothache (pp. 37-40). Another
woman comes to an untimely end because her fiancé photo-
graphs her asleep with a flashlight bulb. Not unexpec-
tedly Starusch identifies himself with this photographer
(pp. 44-45). Another story-- once again presumably an
invention conjured up by his reading of one of the illus-
trated magazines-- allows him to project himself in the
role of a taxidriver who in rapid succession bumps off
his noisy son, his fiancée named Linde and his future
mother-in-law. The taxidriver is suffering, as might be
expected, from the customary toothache (pp. 53-55). Even
after his dental treatment has been completed, Starusch
appears on the island of Sylt as a baths superintendent
and operates a wave machine against Linde, Schlottau (her
husband by then) and family with its full tidal fury (pp.
188-191).

The dentist acts as father-confessor and psychologist
who explains the nature of his patient's fanciful aber-
rations: "das macht Ihnen doch Spaß, nicht wahr, dieser
selbstherrliche Umfang mit Fahrradketten und Blitzlicht-
lampen." (p. 50). Starusch's attempts at self-glorifica-
tion remind the reader of Oskar Matzerath's delight in
committing murders. Ultimately the dentist unmasks Starusch totally as a liar and impostor: he claims that his
patient was not an engineer at all in the years 1954 and

1955, that Sieglinde was not the name of his fiancée and indeed that no engagement took place at all (p. 178). The history teacher is thereby established as belonging to the long line of unreliable narrators, whom Grass has introduced into German literature.

If Starusch's instrument for dispatching his fiancée is a bicycle chain (see p. 39, p. 85, and elsewhere), his principal method of revolutionary change is the bulldozer (p. 73, p. 78, p. 86 and p. 89). His revolutionary bulldozer does occur in the play, but the teacher mentions it with greater insistence in the novel. In conversation with his dentist Starusch often speaks of the temptation to sweep aside existing society and start afresh (see pp. 86-87). The dentist, however, demands that his patient rid his mind of the idea of bulldozers destroying the consumer society and its attendant evils, advises him to trust in the principles of moderation and progress and insists on his renouncing violence. He has a counter-measure calculated to elicit the correct response: he will refuse to anaesthetize his patient's lower jaw if he does not comply (p. 74). As an image it is singularly appropriate, for it recalls an attitude of mind characteristic of the student rebellion of the late sixties. R. Hinton Thomas and Keith Bullivant describe the students of the late sixties as a generation which was "now

accustomed to the idea that, on the analogy of many an industrial product, there was nothing that could not in
principle be quickly changed and improved."[14]

As has been already suggested, Günter Grass accen-
tuates the panoramic sweep of the novel and its allusive
quality vis-à-vis the play by introducing other characters
into the narrative. Some of these characters are ones
who make frequent appearances on the dentist's television
screen, the impact of which is exclusively controlled by
Starusch's hyper-active imagination. The pictures he produces on the screen show in particular the interaction
between Sieglinde Krings, the fiancée with whom Starusch
provides himself as a compensation for under-achievement
in the amorous realm, and her father Field Marshal Ferdinand Krings. The Field Marshal in question who according
to Starusch's imaginative account is supposed to have
played a dominant role in the German military campaigns
of the Second World War, returns from Soviet captivity to
his native Rhineland in 1955 and manages to evade the
jeering welcome of some of his former soldiers at the
station in Koblenz by alighting from the train at another
station (pp. 29-31). In the television film one person
is particularly disappointed by Kring's non-appearance
and that is a certain Heinrich Schlottau whom Starusch
has created as a fictitious competitor to externalize his

all-pervading sense of inadequacy and who wishes to settle
accounts with his former general. Krings has a sand-box
('Sandkasten') set up in a barrack by Schlottau with all
the necessary electrical gadgetry so that the battles of
the Russian campaign in all their complexity can be stra-
tegically simulated in miniature (p. 51). Linde takes it
upon herself to act as her father's opponent in these re-
constructed battles of history. He is obsessed by his
own military defeats and those of others during the war
(see p. 49). His daughter's objective is to defeat her
father in these simulated battles and in effect to force
him to accept his own failures and failings in the same
sense that Germany and her people have to come to terms
with the consequences of Hitler's war. She is allegedly
attempting to rid her father of his illusions and to restore his mental balance.

When Grass describes Starusch's dental treatment, he
places it in juxtaposition with Linde's attempts to defeat her father's military adventures in the sand-box.
By then the connection between the two characters is
clear: both Starusch and Krings are in need of cure.
The teacher must leave his emotional puberty behind (his
"Milchzahnalter"-- p. 66) and have his wisdom teeth re-
paired; and the General must be jolted into the reality
of the present.

Grass mentions the idea of "Sandkastenspiele" and "Sandkastensiege" elsewhere both in *Der Bürger und seine Stimme* (pp. 56-57) and in *Aus dem Tagebuch einer Schnecke* (p. 180). In a speech entitled "Rede von den begrenzten Möglichkeiten" he says that the Germans have never had any difficulty in beginning wars and in wishing to bring salvation to the world.[15] They have found it impossible, however, to admit defeat and to accept the consequences of a lost war. Accordingly, he maintains, it is not unusual for people to indulge in 'games in a sand-box' and surrender themselves to the illusion of a German victory. The strategists who play these games could not, for example, recognise the finality of the Oder-Neisse frontier. Adenauer's policy of strength encouraged such escapism and was based on the illusion that the clock of history could be turned back. Ferdinand Krings in *Örtlich betäubt* is an example of the kind of sand-box strategist whom Grass condemns in his theoretical writings and speeches.

In part III Grass contrasts another two scenes with an effect similar to the one achieved by the juxtaposition of Krings' defeat by his daughter and Starusch's dental treatment (pp. 51-52). In the last part Starusch's fantasy has taken flight again, ably assisted by his innate predisposition to violence, and he plays the part of the student setting his dog alight in front of the Kempinski

hotel. This episode is placed side by side with the re-
enactment of the battle of Stalingrad in Krings' sand-
box. The montage of this type is facilitated by the fact
that Starusch is 'showing' these contrasting events on
the television screen-- thoughtfully left blank so that
he may project onto it the convoluted figments of his
imagination ("krause(n) Fiktionen"-- p. 170). Sections
describing these two disparate events alternate. The al-
ternating elements within the film interpenetrate each
other, producing a new quality of meaning. The two 'defeats' are contrasted, for example, in the following manner: "Auf dem Kurfürstendamm blutete ich (meine rechte
Braue war aufgeschlagen) und in der Zementbaracke D war
ich mit Schlottau Zeuge, wie Linde ihren Vater im Sandkasten besiegte." (p. 180). The montage of these two
elements generates a new awareness. The impression is
created that both these events stem from a mind inflamed
by an imagination which has no longer remained in contact
with reality. Both protagonists have plunged into the
depths of irrationality and both need to acknowledge the
claims of reason and moderation. Restructuring the past,
illusionary hankering after unattainable objectives on
the part of the sand-box strategist, and the extremism and
inhumanity of the utopian revolutionary have much more in
commom and deserve to be condemned in equal measure, for

both actions are apolitical and irresponsible. By contrasting these two events Grass highlights the element of
continuity in the German development-- the cult of unreason at whose altar people still worship. At the same
time it is clear that Starusch, the ostensible advocate
of non-violence, has still not come to terms with his own
complexes and with his own past. In short, the dentist
has not been successful in persuading his patient to abandon his 'confused fictions'.

Even on the dental level the efforts to restore the
patient's health remain inconclusive, if not ineffectual.
The novel ends on the following note: "und bei mir bil-
dete sich unten links ein Herd. Die Degudentbrücke wurde
durchgesägt. Minus sechs mußte gezogen werden. Der Herd
wurde ausgekratzt. Mein Zahnarzt zeigte mir ein an der
Wurzelspitze hängendes Säckchen: eitrig-wässriges Ge-
webe. Nichts hält vor. Immer neue Schmerzen." (p. 192).
The dental operation has proved to be a failure, the dentist is forced to destroy what should have emerged as a
significant achievement. The ending is ambivalent and
also depressing but it is in no way unrealistic, for
throughout the novel the idea is presented that progress
is frequently minute and elusive and that man's control
over reality is insecure. The dentist is acutely aware
of the snail-like pace of progress and accepts this fact

both rationally and emotionally: he is described on one
occasion as "jemand, den Niederlagen nicht umwerfen." (p.
166 *Örtlich betäubt*). The dentist's unsuccessful operation, Starusch's inability to come to terms with his own
complexes, and the possibility of his withdrawing into
the private sphere, and Scherbaum's social acclimatiza-
tion, all contribute to the general atmosphere of ambivalence and dejection-- the sensation that all human labours
might well be futile. When questioned about the depressing ending of the novel in an interview, Grass replied
that he himself would continue his political work "despite all scepticism," that he was not quite sure whether
Starusch would not lapse into resignation, and that he
was not optimistic about Scherbaum.[16] The ambivalence of
the ending is in line with Grass's view of history as expressed, not only in the Danzig Trilogy, but also in later
novels such as *Der Butt* and *Das Treffen in Telgte*, and is
also in keeping with one of Grass's avowed objectives in
writing the novel, that is, his interest in "die Verwand-
lung eines jugendlich lustig-anarchistischen Täters zu
einem vernünftig melancholischen Bürger und Studienrat."[17]
Grass has also stated that he wished to show "den jungen
Störtebeker, der in seiner Jugend dieses Amoralische hatte, nun als den gebrochenen Mann der Aufklärung, konfron-
tiert mit der Mühsal der Aufklärung..."[18] Such intentions

restrict the author in advance and scarcely allow the novel to bound with limitless optimism. The presentation of
Starusch as the broken man of the enlightenment seems to
be entirely realistic, and corresponds quite understandably to what might well be the predicament of the so-
called liberal in present-day German society.

Örtlich betäubt has not fared well at the hands of
the critics. Hellmuth Karasek summarises the complaints
which have been raised against Grass's novel:

1. Grass ist nicht mehr 'der Alte'.

2. Grass hätte diesen diesen Roman nicht im Moment
    des Wahlkampfes erscheinen lassen sollen.

3. Grass' Roman ist uninteressant, weil seine Fi-
    guren uninteressant sind.

4. Grass' Roman ist zwar uninteressanter als seine
    bisherigen, das liegt aber an unserer verflixten
    farblosen Gegenwart.[19]

Örtlich betäubt has certainly suffered from being
compared almost automatically with *Die Blechtrommel*. Even
though the use of a first person narrator and the view of
history have much in common with earlier-- and later--
novels, the narrative élan which one associates with Grass
is lacking, though it would be wrong to say that this novel marks the beginning of a deterioration in the narrative
ability of its author, for both *Der Butt* and *Das Treffen*

in Telgte could be cited in order to disprove such a contention. It is certainly true that the narrative perspective, i.e. the change from the view from below or from
outside society to one which is located within society,
does diminish the novel's appeal particularly since both
the comic and the grotesque have thereby been eliminated.
Equally true is the fact that the 'Müdeheldensoße' which
the narrator defines as "eine Stimmung trübe gemischt aus
wohldosiertem Mitleid und männlicher Melancholie." (p. 156)
can scarcely by its very nature constitute the basis for
a dynamic novel. In other words, the theme of the novel
diminishes its narrative impact. Furthermore the characters who are presented in the novel are more colourless
and less interesting than those in other novels. Presumably this stems from the fact that with *Örtlich betäubt*
Grass has concentrated more on present-day reality, taken
a step away from the petty bourgeois milieu of, for example, *Die Blechtrommel* and entered an environment which
is populated by the members of the enlightened academic
bourgeoisie.[20] Nevertheless, having said all that, it
must be stressed that *Örtlich betäubt* is a novel which is
different from the other novels of Grass and should be
judged on its own merits. Suffice it to say, in conclusion, that the themes and the narrative technique of the
novel allow us to gain insight into attitudes and

responses which might not be untypical of certain sections
of West German society.

Notes

1. Peter Hamm, *Konkret*, February 1969.

2. Page numbering in *Davor* refers to the student edition, Victor Lange, ed. (New York: Harcourt Brace Jovanovich, 1973).

3. Page numbering in *Örtlich betäubt* refers to the paperback edition (Frankfurt/M: Fischer, 1972).

4. "Peter Weiss und Hans Magnus Enzensberger. Eine Kontroverse," *Kursbuch*, No. 6 (1966), pp. 165-76.

5. Günter Grass, *Abendzeitung*, 21-22.9.1968.

6. Paul Konrad Kurz SJ, "Das verunsicherte Wappentier. Zu *Davor* und *Örtlich betäubt* von Günter Grass," *Stimmen der Zeit*, Vol. 184, No. 12 (1969), 377.

7. Günter Grass, *Aus dem Tagebuch einer Schnecke* (Neuwied and Darmstadt: Luchterhand, 1972), p. 121.

8. Günter Grass, "ad lectores 9," (Neuwied and Berlin: Luchterhand, Sept. 1969).

9. Günter Grass, *Der Bürger und seine Stimme* (Darmstadt and Neuwied: Luchterhand, 1974), p. 62.

10. K. H. Bohrer, *Die gefährdete Phantasie* (Munich, 1970), p. 90.

11. As under note 9, p. 61.

12. As under note 9, p. 64.

13. Irène Leonard, *Günter Grass* (Edinburgh: Oliver and Boyd, 1974), p. 67.

14. R. Hinton Thomas and Keith Bullivant, *Literature in Upheaval* (New York: Manchester University Press, Barnes and Noble Books, 1974), p. 38.

15. Günter Grass, as under note 9, pp. 53-66.

16. E. Rudolph, ed., *Protokoll zur Person. Autoren über sich und ihr Werk* (Munich, 1971), p. 72.

17. Paul Konrad Kurz SJ, as under note 6, p. 385.

18. Heinz Ludwig Arnold, "Gespräche mit Günter Grass," *Text und Kritik*, 1/1a (Munich, 1971), p. 72.

19. Hellmuth Karasek, "Zahn gezogen," *Die Zeit*, 5.9.1969, p. 20.

20. Manfred Durzak, "Abschied von der Kleinbürgerwelt. Der neue Roman von Günter Grass," *Basis*, Vol. I (1970), 228.

CHAPTER V

Aus dem Tagebuch einer Schnecke: *Grass versus Hegel*

Unlike the Nobel prize for literature, the title of
praeceptor Germaniae has not been conferred with universal acclaim on any one post-war German author. Rightly
or wrongly, Thomas Mann received the award in the pre-war
period, though it was necessary to ignore 'his intellectual war service with weapon in hand' as evidenced in
Betrachtungen eines Unpolitischen, in which he expressed
support for Germany's struggle against Western democracy.
Heinz Ludwig Arnold has, however, already proposed Grass's
name for the award: he maintains that, wittingly or unwittingly, Grass has become a kind of praeceptor democratiae Germaniae, adding even that the role appears to suit
him.[1] The article concerned appeared interestingly enough
before the publication of *Aus dem Tagebuch einer Schnecke*,
in fact in March 1969.

The present chapter seeks to investigate whether
Günter Grass does achieve a didactic purpose in *Aus dem
Tagebuch einer Schnecke*: it attempts to establish whether
Grass, through the medium of this novel and by the example

of his democratic involvement as described in it, is able
to provide an alternative to the philosophy of the state
as expounded by Hegel, a philosophy which subordinated
the individual to the state and helped to make the 'German Catastrophe' of National Socialism possible. In
short, it tries to show whether Grass is contributing to
the emergence of a new political and social consciousness
which attaches supreme importance to the moral responsibility of the individual.

It is certainly true that even in the Danzig Trilogy
Grass describes "die blinde amoralische Realität mit
ihren elementaren Interessen"[2] and in so doing highlights
many of those aspects which made the plunge into collective unreason possible. Without indulging in moralisa-
tion Grass refers in narrative form to strands in the
German development which J. P. Stern in his book on Hitler has analysed as the basis of the National Socialist
ideology-- in theory and in practice.[3] In *Die Blechtrommel* the cult of unreason, the theme of messianic mega-
lomania, sacrifice as a motivating force and the yearning
for purity and redemption are all part of the narrative
texture. In *Katz und Maus* the Faustian theme of the pursuit of experience as an end in itself is central to the
'Novelle' as are the pseudo-religious associations connected with sacrifice. In *Hundejahre* the relationship

between Jew and Gentile forms the core of the plot.   In
Die Blechtrommel the reader is tempted to draw interesting
parallels between Hitler and Oskar: both are drummers,
both are moral cretins and in a sense both may be regarded
as examples of the representative individual (if one may
use the term which J. P. Stern employs for the title of
his first chapter).   None of these three books pursues a
narrowly moral purpose.   There are no signs of an accusing
finger but the choice of narrative and thematic material
does achieve a critical, if not satiric effect.   The three
books concerned can be most aptly described as a threnody.
As is well known, however, all teachers commence their
harangues by referring in tones of horror and sadness
tinged with appropriate outbursts of sarcasm to what
should never have been.   The moral lesson always follows
the lament.

In laying bare the roots of national socialism and
post-war hedonism Grass usually points to trends rather
than to names of specific individuals.   In describing in
personal and distorted fashion Germany's surrender to irrationality, he does not, for example, mention the name
of Nietzsche, though this name cannot have been far from
his mind, particularly in his references to Apollo and
Dionysos.   However, Goethe's name is mentioned in his
first novel in order to emphasise how reason was undermined

by passion as embodied in the person of Rasputin. A Wag-
nerian hero appears occasionally, Lohengrin for example
in *Die Blechtrommel*, and *Götterdämmerung* provides one of
the leitmotifs of *Hundejahre*, thus pointing to the fascination of self-destruction. One name which occurs frequently in *Hundejahre* is, of course, that of the German
philosopher Martin Heidegger who is accorded a sound linguistic drubbing. In *Aus dem Tagebuch einer Schnecke* it
is Hegel who receives comparable punishment from the pen
of Grass the satirist.

Narrative perspective and content change with the
publication of *Örtlich betäubt* in 1969. The emphasis
shifts from the pre-war to the post-war world. The pessimistic circularity of the Danzig Trilogy recedes in order to allow a faint glimmer of optimistic light to
emerge. The author abandons at least partially his detached pose and enters the narrative fray: author and
narrator join hands in the person of a teacher by the
name of Starusch. The moral lesson begins and the lament
is toned down. In *Aus dem Tagebuch einer Schnecke* author
and narrator enter into a state of blissful union-- Grass
the international novelist and politically involved citizen talks to his children about the 1969 election campaign. He still finds a place for a teacher in his novel, i.e. Hermann Ott, alias Zweifel, and so the reader is

subjected to what is tantamount to a double-barrelled didactic onslaught, the one barrel being fired by the narrator and the other being fired by Zweifel, object of the
narration and at the same time moral example. One of the
targets of this combined assault is Georg Wilhelm Friedrich Hegel.

Before isolating Hegel's role in the novel it may be
appropriate to outline the structure of *Aus dem Tagebuch
einer Schnecke*. The novel consists of three frames of
reference. The first frame of reference is provided by
the events of the present, the present in question being
that which extended from the election of Gustav Heinemann
to the presidency of the Federal Republic on the 5th March
1969 until the federal elections on the 28th September
1969 when the social democrats made sufficient gains for
them to be able to replace the Great Coalition of Christian Democrats and Social Democrats by the Small Coalition
comprising the combined forces of SPD and FDP. During
these seven months Grass was engaged in the election campaign in support of the SPD. In the course of the book
Grass explains the nature of his political activities and
the reasons for his involvement to his four children. In
this sense Grass's novel fulfils the same purpose as the
two volumes which Victor Gollancz wrote for his grandson,
Timothy, and which he described as being an autobiographi-

cal letter. During the election campaign Grass covers
thirty-one thousand kilometres, gives ninety-four speeches
and encourages the setting-up of sixty local action com-
mittees ('Wählerinitiativen') which are intended to pro-
mote interest amongst the electorate for the social democrats and contribute to their ultimate electoral success.
What Grass describes is a grand tour of Germany, a political odyssey which, by kind permission of Laurence Sterne,
might even be referred to as a modern sentimental journey, if by that term one meant a journey occasioned by
sentiment. As one might expect, however, the delightful
whimsicality of Sterne is forced to retreat under the impact of political considerations. On his pilgrimage
through Germany our electioneer encounters a variety of
individuals and provides us with a series of thumb-nail
sketches of politicians: Brandt, Wehner, Ehmke, Eppler
as well as Strauss and Barzel, friend and foe alike, all
dance to the tune of his pen. One person who leaves a
lasting mark upon the autobiographer is a pharmacist by
the name of Augst who commits suicide at an Evangelical
Church Congress which Grass attends. Grass's sentimental
journey takes him abroad to visit Jews in Israel who originally lived, like our author, in Danzig, and to visit a
Czech friend of his behind the Iron Curtain at a time
when the invasion of Czechoslovakia by the Warsaw Pact

countries is still fresh in people's minds. During his
brief visits to his family in Berlin Grass provides us
also with a picture of his own domestic scene as well as
supplying us with advice on the art of cooking.

If the first frame of reference deals with the present, the second frame of reference concentrates upon the
past. In response to the children's questions their father tells the story of the Danzig Jews from 1933 onwards,
how the Jewish community in Danzig is reduced from 10,448
in 1929 to 20 members at the time of the Russian occupation towards the end of the war. He describes how his
fellow-townsmen, acting on the principle that 'the Jews
are our our misfortune' persecute the non-Aryan members
of their society, driving them to suicide or forcing them
to emigrate, and how other Jews of Danzig are shot or
gassed in the concentration camp near Danzig and elsewhere or fall victim to disease during their attempt to
reach Palestine. The reader soon senses that a causal relationship exists between the fate of the Danzig Jews and
Grass's political activities. Our author also introduces
us to a fictitious character whose life is intimately connected with the history of the Jews of Danzig, and who in
his own small way tries to alleviate the suffering of his
Jewish compatriots before he himself is forced to take
flight. Although the character of Hermann Ott (whose

nickname 'Zweifel' is the German word for 'doubt') did
not exist, his life is nevertheless modelled upon that of
Marcel Reich-Ranicki, a well-known literary critic in
West Germany. Zweifel was a student of philosophy and
biology and devoted much of his time to the analysis of
snails and slugs and their behaviour. *The Oxford Companion to German Literature* reminds us that this creature,
i.e. the snail, "is generally regarded more amiably in
Germany than in Britain and figures in many children's
books." Hermann Ott soon comes into conflict with the
National Socialists, simply because he wishes to treat
the Jews in the way one would wish to treat any other human beings, and is forced to take flight in order to save
his own skin. He takes refuge in a bicycle repairer's
cellar and spends the war years there. He is subject to
the whims of his uncouth and often brutish, though basically amiable host, for both of them wish to survive National Socialism and are dependent on each other, their
dependence varying in relationship to the military-- and
political-- situation at the time. Zweifel tries to humour and divert his Kaschubian host by the typical Grass-
like expedient of relating stories. During his underground sojourn the snail-philosopher falls in love with
his host's daughter, Lisbeth Stomma, who has been a victim of melancholy and condemned to dumbness since she lost

both her son and her son's father in the opening stages
of the war. Lisbeth remains cold and unresponsive until
one day Zweifel applies a snail to her which in the manner of a leech sucks the melancholy out of her. From
that moment onwards he is subjected to both a linguistic
and a sexual onslaught. Ott believed that love could
overcome hate, such a belief, contrary to his philosophical attitude, being absolute. When in the post-war years
he finds that love is not the panacea for the woes of the
world and that it does not automatically compensate for
human frailty, he himself falls prey in his disillusionment to melancholy and spends a period of 12 years-- from
1947 to 1959-- in a mental asylum, as did Oskar, the hero
of *Die Blechtrommel*.

The third frame of reference is formed by Grass's
lecture on Dürer's etching 'Melencolia I' which he gives
in 1971 on the occasion of the five-hundredth anniversary
of the birth of Dürer in the town of Nuremberg and which
is reproduced in full in the final pages of the book.
Grass makes the connection between the election campaign
and his lecture abundantly clear in his introductory remarks: "Vom 5. März bis zum 28. September war ich unterwegs auf Wahlreise und gleichwohl auf der Suche nach Stoff
für meinen Dürervortrag." (p. 341).[4] The reader is hence
not surprised to find that before the lecture begins a

number of anticipatory remarks and the presence of inter-
related themes which constitute the basis of the talk
have prepared him in advance for its content. Grass describes utopianism and melancholy as kindred souls and
finds examples of melancholy in the everyday life of the
modern world. Both attitudes of mind can lead to a retreat from reality, especially if coupled with resignation. Nevertheless Grass interprets Dürer's etching not
as the embodiment of a dull, all-embracing, nihilistic
melancholy but as one which stems from knowledge of oneself and of the world and hence can be harnessed to serve
a positive purpose. Such melancholy may be viewed as a
kind of breathing space during which one pauses, reviews
the situation, regains one's strength and perspective in
order to sally forth once again in the name of progress
which proceeds in any case at a snail's pace. In his
closing remarks Grass thus makes a plea for the acceptance
of melancholy and the snail philosophy as productive allies: "Nur wer den Stillstand im Fortschritt kennt und
achtet, wer schon einmal, wer mehrmals aufgegeben hat, wer
auf dem leeren Schneckenhaus gesessen und die Schattenseite der Utopie bewohnt hat, kann Fortschritt ermessen."
(p. 368).

The three frames of reference coexist in juxtaposition, a technique to which Grass has frequently and

successfully had recourse. There is a stimulating and
fruitful interaction between past and present, the one
moulding and being moulded by the other. Common themes
and images interlink the three frames of reference: the
image of the horse, which is intended to represent Hegel's
world spirit, and especially the image of the snail as
well as the complex of ideas associated with them serve
as cohesive bonds throughout the novel. The snail makes
its début on the second page of the novel and by the third
page it has already been apostrophized as the symbol of
progress. Both Grass and Ott whose views largely coin-
cide and who believe in gradual evolutionary change regard the snail as the metaphorical representation of the
democratic principle. It is the affirmation of compromise and moderation as a means of making progress. It
stands for the middle way in politics and society, edging
its slow pace between utopianism and melancholy and steer-
ing past the pitfalls of absolute thinking, whether of a
left-wing or right-wing vintage, with its maximum demands
and heroic appeal for sacrifice. By its connection with
the personalities of Grass and Zweifel it incorporates
the principle of scepticism as the antidote for unreason
and as the counter-weight to those flights of fantasy
which lead away from the ordinary world into the sphere
of the superhuman. It contents itself with limited

objectives and partial successes rather than with grandiose schemes and total success or total failure. It operates in accordance with pragmatic rather than theoretical
considerations. The snail represents not only an attitude of mind but also one particular mind, i.e. that of
the author, narrator and electioneer, Günter Grass, as is
evidenced in the title of the book. The fact that the
diary is written by *a* snail suggests that Grass makes no
unique claims for himself and that his example may be imi-
tated by other like-minded individuals. The snail's adversary in life's confrontations is, of course, the horse,
the metaphorical representative of Hegel and his world
spirit.

It is not difficult to understand why Hegel should
be singled out for attention. Bertrand Russell in his
History of Western Philosophy, maintains that Hegel ad-
vocated a doctrine of the state which "justifies every internal tyranny and every external agression that can possibly be imagined." Statements such as "The State is the
Divine Idea as it exists on earth" (p. 767) or "War has
the higher significance that through it the moral health
of people is preserved in their indifference towards the
stabilizing of finite determinations" (p. 768) ought to
be sufficient to spawn whole generations of Hermann Otts
or sceptics, particularly if they have been nurtured on

the political philosophy of John Locke or brought up within the implications of such a philosophy. Hegel's attitude to freedom is also unlikely to meet with much approv-
al from the would-be democrat, in that it consists largely in the right to obey the law. The principle of 'insight into necessity' which is so popular in the GDR, and
which is the individual's substitute for freedom, allowing him to accept with good grace whatever authority pro-
poses, would appear to proceed from the Hegelian state.
One cannot help oneself: anyone with a democratic blood-
stream inevitably and automatically treats such ideas
with derision. Grass is subject to the same temptation
and one has to admit that derision can be a very effective
weapon for the teacher. One's natural reaction to Hegelian propositions-- at least in the political sphere-- is
not to engage in long-winded counter-arguments, for it
seems self-evident that the state should exist for the
sake of its citizens and not vice versa.

In a conversation with Gertrude Cepl-Kaufmann Günter
Grass produced a generalised statement indicating the nature of his objection to the doctrine of the state as set
out by Hegel. His objection is in essence the same as
that of Bertrand Russell, but he does not concern himself
with any detailed analysis of Hegel's theories: "Ich bin
ein Gegner der Hegelschen Geschichtsphilosophie, und wenn

man das erweitern will auch seiner Staatslehre, die ich

für ein geeignetes Instrumentarium für Diktaturen halte.

Absolutsetzen des Staates... Das sind für mich Gründe,

Hegel abzulehnen."[5]   He goes on to say that both left-

wing and right-wing interpreters of Hegel make use of him

as a basis for the totalitarian state.   In *Aus dem Tage-*

buch einer Schnecke Grass is equally reluctant to produce

a systematised account of his objections to Hegel's phi-

losophy of the state.   His weapons of attack are of a

different nature.   Throughout his narrative works Grass

has been intent on those images which in the past have

had an insidious effect upon the formation of the national

consciousness.   One needs only to look at the covers of

Grass's novels to realise that in his first three novels

he is concerned in demolishing nationalistic imagery,

whether it be that of the Knight's Cross in *Katz und Maus*;

the Hitler salute in the form of the raised black arm,

only the bones of which stand out and the hand of which

is shaped in the head of a dog as can be seen on the front

cover of *Hundejahre*;   or the blue-eyed drummer-boy messi-

anically beating the retreat from reason in the case of

Die Blechtrommel.   In these instances Grass sets out to

undermine the significance of such complexes of imagery

and attitudes.   They are in essence negative images.   On

the covers of *Örtlich betäubt* and *Aus dem Tagebuch einer*

Schnecke Grass has for the first time imagery to which he
attaches a positive value. In the second of these two
novels Grass places a negative image, that of the horse--
and its rider-- alongside a positive image, that of the
snail (or slug), as can be seen from the following quotation which refers to Hegel: "In Jena, Kinder, hat er den
Kaiser Napoleon hoch zu Roß und in der Einheit Roß und
Reiter etwas gesehen, das er Weltgeist nannte;   seitdem
galoppiert er-- während ich auf das Bewußtsein der Schneck-
en setzte." (p. 51). Hegel's admiration for Napoleon is
well-known, as is the fact that he rejoiced in the victory of French arms at the battle of Jena in 1806. It is
also known that Hegel did see the military dictator of
France in Jena, as the following letter to Niethammer reveals: "I saw the Emperor, this world soul, riding out
of town in order to engage in reconnaissance;-- it is indeed a wonderful feeling to see such an individual who on
horseback and concentrated on one point reaches out over
the world and dominates it."[6] Later he describes Napoleon
as "the great teacher of constitutional law."[7] Georg
Lukas in his book entitled *The Young Hegel* confirms the
importance which Hegel attached to Napoleon in his philosophical thinking.

It is clear from the last quotation from Grass's
novel that the positive image of the snail has as its

counterpart the negative image of the horse. It is this
image of the horse which is meant to represent the complex of ideas associated with Hegel's political thinking
and to give allusive expression to the impact which such
thinking has made upon German history and culture. The
image of the horse-- and its rider-- is one which recurs
frequently throughout Grass's novel and it is one which
has played a significant role in German national history.
This image may well have its origins in the Book of Revelation in which a mounted rider prepares the way for the
coming of the Holy City, whilst an Angel imprisons Satan
for a thousand years: "And I saw heaven opened, and be-
hold a white horse; and he that sat upon him was called
Faithful and True; and in righteousness he doth judge
and make war." (Chapter 19, verse 11). Perhaps such a
description provided the inspiration for the stonemason
who created the Rider to be seen in Bamberg cathedral.
Such a statue may have been based on a likeness of a German Emperor, Frederick II, but it acquired nationalistic
overtones at the beginning of the twentieth century when
it was viewed as being a symbol of the ideal aristocratic
ruler. Its nationalistic significance was also enhanced
when a cavalry regiment was named after it. An equally
famous horse and rider is the one depicted in the drawing
entitled 'Ritter, Tod und Teufel" which Dürer produced in

1513, one year before his 'Melencolia I'. It is said
that some writers in Germany interpreted this work in a
nationalistic manner, claiming that this picture represented the situation of the German people beset by dif-
ficulties-- riding through the shadow of the valley of
death (the 23rd Psalm is the one which is read at Augst's
funeral-- see p. 246)-- but pressing forward to a distant
vision of salvation. In 1924 Hans F. K. Günther who was
later to become a leading theorist of National Socialism
published a book entitled *Ritter, Tod und Teufel: der
heldische Gedanke*, attempting to explain this drawing as
an allegory of the German 'Volk'. Another well-known
horse and rider is to be found at the moment in front of
the Charlottengurg Palace in West Berlin: that of the
Great Elector, who in the seventeenth century laid the
firm foundation for the later expansion of Prussia. In
passing it may be mentioned that Kleist's *Prinz Friedrich
von Homburg* in which the Great Elector appears as a character, and which was held in high esteem by the Nazis, is
a play which Zweifel performs in his cellar theatre (p.
234). Grass does in fact refer in passing to his lecture
entitled 'Rede wider die Kurfürsten' in the section which
deals at length with Hegel (pp. 51-52) though he does not
single out the Great Elector for special mention, neither
in his novel nor in the lecture itself. It is not

inappropriate to note that in Kleist's play Friedrich
Wilhelm is described as appearing in the thick of the battle of Fehrbellin on his horse and it is rumoured initially that both horse and rider have been killed (Act II,
Scene 5). However, the Elector of Brandenburg, absolute
ruler of his domain, returns from battle to sit in judgement on the Prince of Homburg. Both Luther and Bismarck
visualised Germany in equestrian terms: the father of the
German Reformation described Germany in his Table Talk as
a beautiful and mighty stallion which had everything it
needed apart from a rider; in March 1867, one year after
his victory over Austria-Hungary and three years before
his equally triumphant war against France, Bismarck, the
founder of the German empire, varied the imagery slightly
by stating that Germany should be put in the saddle, and
expressed his confidence in its capacity to ride. It is
clear that the image of the horse and rider exercised an
appeal on the popular imagination in Germany long before
the Nazis came to power. It does not seem inappropriate
in the light of these preceding remarks for Grass to visu-
alize Hegel in terms of an image which has nationalistic
overtones and to satirise this "Weltgeist in Kleppergestalt" (p. 357) or "diesen durchgegangenen Gaul" (p. 52).

The image of the horse also figures in a literary
work whose main character along with his attitudes Grass

ridicules both in *Aus dem Tagebuch einer Schnecke* (p. 317)
and in *Der Bürger und seine Stimme* (p. 240): in this instance it is Michael Kohlhaas who is the main character
in the 'Novelle' of that name by Kleist, whose horses are
ill-treated and who in his quest for justice becomes a
robber and murderer. The symbolical significance of these
horses is of a different nature to that of the horse which
Napoleon rides and which by allusion Hegel also rides.
They are, however, associated with Hegelian modes of
thought: Kohlhaas's absolute demand for restitution has
much in common with the all-or-nothing, black-or-white
mentality of the National Socialists and-- Grass would
claim-- with that of the revolutionary students of post-
war Germany. Grass makes his position quite clear in *Der
Bürger und seine Stimme* when describing the attitude of
Kohlhaas and those who are following in his footsteps:
"Sein Anlaß-- war es ein zerbombtes Grundstück, ein Ren-
tenanspruch oder auch nur ein Gärtchen mit sieben Sauer-
kirschbäumchen-- hat Jahresringe angesetzt, hat Dimen-
sionen gewonnen: Der Mensch, die Gerechtigkeit, Sein oder
Nichtsein sind in Frage gestellt. Es geht nicht um lappig
gewordene Scheine, sondern ums Ganze. Kohlhaas und seine
Pferde. Er will sie wiederhaben und sei es als Kadaver."
(p. 240).

One final horse-- and its rider-- may be mentioned,

one, however, which does not exist in *Aus dem Tagebuch einer Schnecke* but whose existence is implied. Grass states that he likes to think of Herbert Wehner as Moses dividing in this instance not the waters, but what he refers to as "den Mief" (see pp. 264-65). His main description of Wehner is also preceded by a section which deals with an updated version of the Exodus story and the dividing of the sea. Anyone who has had the good fortune to sing or listen to Handel's 'Israel in Egypt', or, more pertinently, any Jew-- and one must remember that one of the narrative strands in Grass's novel deals with the exodus of the Jews from Danzig-- will immediately recall that the parting of the waters coincided with the drowning of the Egyptians. Moses and the children of Israel sing a song of praise to the Lord, "for he hath triumphed gloriously: the horse and his rider hath he thrown into the sea," (*Exodus*, Chapter 15, verse 1). The rider in this instance is another tyrant of history, not Napoleon, nor Hegel with his Napeolonic hat (cf. p. 176) but Pharaoh. Wehner's objective in his political activities as one of those who has led the social democrats out of the wilderness is to do battle with that complex of ideas and prejudices, for which Hegel is in some measure responsible, that collective fug of nationalistic sentiment which led "zu einer Ortschaft, die Auschwitz heißt, aber auch

Treblinka heißen könnte." (*Der Bürger und seine Stimme*,
p. 90). In figurative language one might say that Wehner's-- and Grass's-- aim is to triumph gloriously over
horse and rider, that combination which, according to
Grass, Hegel visualised as the world spirit. Grass sets
himself the task of finding a middle road between the po-
larised extremes of German political thinking and behaviour. He has to cut a path through a series of obstacles
which is presented by the implications of Hegelian philosophy. Like every good praeceptor Germaniae he is pursuing a didactic objective.

One critic of Grass's political attitudes comments
upon his failure to produce a systematised analysis of
his own political philosophy, claiming that new political
thinking is what the Germans stand in need of: "Seine
Überzeugungen politischer Natur decken sich gewiß mit
denen von mehr als 30 Prozent der deutschen Wähler. Aber
in der Tatsache einer solchen von vielen geteilten Erkenntnis und Beurteilung liegt eben nicht allein das We-
sentliche, das dieser politischen Landschaft gut täte:
nicht an sprachlich perfekt, plastisch und bildhaft pla-
kierten Überzeugungen fehlt es uns, sondern am politischen
Denken. Nicht die Erziehung zu Überzeugungen führt uns
weiter, sondern die Erziehung zu differenziertendem Denken,
das Ressentiments auflöst."

He also maintains that even though Grass fits into his
role as a kind of a praeceptor democratiae Germaniae very
well, his role has "a moral and unfortunately not a political function." Admittedly this article by Heinz Ludwig
Arnold was published in 1969 but was reprinted in a collection of essays in 1973.[8] Nevertheless its general pre-
suppositions seem to miss the democratic mark completely
in that they ignore the moral basis of democratic thinking and democratic participation. Even Gertrude Cepl-
Kaufmann who refers to Grass's rejection of Hegel's philosophy in *Aus dem Tagebuch einer Schnecke* in her book
appears to be uneasy about the lack of historical relativ-
isation, sober analysis and differentiation (p. 118).
Dieter E. Zimmer, commenting in *Die Zeit* on *Aus dem Tagebuch einer Schnecke* (Nr. 39, 29.9.1972) makes the following observation about Grass's political activities: "Aber
von einem derartigen Buch erwartete ich doch einige nähere
Aufschlüsse darüber, um welcher Ziele willen diese Placke-
rei denn nun unternommen wird. Nicht unbedingt umfassende
politische Theorien, von mir aus bruchstückhafte pragma-
tische Binsenwahrheiten-- aber doch auf jeden Fall einen
Versuch zu Analyse und Folgerung."

The critics of Grass's political attitude appear to
be still partially influenced by the age-old German belief that a political orientation must have its foundation

in a specific theoretical viewpoint. Grass's response
would be in effect to stress the personal and moral aspect of his thinking and his behaviour, and be prepared
to claim that pragmatic adaptation to events in a sensitive and enlightened manner was more appropriate in the
sphere of politics than predetermined adherence to principle and programme. It is, of course, possible that
Grass might be over-reacting to the ideological, theoretical approach to politics. Nevertheless it is clear in
Aus dem Tagebuch einer Schnecke-- and this is the case in
his other novels-- that his motivation within the sphere
of politics is based upon the negative reaction or a moralist to the course of German history up to 1945 and to
aspects of the German mentality which continue to exist
since 1945, as he himself states in *Der Bürger und seine
Stimme* (p. 265). In the novel Grass tells us how during
the election campaign of 1969 he explains the nature of
his current literary activities to a group of monks at
the monastery of Maria Laach: "Ich verriet den nahezu
sozialistischen Mönchen, daß ich dabei sei, euch um-
schweifig zu erzählen, wie es zu all dem gekommen ist,
warum ich so oft unterwegs sein muß, und wieviele Niederlagen Zweifel hat einstecken müssen, bis er seine Flucht
zu erwägen begann." (p. 145). From the context it is
clear that "all dem" refers to the history of the Jews in

Danzig as the microcosm of Germany. Elsewhere he also
emphasises that the starting point for his political activity is a reaction against the past and against the attitude of mind as represented by certain individuals: on
one occasion he states that he is concerned with preven-
tion (p. 39) and on another occasion he claims that he is
greatly indebted to Franz Josef Strauss for the realisation that his rise to power must be prevented (p. 327).

In Nazi Germany, and in that part of Europe occupied
by German troops, a minority group was exterminated.
Grass was so horrified by the crimes that were committed
in the name of the German people that he must involve
himself in political affairs in order to prevent the repetition of crimes of comparable nature directed against
the individual. The murder of the Jews was prepared long
before Hitler came to power, for, as Grass says, ideas
pave the way for violence. Hence, he goes on to claim,
ideas must be resisted before they are converted into
violent action (p. 173). One core of ideas which made
the dictatorship of Hitler possible is associated with
Hegel and German idealism. Before Grass-- and those who
share his attitude to democracy-- can create a new political climate, he has to clear the gound of those idealistic weeds which have choked the growth of reason in the
past. Grass expresses the sisyphean nature of the task

in the following sentence (Brandt is described on one occasion as though he were a Nordic Sisyphus-- see p. 303):
"Wenn ich den deutschen Idealismus, der dem Spitzwegerich
gleicht, mißmutig jäte, doch unentwegt wächst er nach.
Wie sie immerfort eine Sache-- und sei es die Sache des
Sozialismus-- um ihrer selbst willen betreiben..." (pp.
39-40). In doing battle with German idealism Grass is
not attacking a remote manifestation of the past which
was somehow miraculously eradicated in the year zero of
the German history, but he is engaged in a struggle with
an aspect of the German continuum. The break with tra-
dition-- the 'Kahlschlag' is still not complete, even
though this was part of Grass's purpose in his first three
narrative works.

In attempting to clear the ground for a new democratic ethos, Grass directs his attention at the images which
almost subliminally provided the fertile basis for the
rule of a dictator and the glorification of the state. It
may be claimed, as does Hulme, a Bergsonist, in a paper
published posthumously by Eliot in his *Criterion* (July
1925) that an analogy is "a way of expressing and knowing," that it precedes thought and feeling and hence
creates them.[9] Poets, novelists such as Grass-- and ad-
men-- would certainly agree with such a proposition.
Ezra Pound regards an image as a "node or cluster or

vortex from which and through which and into which ideas constantly rush."[9] If one accepts Hulme's definition of an analogy as antedating thought, then to satirise an image is to ridicule thought in its embryonic form and is at the same time the obvious method for exposing the irrationality and inconsequentiality of a philosophical system. Accordingly, poking fun at Hegel by means of an analogy is a most effective way of reducing the stature of Hegel, the philosopher of the state. The following description of Hermann Ott's denunciation of Hegel is an example of this technique of reduction: "Als er zu Beginn der dreißiger Jahre den Weltgeist in einer Seminararbeit als ein Gespenst beschrieb, das in Kleppergestalt dem Kopf eines spekulierenden Roßtäuschers entsprungen sein müsse, befeindeten ihn gleichlaut die intim verfeindeten Linkshegelianer und Rechtshegelianer; denn die Linken und die Rechten wollten den Weltgeist beritten und galoppieren sehen-- und wenig später galoppierte er auch." (pp. 54-55).

In lampooning Hegel Grass aims at replacing the positive associations attached to Hegel and his idealistic philosophy by negative ones of disapproval. References to Hegel as a horse-dealer, as 'Spekulatius' or 'Mystifizierfritze' is presumably a reference to Hegel's early interest in mysticism which led him to believe in the

unreality of separateness and in the reality of wholeness. The whole, according to Bertrand Russell, is called
by Hegel the "Absolute" (p. 758) and "the Absolute Idea
is pure thought thinking about pure thought." (p. 761).
One is not surprised to find that the key-words of Hegel's
philosophy are also knocked off their pedestals in the
course of Grass's novel, that they are converted into
terms of disapproval. Accordingly Grass describes how
Zweifel "zerlachte Systeme und ließ jedes absolute Gehabe
über seinen Witz springen." (p. 54), and this principle
of jibing at absolute standards and absolute behaviour is
constantly in evidence. Words such as 'total', 'whole',
'absolute', 'pure', 'world spirit', all are subject to an
attack which aims at denting the gloss of their previously positive associations. Grass offers the following advice to his children (and those who, childlike, listen to
the words of the teacher): "Glaubt nicht den Spekulanten.
Da sie nicht hinsehen, sehen sie alles total, urteilen
sie total. Ihr Schwindel heißt Ganzheit. Da stehen sie
deutsch und gesendet: wollen dem Meer bis zum Horizont
den dialektischen Materialismus einpauken; es möge sich
dem System fügen..." (p. 210). For students of German
history the word 'total' ought to have been made unusable
by Goebbel's question to the German people: "Wollt ihr
den totalen Krieg?" Grass establishes a clear and

alarming connection between the attitudes of the Nazis
and those post-war followers of revolutionary communism.
Grass describes how the work of Jewish students was made
impossible by S.A. students, for example, by the fact that
they tipped ink on their technical drawings. When questioned persistently by his children, Grass has to admit,
somewhat reluctantly, that Maoists might well do the same
thing nowadays (pp. 30-31). The attitudes which facilitated the murder of the Jews are still a part of the present German reality. Grass, the pedagogue, issues the
fatherly warning that the just and the violent suffer from
defective hearing and implores his children not to be too
just. Grass lists some of the components of the language
of extermination and of totalitarianism and describes
these words as "the Freisler finger on Lenin's hand"
(p. 20), thus linking together those representatives of
the left- and right-wing who accept Hegel's belief that
all 'Staatsgewalt' is historically necessary (see p. 55).
It is a disturbing linguistic fact that the German word
'Gewalt' refers both to power and to violence. The repetition of Hegel's favourite words in negative contexts
produces a cumulative effect. It begins to deprive such
words of their aura of respectability. One is reminded
of Döblin's dictum which Grass quotes in his essay on his
master: "Im Roman heißt es schichten, häufen, wälzen,

schieben."[10]

A series of very brief references to a person by the name of Bettina who is possibly a student and is helping out in the Grass family suggests in a simple and very concise manner the extent to which Hegel's doctrine encourages intolerance towards the non-believer. We are told: "Bettina, geduldig bei den Kindern, ist, weil ihr Freund sie politisiert hat, neuerdings streng mit mir." (p. 5). In the same section we learn that she is reading Hegel in a study group and a short time later that she now only speaks factually with Grass-- in effect personal relations are restricted, because he does not belong to the same philosophical and political community. (p. 25).

If one asks, as Gertrude Cepl-Kaufmann does in her book, what is to replace Hegel's image of horse and rider, his concept of the state and his way of thinking, then one thinks first of all of Grass's image of the snail and its cluster of associations and also of those confessions in his book which may be regarded as statements of intent-- since Grass is highly suspicious of belief, one has to avoid its use as well as that of creed. Gertrude Cepl-Kaufmann refers to the section in his novel in which he states that he does not believe in any doctrine, does not know any panacea, but offers scepticism and concludes with the plea that we should be sensitive (p. 177). Another

confession which is slightly more revealing is to be
found sandwiched between two attempts to locate himself
in the political spectrum: "Wo beginnt die Enthäutung
einer Person? Wo sitzt der Zapfen, der die Bekenntnisse
unter Verschluß hält? Ich bekenne, schmerzempfindlich zu
sein. (Schon aus diesem Grunde bemühe ich mich, politische
Verhältnisse zu verhindern, die mich mir unerträglichen
Schmerzen ausliefern könnten: Nacktschnecken verkürzen
sich, sobald sie berührt werden)." (p. 86). He precedes
this revelation of the core of his being by maintaining--
after much insistence from his children-- that he is a
revisionist, who, like Eduard Bernstein, one of the leading social democratic theorists in the nineties of the
last century, denies the existence of a final objective
and approves Bernstein's "Hinweise auf einen evolutionären,
in sich verzögerten, phasenverschobenen, insgesamt
schneckenhaften Prozeß..." (p. 85). He completes the
triadic, almost dialectic progression of confession by
concluding: "Ich bin Sozialdemokrat, weil mir Sozialis-
mus ohne Demokratie nichts gilt und weil eine unsoziale
Demokratie keine Demokratie ist." (p. 87).

Such statements constitute almost those truisms which
Dieter Zimmer is demanding in his article. They are what
he is requiring-- 'fragmentary pragmatic truisms'.
Grass's sensitivity to pain and his wish to reduce the

extent that he can be exposed to pain is the springboard
for his desire to prevent those political circumstances
which cause suffering. Egoism and altruism overlap in
the same way that the two beer mats representing political and literary work can overlap in Grass's discussion
with writers concerned about his excessive involvement in
politics and its adverse effect on his literary activities
(see p. 338). The same, on occasions, almost inextricable
intertwining of egoism and altruism occurs in Christ's
commandment that we should love our neighbours as ourselves, and no one could deny that Grass's moral attitude
has a strongly Christian basis. Schweitzer explains moral
action in terms of being sincere with oneself. Egoism
may not be a very edifying basis for a moral philosophy
but our ego is the only means through which we have contact with reality and our reason is capable of recognising
when egoism and altruism cease to overlap, as Grass's
quotation from Laurence Sterne's *Sentimental Journey* amusingly suggests: "Ich fühle mein Ich zu sehr, um zu sagen,
es geschähe um anderer willen." (pp. 231-32).

Grass's moral and political attitudes are similar in
essence to those of John Locke, whose philosophy has as
its basis enlightened self-interest. Bertrand Russell
goes so far as to claim that "on the whole, the school
which owed its origin to Locke, and which preached

enlightened self-interest, did more to increase human happiness, and less to increase human misery, than was done
by the schools which despised it in the name of heroism
and self-sacrifice." (*History of Western Philosophy*, p.
672). As J. P. Stern demonstrates, Hitler's Germany did
pursue the principle of heroism and self-sacrifice to its
ultimate-- and absurd-- conclusion. Unfortulately, Hitler, that 'world-historical individual', in his orgy of
destructiveness, left the principles of idealism intact
according to Grass who introduces his children to Augst,
father and son: "Auch kannte ich, da beide alterslos
sind, den jungen Augst, bevor der ältere zu sprechen begann. Beide sind Zeugen des Absoluten. Beide sind süch-
tig nach Untergang und Erlösung. Beide wollen die Wahrheit und nichts als die Wahrheit dringlich durch Hervor-
pressen zum Ausdruck bringen: ein mühevoller, ausbleiben-
der Stuhlgang." (p. 192). Ott makes quite clear his repudiation of Hegel's philosophical methods and his pref-
erence in effect-- though this is not stated-- for Locke's
empirical mode of approach, as the following quotation
reveals: "Schon vor dem Beginn der Studienzeit soll
Schopenhauer den Schneckensammler Ott gelehrt haben, vor
dem Erkennen anzuschauen und niemals nach Hegelscher
Methode vorgefaßter Erkenntnis die Beweise der Anschauung
nachzuliefern." (p. 54). Perhaps Grass is a latter-day

Voltaire introducing English philosophy-- in disguise--
not to France, of course, but to Western Germany!

Grass's starting point for his political involvement is a moral one. If the principle of the absolute
state and the principle of the amorality of the world
historical individual, hero or genius, have been proved
morally wrong-- presumably by the world spirit himself--
then there remains only one other alternative-- to produce another focus of power, that is a grouping together
of individuals who are sensitive to their own needs and
to the needs of others and by their democratic participation produce a greater measure of social justice. The
creation of such a democratic ethos presupposes, obviously, political involvement, personal responsibility,
reverence for life (to use a Schweitzer term), critical
awareness, tolerance, a positive attitude towards compromise as a means of (partially) solving problems and a
belief in evolution. All such principles are preached in
Aus dem Tagebuch einer Schnecke, either by statement or
example. And there could scarcely be a better set of
democratic platitudes! Dieter Zimmer ought to be well
satisfied! Furthermore Heinz Ludwig Arnold's criticism
that Grass's function is moral rather than political
appears to me to stem from a misunderstanding of the nature of democracy.

Unfortunately democratic platitudes-- vital though
they are in political life-- do not make for very interesting reading in a novel (this presupposes, of course,
that *Aus dem Tagebuch einer Schnecke* belongs to this
category). Grass deals with this problem by employing
a time-honoured method, one which was used by a teacher
of morality nearly two thousand years ago. Christ, when
asked who is our neighbour, produced the parable of the
Good Samaritan. Grass, when asked what is a good social
democrat (or how can Hegel's influence be reduced), produces, as we have seen, three stories: one, a negative
parable, the history of the Danzig Jews, and two positive
or normal parables, the story of Hermann Ott and Grass's
electioneering campaign. Grass has stated, as we have
noted, that he draws his political impetus from German
history. Accordingly, he fills his readers with that
degree of horror and revulsion which has formed the
spring-board for his own political involvement. He does
this by telling the story of the exodus of the Jews from
Danzig-- an exodus which was caused by the kind of thinking to be found in Hegel's philosophy. Danzig is taken
to be the microcosm of Germany. From the outset he states
the relevant sections from the Danzig constitution, indicating that all citizens were equal in the sight of the
law and that they had the right to freedom of religion

and conscience (p. 17). The political theory was fault-
less; the political practice-- and the political attitudes of the citizens-- were, however, at variance with
the theory. For Grass theory and practice form "eine
Einheit"[12] in the same way that horse and rider did for
Hegel. Grass describes the increasing divergence between
theory and practice and in the course of this he de-
scribes-- in narrative but not theoretical fashion-- that
history is made by individuals and that the state does
not exist apart from those individuals who constitute it.[5]
Grass relates, for example, how Zweifel is jostled by a
mob of women, pensioners and youngsters, when he buys a
lettuce from the stall of a Jewish friend of his, and how
"eine alte, als Oma liebenswerte Frau" sticks her hat-
pin through the lettuce shouting, "Pfui Deibel" as she
does so (p. 100). By her action the grandma is glorify-
ing the state which without her and the some four hundred thousand others does not exist. The city of Danzig
is ironically a free state and its citizens cannot even
blame Hitler or Germany for their misdemeanours, the year
being 1937. Even the 'Kristallnacht' is enacted in
Danzig in the same way as in the Reich in November 1938
(p. 108), for during that night synagogues were set on
fire in Danzig as in Germany itself. Immediately after
the incorporation of Danzig into the German Reich it even

acquired its own concentration camp, Stutthof (p. 132).
Grass also mentions the last emigration of Jews from
Danzig in August 1940; he refers to the name of the SS-
Obersturmführer who is in charge of the operation and
tells us of the way in which many Danzig citizens bid
their fellow humans beings a derisive farewell (p. 181).
The theory of world history, "in der (wie Hegel sagt) nur
von Völkern die Rede ist, welche einen Staat bilden..."
(p. 57), and which measures people by the sacrifices they
make, reduces individuals to insignificance and has to be
replaced, in Grass's estimation, by a framework of reference in which personal morality and responsibility are
placed in the foreground. As we have already seen, Grass
draws a parallel between the inhumanity which produced
the final solution and the bigotry which political fa-
natics exhibit today.

Grass's anti-Hegel parables centre on Zweifel's
career and on the author's own political activities.
Like Grass Hermann Ott has the makings of a pedagogue and
does in fact work as a teacher in a Jewish school which
employs some non-Jewish teachers-- like Ott-- who have
made critical remarks about National Socialism (p. 42).
Like Grass he proclaims doubt as the new creed (p. 24),
is opposed to Hegel's teachings and is a keen student of
snails. Ott, who likes to be known by his nickname of

Zweifel, is horrified to learn of the suicide of a Jewish
pupil who has been persecuted by his fellows, and criti-
cises colleagues at this state school who have been setting essays such as 'Die Juden sind unser Unglück' (p. 32).
He frequently assists members of the Jewish community in
Danzig, for example, doing office work in a Jewish tran-
sit camp (p. 23), helping with preparations for trans-
porting Jewish children to England (pp. 114-15), and
being involved in fitting up a warehouse which is to become a ghetto for the few remaining Jews from Danzig (p.
134), shortly before he, the born sceptic, goes underground soon after the beginning of the war. Zweifel,
who is the counterpart of Augst, both father and son, is
Grass's updated version of the Good Samaritan. For him,
as for Grass, theory and practice form a unity.

Grass obviously attaches exemplary importance to
his own political activities during the 1969 electioneering campaign. He and other like-minded individuals de-
cide to set up voters' clubs in fifty constituencies during the period before the election, and they set themselves not an ultimate objective, but an objective for
the election campaign: replacing the Great Coalition by
a FDP-SPD coalition (pp. 68-69). In such a context it is
possible for anyone to find a task which would correspond
to his ability, energy and the time at his disposal.

Grass mentions with great respect a long-serving social
democrat who supports his political party and its objectives by collecting subscriptions. Each can operate
worthily in accordance with his own talents: but each is
contributing to the establishing of a democratic ethos
and to the practical repudiation of Hegelian principles.
Grass's task of clearing the ground, eradicating the
roots of authoritarian thinking and encouraging the
growth of socially-oriented democratic attitudes is exceptionally difficult, for he is operating in the limited
sphere between the two extremes. He is of the opinion
that "the Christian doctrine of salvation and the ideology
of Marxism-- both with their absolute demands-- have
failed." (*Der Bürger und seine Stimme*, p. 160). He is
aware of the fascination which both doctrines of salvation exercise. Being hedged in by these two visions, he
is reluctant to employ the vocabulary of either school of
thought, even though his moral attitude has strong affini-
ties with Christian morality, as a number of observers
have pointed out.[12] So concerned is he to avoid the dog-
matic approach that he avoids categories, for example,
such as right and wrong, and he is equally loath to set
up a counter-theory which could then deteriorate quite
quickly in the German context into yet another one and
only truth. Those who criticise his lack of theory do so

in accordance with that attitude of mind which is specifically typical of the German cultural and political
climate (see p. 172) and from which Grass, the praeceptor
Germaniae, is attempting to wean his fellow-countrymen.
Grass's weapons in his jousting with the horse and rider
are narrative, satirical and figurative.

Though disinclined to indulge in the language of
Christian morality Grass does provide himself with dimly
outlined messianic associations. He refers to himself on
one occasion as "die zivile, die menschgewordene Schnecke"
(p. 76), thus conjuring up religious associations. Much
later he relates how Lisbeth Stomma crushes a snail with
her foot, an action which prompts Grass to speak of nail-
ing the snail to the cross (p. 314). On the following
page he tells his reader of a threat to his life in the
form of the words spoken on the phone to one of his sons,
obliquely hinting at the possibility of crucifixion by
shooting. It is to be hoped that Grass does not take his
role as mentor too seriously, for excessive emotional in-
vestment can swing too easily, as he himself knows, into
apolitical resignation. It would be a pity if this were
to happen, for Grass and those who share his attitudes
ought to triumph gloriously over horse and rider.

Nevertheless in *Aus dem Tagebuch einer Schnecke*
Grass shows how he has entered into battle with Hegel,

whom he regards as the enemy of democracy and of individual responsibility. The weapons he wields in his struggle against this adversary are figurative and narrative
and in the process he counters the one image, that of the
horse, with another image, that of the snail. In the same
way that water slowly undermines rock, the snail, the
symbol of compromise and slow-moving but sure progress,
emerges victorious over the Hegelian horse, the symbol of
black and white thinking, absolutism and of impetuous
action, which sweeps all obstacles aside in total disre-
gard of reality and of men's sensibilities. Grass not
only does battle in the metaphorical sphere but also in
the narrative sphere: he provides us with examples of
democratic involvement, his own and that of Zweifel, and
it is also clear that such exemplary behaviour belongs
to a pattern of political orientation which is absent
from the German historical tradition. Grass's purpose is
to help the partially obscured tradition of enlightenment
and social political responsibility to assume a more dominant role in the German political and cultural landscape.
In strengthening this trend Grass is setting himself up
as an educator of public opinion: he is an emergent
praeceptor democratiae Germaniae. It is hoped that Ger-
mania heeds his moral and democratic lesson. Of the two
souls fighting within her breast the autocratic one needs

to be jettisoned and the democratic one cherished and
nurtured. This is the message of Grass, novelist and
mentor, who in *Aus dem Tagebuch einer Schnecke* gives us
unique insight into his world and the nature of his political involvement.

It would, however, be wrong to view Grass's novel
solely in terms of a series of political confessions, for
it is an interesting and stimulating interplay of literature and politics. Political statements are constantly
being illuminated and exemplified by the narrative and
non-discursive elements. Political author and narrator
have become one-- politics and literature co-exist in
perfect harmony.

Notes

1. "Großes Ja und kleines Nein," *Frankfurter Rundschau*, 8.3.1969;   also in Heinz Ludwig Arnold and Franz Josef Görtz, editors,: *Günter Grass-- Dokumente zur politischen Wirkung* (Edition Text und Kritik, 1971), p. 148.

2. See Günter Grass, *Über das Selbstverständliche* (1968), p. 175.

3. J. P. Stern, *Hitler, the Führer and the People* (1975).

4. Page numbering in connection with *Aus dem Tagebuch einer Schnecke* refers to the Luchterhand edition, Neuwied and Darmstadt, 1972.

5. Gertrude Cepl-Kaufmann, *Günter Grass: Eine Analyse des Gesamtwerkes unter dem Aspekt von Literatur und Politik* (1975), p. 302.

6. *Briefe von und an Hegel*, Vol. I (Hamburg, 1952), p. 120.

7. Georg Lukács, *The Young Hegel* (London, 1975), p. 454.

8. Heinz Ludwig Arnold, see note 1, p. 148.

9. See William York Tindall, *The Literary Symbol* (Bloomington and London, 1955), pp. 102-03.

10. Günter Grass, *Über meinen Lehrer Döblin und andere Vorträge* (Berlin, 1968), p. 11.

11. See G. Cepl-Kaufmann, p. 303.

12. See G. Cepl-Kaufmann, p. 126.

CHAPTER VI

Der Butt: *the fairy-tale which becomes reality*

Der Butt was published in 1977 and within two years
it had achieved considerable popularity in that it had
sold 450,000 copies.[1] At the same time it was for Grass
a huge financial success, netting with its first edition
a profit of some three million marks. In 1978 Grass
established the Alfred Döblin prize with income derived
from this book, explaining its foundation in the following terms: "Ich habe mit dem *Butt* mehr Geld verdient,
als ich für mich persönlich benötige. Ich sehe nicht ein,
daß ich mich durch einen Bucherfolg etwa zwingen oder ver-
führen lassen sollte, meinen Lebensstil zu ändern. Ein
Rolls-Royce, da ich nicht Auto fahren kann notwendiger-
weise mit Chauffeur, käme mir über die Maßen lächerlich
vor."[2]

Generally the novel was greeted in a positive, if
not enthusiastic manner and comes close to *Die Blechtrommel* in ranking as Grass's major work. Fritz J.
Raddatz spoke of it as "die wichtigste deutschsprachige
Prosa seit vielen Jahren"[3] and Rolf Michaelis was equally

complimentary ("Schon lang nicht mehr so Schönes gelesen").[4] Wolfgang Hildesheimer referred to it as "ein Jahrhundertbuch".[5] Manfred Durzak was of the opinion that *Der Butt* achieved "eine erzählerische Vitalität und ästhetische Vielfalt der Darstellung..., die die spontane Lobesformel in der Tat zusammenfassen könnte: ein märchenhafter Roman."[6] Peter Russell described the novel as having "a brilliant prose style even richer in mischievous idiosyncrasy than those of his previous novels" but then went on to complain about its "confused and unsatisfactory message".[7]

Grass has already announced his intention of writing a new novel in *Aus dem Tagebuch einer Schnecke*, though there was no hint at that stage that the fish was to assume a dominant role: "Bevor ich mal alt bin und womöglich weise werde, will ich ein erzählendes Kochbuch schreiben: über 99 Gerichte, über Gäste und Menschen als Tiere, die kochen können, über den Vorgang Essen, über Abfälle..." (p. 212). Advance notice was also given of the Fathers' day episode: "Werde mal, weiß nicht wann, ein Buch-- 'Vatertag'-- schreiben, das in Berlin siedelt und am Himmelfahrtstag nur von viereckigen Männern handelt..." (p. 220). In *Der Butt* Grass combines the two promised books into one. The reader is also prepared by *Aus dem Tagebuch einer Schnecke* for the author's reference

to the speaking fish as 'Weltgeist' (see p. 188, p. 407,
p. 495, p. 515 in *Der Butt*). Grass's *Aus dem Tagebuch
einer Schnecke* anticipates *Der Butt* in at least four other
ways. In *Aus dem Tagebuch einer Schnecke* narrator and
author may be regarded as largely identical as Grass himself has observed.[3] In *Der Butt* Günter Grass continues
this convention, whilst at the same time projecting a
fictional narrative ego into the past, so that a wide-
sweeping historical survey may be allowed to unfold.
Accordingly Grass includes detailed descriptions of events
in which he himself has participated: his visit to
Poland (pp. 140-61) and to India (pp. 221-38), the congress of Bièvres on the future of democratic socialism
(see pp. 425-26) and, of course, the birth of his daughter, Helene Grass, to whom the book is dedicated. In
both novels the action takes place in three different
places. In *Aus dem Tagebuch einer Schnecke* the author
converses with his children in Berlin, conducts an election campaign in West Germany and has the story of Zweifel
and the history of the Jews situated in Danzig. A similar
pattern is developed in *Der Butt*: the author talks to
his wife, Ilsebill, in his new home in Wewelsfleth near
Glückstadt, describes a case being conducted against the
turbot by a women's tribunal in Berlin and as a fictional
narrator ranges to and fro in history from the beginnings

of time to the present day, taking Danzig as his focal point.[8] Thus the narrative structure in both novels has much in common. There are some interesting links between the imagery in *Aus dem Tagebuch einer Schnecke* and that in *Der Butt*. One need only look at the cover of the two books to realise that the head and the snail have been replaced in *Der Butt* by a head and a fish. Finally, it will be quickly evident that the theme of history-- one which is not restricted to *Aus dem Tagebuch einer Schnecke*-- assumes major proportions in *Der Butt*. In one sense it could be maintained that *Der Butt* is complementary to *Die Blechtrommel* and *Hundejahre* in that they deal mainly with the twentieth century whilst *Der Butt* provides the panoramic sweep of four thousand years, from the early Stone Age onwards.

Themes

Having provided an indication of the content of his future novel in *Aus dem Tagebuch einer Schnecke*, Grass describes in *Der Butt* itself how the idea of "ein erzählendes Kochbuch" acquired further dimensions: "Anfangs hatte ich nur über neun oder elf Köchinnen eine Art Ernährungsgeschichte schreiben wollen: zum Schwadengras über die Hirse zur Kartoffel. Aber der Butt sei gegengewichtig geworden. Und der Prozeß gegen ihn." (pp. 184-

185). In his conversation with Heinz Ludwig Arnold,
Günter Grass supplies further insight into the origins of
his novel. He states that in collecting material for his
history of food and of cooking he became aware of "women's anonymous contribution to history" and this reali-
zation was accompanied, after a year's preparatory work,
by the discovery of Grimm's fairy-story 'Von dem Fischer
und syner Fru'. Grass refers to the fairy-story as "ein
irritierendes Moment, das dann sehr rasch eine zentrale
Position gewann und zum ordnenden Faktor dieser Stoff-
masse gegenüber wurde." (p. 31). Then Grass goes on to
mention a third factor: "Hinzu kam auch Privates, be-
stimmte Verletzungen, Verzweiflungen, Konfrontationen mit
Wünschen, meinen und anderen, Unerfüllbares-- und ein
Kind." These then are the three interweaving themes in
Der Butt: the cooks and their contribution to history,
the fish and his trial, and the birth of a daughter.
Each theme has its own particular narrative location:
the birth in Wewelsfleth, the trial in Berlin and the
history of the cooks mainly in Danzig, apart from the
Fathers' Day episode. The birth of the child determines
the structure of the novel, which is divided up in accordance with the nine months of the pregnancy. The turbot--
along with the fairy-tale-- interlinks the various episodes in the novel, constitutes a central image to which

many stimulating associations are attached, and makes its
contribution to the unfolding of the cooks' history. The
history of cooks and cooking provides the chronological
sequence in the novel, is at the same time a history of
the sexes, of the emancipation of man from woman and of
woman from man, and allows a survey of history to take
place, which is the counterpart to the official version
as presented in the text books. The cooks provide an
additional cohesive element within the book in that food
and recipes are constant ingredients within the novel and
that each of the nine parts contains one chapter or at
least the conclusion of a chapter in which a meal is described, as Grass observes in his conversation with Heinz
Ludwig Arnold.[11]

Even in the first short paragraph of the book the
three themes we have just mentioned are rapidly drawn to
the attention of the reader. Admittedly a reference to
the fish is not included, but the wife of the author-cum-
narrator is called Ilsebill, which is the name of the
fisher's wife in Grimm's fairy-tale: "Ilsebill salzte
nach. Bevor gezeugt wurde, gab es Hammelschulter zu Boh-
nen und Birnen, weil Anfang Oktober. Beim Essen noch,
mit vollem Mund sagte sie: 'Wolln wir nun gleich ins Bett
oder willst du mir vorher erzählen, wie unsere Geschichte
wann wo begann?'" (p. 9). Thus the themes of eating,

procreation and history make their entrance onto Grass's stage in a startling and amusing manner and usher in a pageant of cooks and associated characters, the majority acting in accordance with the advice of the speaking fish.

In the first part, the first month, of the book, the central themes are made more and more explicit. In the second chapter of the book, which is entitled 'Neun und mehr Köchinnen', we are introduced, for example, to Grass's representative cooks and in the course of twelve pages we are presented with a potted version of their characters and lives. The narrator who has been granted nine months to give birth to his cooks (see p. 14), allocates each one to a specific period of time: Aua, the first cook, belongs to the Stone Age, Wigga to the Iron Age, Mestwina to the Tenth Century, Dorothea von Montau to the Gothic Age of the Fourteenth Century, Margarete Rusch to the Reformation, Agnes Kurbiella to the Thirty Years' War and the Seventeenth Century, Amanda Woyke to the Eighteenth Century with its introduction of the potato into Prussia after the Second Partition of Poland, Sophie Rotzoll to the age of Revolution associated with Napoleon and Lena Stubbe, the ninth cook, to the period of the Franco-Prussian War and the two World Wars; and then to complete the picture Sibylle Miehlau, who died on Fathers' Day in the sixties, and Maria Kucyorra who was born into post-war Poland. In this way Grass ensures that the reader does not run the risk of losing his orientation in the highways and byways of his unofficial version of history. After having made the acquaintance of the cooks, we are introduced in the next three chapters to the turbot and his history: the content of Grimm's fairy-tale is outlined and the narrator catches the fish back in the Stone Age ('Wie der Butt gefangen wurde'); then the three lesbians catch the turbot a few months before the oil crisis ('Wie der Butt zum zweiten Mal gefangen wurde'); and finally the fish is put on trial by a tribunal of Ilsebills for having aided and abetted man throughout the course of history ('Wie der Butt von den Ilsebills angeklagt wurde'). The rest of the first month deals with the first three of the narrator's cooks and by the end of it the reader is aware that each cook is a projection of Ilsebill into the past and that each man with whom the cook associates is the narrator in a different guise. In short, each narrator and each cook are united by the bonds of food and sex.

Narrative Perspective

The role of the narrator in *Der Butt* needs some elaboration-- particularly in the light of the observations made in the previous paragraph. On the first page of the

book immediately after having introduced the three main
themes, the author states the principle underlying the
narrative perspective: "Ich, das bin ich jederzeit. Und
auch Ilsebill war von Anfang an da." (p. 9). Günter Grass
thus makes use of a narrative technique which has already
been employed successfully in Virginia Woolf's *Orlando*,
an Elizabethan who appears in a succession of guises
throughout the centuries that follow. This device is perhaps initially a little bewildering for the reader, but
by no means totally unrealistic, particularly given the
fact that the use of a fairy-tale as a focal point for
the novel releases the momentum which allows the imaginative investigation of reality throughout the centuries to
take place. It is realistic in the sense that each individual existing in the present is a continuation, almost
a summary, of those characteristics which have been passed
on, generation by generation, by a series of ancestors,
who have lived their lives in preceding centuries. The
sentence "Das Leben geht weiter" which occurs in various
forms throughout the novel can suggest the idea that the
torch of life is handed down the centuries from individual
to individual. The narrator in Günter Grass's *Der Butt*
dons the mantle of a succession of representative individuals who are related, not by consanguinity, but by the
similarity of their attitudes and behaviour. In each

stage of reincarnation he usually sires the children of
the cook with whom he is associated at the time. Each
narrator and cook constitutes a reenactment of the relationship between the present-day narrator-cum-author and
his Ilsebill which is depicted on the first page of the
novel.

In accordance with this narrative scheme the narrator
first enters life as Edek and in keeping with Grimm's
fairy-tale he is a fisher who catches the turbot, and
egged on by his adviser, sets in motion that process
which has been variously described in official history
books as progress or the course of civilisation. He is
reincarnated in a number of personalities, frequently
assuming more aggressive roles in society, though not reluctant on occasions to pursue his artistic inclinations--
the first Edek earns himself the title of "baltischer
Dädalus" (p. 122). Sometimes he leads a double, if not
triple existence: during one sojourn on earth ('Zeitweil'
is the term used to describe his period of reincarnation),
he is not only the man of God, the Bishop Adalbert of
Prague, who is murdered by Mestwina in the year 997, but
also the shepherd who betrays her to the Bohemians and is
thus instrumental in having her executed. He explores
his dual personality in the following terms: "Der
Schäfer-- der Bischof: zum erstenmal zeitweilte ich

doppelt, war ich gespalten und dennoch ganz heidnischer Schafshirt, ganz christlicher Eiferer." (p. 131). Subsequently, he becomes a swordmaker by the name of Albrecht Slichting, and enters into a not unduly successful marriage with Dorothea von Montau, who, suffering from aspirations to saintliness, has herself immured in the cathedral of Marienwerder in 1393; then he is simultaneously monk, Lutheran preacher, mayor, and abbot; in the seventeenth century he assumes the shape of artist (Anton Möller) and poet (Martin Opitz) and receives comfort and inspiration alternately from Agnes Kurbiella; in the eighteenth century he impregnates Amanda Woyke in the intervals between the battles of the Seven Years' War; during the Napoleonic era he enjoys a triple existence of youthful revolutionary, priest, and French Governor of the Republic of Danzig; then becomes the first and second husband of Lena Stubbe; and finally slips into the role of the first-person narrator of the present, initially as a partner of Sibylle Miehlau, and then as the half-cousin of Maria Kuczorra.

Thus the narrator consists, as we have already noted, of a fictional ego and yet may correspond at the same time to the author himself who sometimes intervenes in the narrative and reports upon his activities in the personal and political sphere and even comments upon his artistic labours as the author of *Der Butt*. Following a conversation which he has with the artist, Strya, during the course of his visit to Gdansk in the summer of 1974, the author mentions the advantages which stem from his narrative technique: "Wir sind immer nur zeitweilig gegenwärtig. Uns nagelt kein Datum. Wir sind nicht von heute. Auf unserem Papier findet das meiste gleichzeitig statt." (p. 156). In other words, the use of a narrator who can flit to and fro through history allows the author the maximum degree of flexibility. He can place past, present and future in juxtaposition and mingle them in whatever proportions he pleases. He makes a further comment upon the way in which he can break through the chronological sound barrier of time and history. He produces his observation in reply to a member of a works committee in Kiel who asks why Grass writes in a complicated manner for the priveleged middle class and not for the working class: "Ich schreibe gestauchte Zeit. Ich schreibe, was ist, während anderes auch, überlappt von anderem, neben anderem ist oder zu sein scheint, während unbeobachtet etwas, das nicht mehr da zu sein schien, doch, weil verdeckt, blöd dauerte, nun einzig noch da ist: zum Beispiel die Angst." (p. 543). The author may be pulling the leg of his fellow worker by stressing the complexity of the writing technique, but he is nevertheless highlighting

the simultaneousness of the various periods of time and
their interlocking and yet deceptive effect. The word
'gestaucht' suggests that the process of writing almost
inevitably involves a compression of time: four thousand
years in six hundred and ninety four pages is an obvious
example of this. If one were to examine the section in
Hundejahre in which Walter Matern throws a stone into the
Vistula, then one could also claim that a writer like
Grass also indulges in the extension of time, retarding
it as though one were watching a slow-motion picture. In
the chapter entitled 'Vatertag' it could be claimed that
Grass subjects the episode virtually to a double compression process: by his constant references to the Thirty
Years' War and the battle of Wittstock an der Dosse in
particular, he kaleidoscopes seventeenth and twentieth
century together, and in the course of one day demonstrates how female behaviour can degenerate if pressurized
by the accelerating effect of man's violent example, a
pattern which has become the norm over the course of four
thousand years. The narrator as the repository of past
and present can range freely over time by virtue of his
magic narrative carpet, making comparisons as any good
historian should, between one era and another, and one
person and another, whilst also enjoying the possibility
of accelerating the sluggish flow of time and of landing

in various locations, Wewelsfleth, Berlin, Danzig or even
Calcutta. In the first chapter of the book, for example,
the author assures himself that their act of procreation
might have been a success, promptly escapes into the past
("Ich lief, die Zeit treppab, davon", p. 10) and proceeds
to tell Ilsebill about Aua and her three breasts. Trans-
port over four thousand years in five sentences.

Comparisons between the various epochs, events and
people abound throughout the novel and produce an impression of repetitiveness, if not of circularity. One
critic, Hanspeter Brode, has referred to Grass's story-
telling as "die Grassche Geschichte des Immergleichen."[12]
An interrelationship is constantly being established between revolts which took place in Danzig in the Middle
Ages and which were brutally suppressed and the dock
workers' strike in Danzig in 1970 in which Jan Ludkowski,
Maria Kuczorra's fiancé, was killed (see p. 144, p. 146,
p. 151, p. 154, p. 181, p. 641, pp. 644-48). In drawing
this parallel the author comes to the melancholy conclusion: "Seit 1378 hat sich in Danzig oder Gdansk soviel
verändert: die Patrizier heißen jetzt anders." (p. 152).
Our roving reporter compares the situation of August Bebel
and his respect for a young supporter who later becomes
a fascist, and the situation of Willy Brandt, who found
his trust in Guillaume betrayed in 1974 (p. 560). The

author also likens a member of the tribunal, the prosecutor Sieglinde Huntscha to his own present-day Ilsebill
and also to Dorothea von Montau: "Auch hat die Anklägerin
des Hohen Gerichts erschreckliche Ähnlichkeit nicht nur
mit meiner Ilsebill. Beide sind Schwestern der Dorothea
von Montau: von bezwingendem Ausdruck, mit starkem
Willen geimpft, der alles engführt und auf plattem Land
Berge versetzen kann. Entsetzlich blond sind sie (alle
drei), strenger Moral verpflichtet und von jenem Mut be-
sessen, der immer nur geradeaus geht, komme was wolle."
(p. 170). In fact all the eleven cooks have their counterparts in the eleven members of the tribunal, although
the references to the similarities between the cooks and
the members of the tribunal are few and may easily escape
the attention of the reader.[13] And, of course, as we
have already indicated, Ilsebill is reincarnated in each
of the individual cooks. In passing it might also be
mentioned that in each sojourn the narrator has one particular friend, whose name is usually a variation on Lud
(see p. 629), but here again, as with the pairing of
cooks and tribunal members, this linking is undertaken in
a circumspect manner, so that the artificiality of this
arrangement does not obtrude.[13]

The future also is woven into the description of
things past. In the second part which is devoted to the

life and death of Dorothea von Montau, the author gives
us a preview of the end of the novel: he describes how
Maria Kuczorra wades out into the Baltic Sea and calls
out the name of the fish (p. 160). In addition to describing the future in the context of the time scale of
the book, Günter Grass gives some indication of the future
in relationship to the actual present of to-day. Not
content with being a monk, Lutheran preacher, mayor, and
abbot, the narrator also assumes the garb of Vasco da
Gama and goes by plane to India. Having arrived in Calcutta, he once again explains his narrative technique, on
this occasion, of course, to the Indians: "Wohlgenährt
leidet Vasco am Welthungerproblem. Wieder- und wiederge-
boren ist Vasco jetzt Schriftsteller. Er schreibt ein
Buch, in dem es ihn zu jeder Zeit gegeben hat: stein-
zeitlich, frühchristlich, hochgotisch, reformiert, barock,
aufgeklärt und so weiter." (p. 222). He also categorises
his book as a history of food which is enacted near the
mouth of the Vistula, adding that it could just as well
take place near the mouth of the Ganges (p. 232). The
suggestion emerges indirectly that he ought to write a
history of hunger, either as an addition to or instead of
his present work: "Man müßte historischen, gegenwärtigen,
zukünftigen Hunger ins Verhältnis setzen." (p. 222). He
then proceeds to relate examples of starvation in the

fourteenth and sixteenth centuries to the present-day
situation in Asia. At a much later stage the fish blames
Western civilisation for the rampant malnutrition in many
parts of the world and, diverting attention from himself,
places European man on trial: "Es hat das Prinzip der
Freien Marktwirtschaft die permanente Unterernährung von
Millionen zur Folge: auch Hunger ist Krieg!" (p. 661).
In this way Grass extends the European context of his
novel to embrace the non-European world (and incidentally
builds the Brandt report into his book!). In that the
unsolved problems of to-day constitute the future of the
next generation and subsequent generations the author is
incorporating the future, alongside the past and present,
into the narrative landscape of his novel. At the same
time he is giving us a foretaste (to use a gastronomic
term) of what is to become a central theme of his most
recent 'narrative' work-- *Kopfgeburten oder Die Deutschen
sterben aus*. And in the sense that *Der Butt* is open-
ended in its portrayal of the war of the sexes-- the book
ends with the turbot being transferred as consultant to
the woman-- the future enjoys parity of esteem with past
and present and has a constant right to be involved in
Grass's survey of history.

Our protean narrator revels in the delights of trans-
mogrification-- and the reader enjoys his escapades.

This narrative 'Wanderlust' includes even the possibility of entering into the soul of Vasco da Gama in 1492 and, then complete with new identity, flying by Jumbojet into twentieth-century India. There are certain rules which he seems, at least officially, to observe. On the one hand he prefers resurrection in the shape of a fellow-man and on the other hand he avoids transfer to the realm of animal or fish (for reasons which will be obvious later). Nevertheless there is a close affinity between narrator and Ilsebill and by implication between the partners of each individual pair throughout the centuries. The present-day Ilsebill conforms to the behavioural pattern which is in keeping with the official version of Grimm's fairy-tale. Man in his various guises has been and is as insatiable as is the fisher in the unofficial version of the fairy-tale. Both man and woman are equally voracious in the demands they make, in their hunger for things material and things spiritual. In the poem 'Hinter den Bergen' (p. 450) Grass expresses the basic similarity in their temperament and in their attitudes-- and it may be noted that the reference to the 'fisher' suggests a general applicability to all partnerships of narrator and Ilsebill:

> Was wäre ich ohne Ilsebill!
> rief der Fischer

zufrieden

In ihre Wünsche kleiden sich meine.

... Immer kommt, wenn ich rufe, der Butt.

Ich will, ich will, ich will wie Ilsebill sein!

The seeming contentment of the first three lines is rapidly converted into the restless craving of the second section. In the fourth and final section of the poem, dissatisfaction, the incapacity to attain a state of content, once again reaches a climax, and wishes take on an independent existence of their own, whilst seeking a medium through which they may be expressed. Whether its vehicle for their realisation is man or woman seems in the terms of the poem to be of no significance, for each is the replica of the other.

Kürzlich träumte ich reich:

alles was da wie gewünscht,

Brot, Käse, Nüsse und Wein,

nur fehlte ich, mich zu freuen.

Da verliefen sich wieder die Wünsche

und suchten hinter den Bergen

ihren doppekten Sinn: Ilsebill oder mich.

Grass alludes to the likeness of narrator and Ilsebill, their virtual indistinguishability with regard to their insatiable desires, by suggesting that each carries-- and gives birth to-- a potential partner. During

Ilsebill's pregnancy-- and, of course, she wants to produce a son-- the narrator is allowed nine months to de-
liver himself of his cooks (p. 14) and on each occasion
when he provides the summary of their lives, he starts by
saying, "die erste Köchin in mir" (p. 16) or "die zweite
Köchin in mir, die raus will namentlich" (p. 17), the
words 'in mir' recurring with each cook. Male and female
are in a constant state of civil war within each individual, as though a sexual complex, like a child in embryo, were in a permanent state of gestation: "Die Köchin
in mir und ich, wir schenken einander nichts. Zum Beispiel hat Ilsebill einen Koch in sich-- der werde wohl
ich sein-- den sie bekämpft. Unser Streit von Anbeginn,
wer als Komplex drall oder mager in wem hockt, fördert
neue Gerichte oder alte, die wieder beliebt sind, seitdem
wir historisch bewußt kochen." (p. 429). The one partner's desire to be the exact reflection of his sexual
opposite, the yearning to be converted in physical terms
into his or her sexual counterpart, is presented as the
height of folly, the final degree of insatiability which,
in terms of the fairy-tale, leads to retribution. The
attempt on the part of the three lesbians to rape Sibylle
Miehlau and sire a son is an axample of this. It is no
coincidence that in the paragraph immediately preceding
this episode on Fathers' Day the narrator should dream of

being a pregnant woman who gives birth to a pregnant
daughter who in turn is delivered of a son with a turbot's head (p. 615). This dream conjures up a picture of
the eternal cycle of immoderation in which the one sex
vies with the other in its incessant craving for satisfaction and for the unattainable. In short, the narrator
preserves his physical separateness from his sexual partner and cook, but in the boundlessness of their desire
they can scarcely be differentiated., By the end of the
novel Ilsebill has abandoned one of her roles: the narrator has become a cook and serves the women. The narrator is also keen to reagrd the turbot as a separate
physical entity-- he has to keep to the rules of the
literary game as far as fairy-tales are concerned. However, in that the fish may be viewed as a kind of 'Kopfgeburt' (see p. 123) or possibly even as an 'Ersatzgeburt'
(see p. 501) the narrator could, if he so wished, lay
claims to paternity. The role and smybolical function of
the turbot is perhaps best left until we discuss the
fairy-tale and its associated imagery shortly.

Though the narrator has plenty of experience as a
story-teller, this should not mislead us into thinking
that his account of history is necessarily objective.
The narrator is allowed into the tribunal as a spectator
and is thus in a position to report on the proceedings

against the turbot (pp. 94-95). However, as he admits to
Ilsebill, he does consider himself to be an unbiased reporter: "doch erwarte bitte von mir keinen korrekten Pro-
zeßbericht: einerseits bin ich kein Jurist, andererseits
(wenn auch schwankend) Partei; schließlich hat man mich
meinen Fall mitverhandelt, ohne daß ich Schlagzeilen
machte." (p. 56). Ostensibly-- in keeping with the fiction of the fairy-tale-- it is the fish who is being
tried; in the terms of the fiction of the novel as a
whole it is the narrator whose case is being investigated,
whilst in reality, that is, in terms of the reality which
exists outside the novel, it is man and especially the
German version of man who is on trial. On another occasion the narrator states in effect that though the speaking fish is the chief defendant, he, the narrator, is the
focal point of the hearing and he creates the impression
that he would like to trumpet forth his guilt in order to
claim more attention for himself: "Denn eigentlich,
Ilsebill, ging es immer um mich. Ich habe versagt und
mich herausgelogen. Ich habe verdrängt und vergessen.
Wie gerne hätte ich mich vor dem Tribunal, vor Frau Dr.
Schönherr, vor Helga Paasch, vor Ruth Simoneit, vor allen
schuldig bekannt: Das tat ich. Und das." (p. 115). He
thinks of himself as exemplary in that he has a representative function to fulfill, and regards his writings as a

form of confession which he makes to Ilsebill: "weil aber
der Butt nicht freigesetzt wurde, kam alles raus, ist die
mündende Weichsel der exemplarische Ort, wurde ich bei-
spielhaft, muß ich mich häuten, beichte ich Ilsebill,
schreibe ich auf, steht hier geschrieben." (p. 52). As
in the Danzig Trilogy, Grass's native town is the microcosm of European, if not world, events. In that the novel
consists of a confession in the present, all excursions
into the past (or into the future) return to the present
as the focal point of the narrative and in that the novel
is the account of a trial, comments and information about
the great historical survey ("die große historische Auf-
und Abrechnung"-- p. 524) are supplied from at least four
different sources, firstly, from the fish, secondly, from
the members of the tribunal, thirdly, from Ilsebill, and,
last but not least, from the narrator who is in any case
the medium through which all information is conveyed--
and coloured. As we have already suggested, however, the
narrator is manifested in two forms. On the one hand he
is a fictional being who flits through centuries and on
the other hand he corresponds very largely to the author
of the book itself. On one occasion the narrator provides
a survey of the lives of his cooks, highlighting the fact
that violence has been a dominant factor in many of their
lives and deaths: "Amanda und Sophie ausgenommen, so viel

gewaltsamer Tod: das vergiftete Blut, der ausgehungerte
Leib, das verbrannte Fleisch, das erstickte Lachen, der
Rumpf ohne Kopf, die erschlagene Fürsorge.   Viel ist da
nicht zu beschönigen.   Addierte Verluste.   Das Konto
Gewalt." (p. 571).   The narrator who is speaking here is
expressing views which are presumably much in keeping
with those of the author himself.   It is not uninteresting
to note that both Ilsebill and the fish promptly produce
their commentaries on the narrator's statement.   The
stimulating quality of the novel proceeds at least in part
from the interaction of the various statements and observations of the four principal purveyors of information.

As in the Danzig Trilogy the narrator is motivated by
a sense of guilt.   The narrator makes no secret of his
desire to forget unsavoury aspects of his past, for he has
a chapter entitled 'Woran ich mich nicht erinnern will'
(pp. 121-34).   What he has in mind especially is the fact
that he betrayed Mestwina to her executioners.   Nevertheless this is but one in a list of incidents which he
would prefer not to have happened (p. 121).   In a more
general sense he feels a sense of complicity for the whole
of the German development, for he has been involved in it,
either actively or passively.   For example, Runge burns
and thus suppresses the version of Grimm's fairy-tale in
which man is depicted as the creature of immoderation and

of boundless ambition and because this version is then
converted into reality, the narrator is overwhelmed by
guilt and feels impelled to write ("Darauf gingen alle
ins Haus zurück. Und ich muß nun schreiben und schreiben."-- p. 450). The turbot, perhaps more so than the
narrator, likes to play the game of being guilt-laden,
so much so that the women in the tribunal have difficulty in determining whether he is being serious or
merely ironical. His exaggerated protestations of guilt
inevitably arouse the suspicions of the tribunal (see
p. 655). He indulges in hyperbole, clearly not as an
expression of genuine sorrow but in an attempt to have
himself released in his native waters: "Man möge ihn,
den Schuldbewußten und zu verurteilenden Übeltäter, damit
er zweckdienlich sühnen könne, in seinem bevorzugten Gewässer, in der westlichen Ostsee aussetzen." (p. 670).
On other occasions he is concerned to demonstrate that,
though his advice has always been sound, man-- in the
shape of the narrator-- has constantly been a failure.
He emphasises this fact in his conversation with the
three women who catch him in the Baltic near Holstein's
Eastern coast: "Wann immer ich zeitweilte, ob während
der Hochgotik, ob im Jahrhundert der Aufklärung, sei ich
ein Versager gewesen. Überhaupt könne er der Männersache,
so leidenschaftlich einseitig er sie betrieben habe,

nichts mehr abgewinnen." (p. 51). The narrator for his
part returns the compliment by blaming his mentor for his
own transgressions. For example, he claims that the
turbot advised him to kill Mestwina (p. 132) and even Aua
(see pp. 37-38). We are told that the fish recommends
that the narrator should have recourse to absolute solu-
tions (p. 19). The fish promotes the cause of man at
every possible opportunity, advising him to learn to
count (p. 39), forge metals (p. 36) and take part in the
migration of the peoples (p. 76). In short, the turbot
ensures, according to the narrator, that the version of
Grimm's fairy-tale which was suppressed is converted into
reality. The narrator defends himself by blaming the
fish for all his own misdeeds, claiming that he, the narrator, was taken in by his adviser when he made him his
original offer of assistance in man's struggle against
the domination of women: "Stimmt. Ich fiel auf ihn rein.
So von ihm angesprochen, fühlte ich mich. Mir kam Bedeutung zu. Dieses Übersichhinauswachsen. Dieses Sich-
bewußtwerden. Schon nahm ich mich wichtig. Doch immer-
hin-- glaub mir, Ilsebill!-- bleiben noch Zweifel."
(p. 34).

The narrator's duplicity and desire to absolve himself from all responsibility reach their climax during
the course of his speech on the occasion of "das große

Buttessen": "In den Bauch haben sie Jan geschossen. Ja,
die Miliz schoß auf Arbeiter. Und das im Kommunismus.
Nein, überall, wo Männer den Finger am Abzug halten. Und
das immer schon. Waffensprache. Materialschlachten.
Vorwärtsverteidigung. Verbrannte Erde. Das hat der Butt.
Sein Rat hieß: Töten! Sein Wort setzte Gewalt. Aus ihm
wirkte das Böse. Ihn zu bestrafen, sind wir versammelt.
Hier, Butt! Hier! Damit du siehst, was von dir bleibt.
Du Todbringer, Lebensfeind!" (pp. 668-69). Such hyperbole is worthy of the turbot himself. Yet it shows most
clearly the extent to which the narrator uses him as a
scapegoat, burdening him with his own guilt.

The turbot and the imagery associated with it
     As with all of Grass's narrative works, the dust-
cover of *Der Butt* draws the reader's attention to the
central imagery of the novel. We are presented with the
picture of a fish which is drawn in full, and the ear of
a person, the rest of whose head is not visible. Given
the fact that the mouth of the fish is pointed at the ear
of the person, one may presume, and certainly once one
realises that Grimm's fairy-tale 'Von dem Fischer und
syner fru' has a central role to play in the novel, that
the fish is speaking into the ear. The fact that the
eyes of the person are not shown in the picture suggests

perhaps that the person is dependent on what the fish has
to say and that he cannot, or does not wish to, see for
himself. Once again we are confronted with a sexual
symbol, i.e. the fish, in the same way that the outstretched arm on the dust-cover of *Hundejahre* may be
regarded as a phallic emblem. The ear as an orifice may
be readily regarded as the female counterpart to the
phallic symbol of the fish. The reader is hence reminded
of the head and tail imagery which can be found in *Die
Blechtrommel* or even of the juxtaposition of drum-stick
and drum. The fish and head have their counterpart in
the snail and the head on the dust-cover of *Aus dem Tagebuch einer Schnecke*.

We have already noted that Grass considers the fairy-
tale of the speaking fish to be 'a unifying factor' within
the novel (see p. 256 of this chapter). Furthermore Grass
had originally wanted to label the novel 'ein Märchen'
just in the same way that he has classified *Katz und Maus*
as a 'Novelle'.[3] This is in itself a clear-cut indication
of the importance which Grass attaches to the fairy-tale
and its role within the novel. Another remark which Grass
has made reinforces this statement, for in the same conversation with Fritz J. Raddatz he maintains, "daß im
Märchen in bündiger Form oft mehr Realität eingefangen ist
als zum Beispiel im angeblich so tief schürfenden

psychologischen Roman." One is also reminded of the comment Grass made in his analysis of the common features of the three works which form the Danzig Trilogy when he referred to the extension of our understanding of reality by "das Einbeziehen der Phantasie, der Einbildungskraft, des Wechsels zwischen Sichtbarem und Erfindbarem."[14] The introduction of Grimm's fairy-tale as a constant factor within *Der Butt* establishes an imaginative framework of reference which, by the interaction of fantasy and seeming reality and by associations which the imagery accumulates, contributes to the extension of our emotional and intellectual horizons and is a constant and most satisfying source of stimulation.

As with the history of the cooks the narrator gives us an abridged version of Grimm's fairy-tale in the first 'month' of the book in an apologetic manner so as not to offend his wife unnecessarily and hence incur her displeasure (pp. 28-29). The official version portrays the wife as lacking all moderation in the excessive demands she makes of the fish. The narrator also refers to the other version of the fairy-tale, which is described as "die andere Wahrheit" which both the fish and his pupil think ought to be published in order to rehabilitate all Ilsebills. The narrator fills in the details of this so-called original version when he relates how a group of

friends, including the brothers Jakob and Wilhelm, meet
in a forester's hut in the year 1807. This version
paints a picture of the fisherman as a man subject to
boundless desires: "im Krieg unbesiegbar will er sein.
Brücken über den breitesten Fluß, Häuser und Türme, die
bis in die Wolken reichen, schnelle Wagen, weder von Ochs
noch Pferd gezogen, Schiffe, die unter Wasser schwimmen,
will er bauen, begehen, bewohnen, ans Ziel fahren. Die
Welt beherrschen will er, die Natur bezwingen und von der
Erde weg sich über sie erheben." (p. 443). It is this
version which the group of friends decides not to publish
and which Runge ceremoniously burns in front of the
forester's house. It is suppressed, so we are told, because of its nihilistic overtones. The realisation that
this fairy-tale was converted into reality nurtures the
narrator's feeling of guilt and compels him to write. In
the poem that follows Grass reminds us that only fairy-
tales are real ("Nur das Märchen ist wirklich", p. 450).
The poem ('Hinter den Bergen') also reinforces the statement of the old woman that both versions of the fairy-
story are correct (p. 443). The artist Philipp Otto
Runge is likewise convinced that two truths may exist
side by side and both be valid.

Peter Russell has described *Der Butt* as "the elabora-
tion on a Joycean scale of a famous fairy-tale."[15] This

description is accurate in that the fairy-tale is a
dominant cohesive element and a constant frame of reference within the novel. It is a unifying factor in that in
the first part of the book the two occasions on which the
fish is caught are portrayed. From that moment onwards
the fish is continually in the forefront of the narrative,
on the one hand because the narrator at each stage in his
development turns to him for advice and on the other hand
because the turbot is placed on trial and the reader is
acquainted with the accusations which are levelled against
him and with the remarks with which he attempts to defend
himself. In this way the fairy-tale casts its fishy net
over the whole of the narrative.

We are even presented with a third, very much updated version of 'Von dem Fischer und syner Fru'. Mäxchen
(or Maxe), a woman by the real name of Susanne Maxen, is
the person who entertains us with this variation on the
story of the turbot. Mäxchen, who has aspirations to
masculinity, tells his version to Billy (Sibylle Miehlau)
as a kind of lullaby before the three 'men' rape her.
Maxe portrays his Ilsebill as being insatiable in the
sexual realm ("Deine Ilsebill kriegt wohl das Loch nicht
voll" is the turbot's comment-- p. 613). When she
finally demands "Olle Beethoven" as a sexual partner, the
fish commands her to be content with her Max (p. 614).

In the Fathers' Day episode the women are satirised because of their attempt to behave in accordance with the
example which men have set them. Their conduct is no
better than that of the rockers who gang-rape and murder
Billy shortly afterwards. The inordinate sensuality of
Billy-- and Max-- in the modernized version of the fairy-
tale prefigures the sexual aggressiveness of both the
lesbians and the rockers. The thugs who ride their motor-
cycles over Billy behave "als sei das Töten die Fort-
setzung der Sexualität mit anderen Mitteln." (p. 661).
The events on Fathers' Day demonstrate what happens when
the contents of Grimm's fairy-tale are updated and converted into reality. In a perverse sense the fairy-tale
is just as real as reality and, as Grass has indicated,
may contain more psychological truth in concentrated form
than the so-called psychological novel.

Grimm's fairy-tale not only makes an early appearance
in the novel but also forms the conclusion of the book.
In the final stages of the novel, Maria wades into the
sea and the fish jumps into her arms: the turbot has, at
least nominally, transferred his allegiance to woman. It
will be recalled that we are given a preview of this incident at a much earlier point in the novel (pp. 160-61).
Thus the fairy-tale is not only an integrating factor
within the novel but it quite literally spans the whole

novel.

The atmosphere of the fairy-tale informs the whole book and its individual parts. It could be maintained that the Fathers' Day episode is a particularly brutal fairy-tale and that Frederick the Great's visit to Amanda Woyke and how she offers him a plate full of soup (p. 392) belongs to a more agreeable variety. It is certainly true that the novel consists of a series of stories, and that many of them are re-enactments of the two versions of Grimm's fairy-tale, with violence and war as constant threads in the narrative. The extremism of the fairy-tale 'Von dem Fischer und syner Fru' is reflected in the individual episodes within the careers of the cooks. Many of the lives of the cooks come to a close through an act of violence, whether this be the murder of Mestwina or the death of Lena Stubbe in a concentration camp. Thus after discussing Jan's death in the 1970 disturbances in Gdansk, the narrator formulates the following generalisation: "Am Ende wurde alles bestätigt. Die Märchen hören nur zeitweilig auf oder beginnen nach Schluß aufs Neue. Das ist die Wahrheit, jedesmal anders erzählt." (p. 692). The word 'zeitweilig' obviously means 'for the time being' or 'temporarily' but, since 'Zeitweil' is the particular word in the novel for each narrator's reincarnation, it acquires the special connotation which stems from this

usage.   In other words, the life of each cook and the life
or lives of each narrator associated with her may be regarded as a fairy-tale and each has a repetitive quality.
Each episode or period, each fairy-tale, is a re-enactment
of the original version of Grimm's fairy-tale, each is
"die andere Wahrheit" (see p. 444), varying not in substance, but merely in detail and in the way in which it
is told.   In one sense each episode is a fairy-tale, and
in another sense the whole novel, the story of man's
development and also the story of woman's development
which is about to unfold is a fairy-tale.   And the history
which is a fairy-tale always turns out badly: "und doch
verlief die Geschichte nicht anders, sondern wie immer
und überall böse." (p. 687).   Even future history seems
haunted by the spectre of past history: "Ach Butt!   Dein
Märchen geht böse aus." (p. 689).   This last quotation,
it may be added, occurs at the end of a paragraph in
which the narrator records the conflicting unfulfilled
wishes of Ilsebill and himself.   The fairy-tale both in-
tegrates and binds together the novel.   It also exercises
a cohesive effect in that the imagery which is linked
with the fairy-tale creates a complex system of interrelationships.   One could trace the occurrences of the
word for 'wishing', to quote but one example of a word
which we have just mentioned and which figures largely

in Grimm's story. However, it would perhaps be more
appropriate first of all to investigate the significance
of the 'Butt' itself and analyse the associations which
it amasses in the course of the novel. During his re-
ception in Calcutta Vasco da Gama alias Grass produces
a number of comments on his own novel. One is particularly interesting in providing some insight into the function
of the fish in the novel: "Es werde dort symbolisch gegen
einen gefangenen Steinbutt verhandelt. Der Butt ver-
körpere das männliche Herrschaftsprinzip." (p. 224).
Elsewhere the fish refers to himself as "das so verhaßte
männliche Prinzip" (p. 408), and Sieglinde Huntscha,
counsel for the prosecution in the trial of the turbot,
melodramatically calls him "das zerstörende, dem Leben
feindliche, das mörderische, männliche, das kriegerische
Prinzip." (p. 658). The fish also acquires the negative
associations which surround the name of Hegel and the
'world spirit'. The reader is well acquainted with
Grass's denunciation of Hegel from his perusal of *Aus dem
Tagebuch einer Schnecke*. In the latter novel the snail
and the 'Weltgeist' are presented as being in conflict
with one another, in *Der Butt* the fish and the world
spirit are shown as being closely linked and are virtually
equated one with another. On one occasion-- significantly
when talking about Lena Stubbe and the second half of the

nineteenth century-- the turbot jocularly refers to his
elevation to the rank of world spirit whilst at the same
time placing it in juxtaposition with the word 'principle':
"Neuerdings zum Weltgeist erhoben, sah ich mich als Butt
(und Prinzip) gelegentlich überfordert." (p. 515). Other
references also allusively interlink the turbot and the
Hegelian world-spirit (see p. 50, p. 186, and p. 407).
Given the fact that the fish views himself or is viewed
as the masculine principle and as the Hegelian world-
spirit, it is not surprising that his powers (and his
associations) should be extended sufficiently to allow
the possibility of his being regarded as a God or a God
substitute (see p. 87, p. 89, p. 90, p. 92, p. 108, pp.
414-416). Though his name may be linked with divinity,
it is open to doubt as to whether he may be considered to
be a benign God, for he is portrayed as an impostor and a
scoundrel who, though he may be favourably disposed
towards man, often achieves an effect, which is malignant
rather than benign.   In this sense the turbot is a 'dia-
bolus ex machina'[16] or 'Mephisto Butt'.[17] The suggestion
which the fish makes that he may be the equivalent of an
extraterrestrial power or fate (p. 661) follows naturally
from his acquisition of divine (and magical) powers. The
turbot's progression from being the incorporation of the
masculine principle into being a phallic symbol is also

obvious. The fish encourages man to shake off the yoke of female bondage and to assert his paternity. In so doing he promotes the triumph of the masculine principle, the victory of the phallic symbol (see p. 333). The narrator comments upon the degeneration of the ideals of the French Revolution through the intervention of Napoleon who is likened to a "Steinpilz" (p. 460) (The fact that the turbot is a 'Steinbutt'-- see p. 41-- is not coincidental). Friedrich Bartholdy thinks of him as, the embodiment of a principle or idea (see p. 451) and, hidden in the section dealing with the Napoleonic era, is a reference to the world-spirit. The narrator points to the betrayal of his ideals in the following terms: "Zwar standen Pilze wie einzig für uns, aber die Idee, unsere, war vergangen oder hieß anders, stand nicht mehr auf einem Bein, war viel-mehr beritten: vom Weltgeist zu Pferde war damals die Rede." (p. 495). In this instance, so we are told, the victory of the phallic principle had disastrous conse-quences for Europe and the world. One of the climaxes in the assertion of man's masculinity is the First World War which is described in the novel as "dieses Meisterstück europäischer Männlichkeit." (p. 521). Another triumph of male prowess is celebrated when the three lesbians attempt to rape Billy by means of a plastic penis. They no longer suffer, according to the narrator, from penis envy ("Kein

Neid auf die Stinkmorchel mehr."-- p. 588).

In *Die Blechtrommel* another sexual symbol, the eel,
devours the head of a horse. In other words, the phallic
principle subdues all reason, in the same way that Raputin,
the epitome of inordinate masculinity, emerges triumphant
over Goethe and the values he represents. In *Der Butt* unreason in the shape of a fish sweeps moderation aside.
The hunger that can never be satisfied brings catastrophe
to the world. The masculine principle encourages "den
Umschlag männlicher Großtätigkeit ins Monströse." (p. 572).
However, though the phallic principle has triumphed and
wrought havoc, the narrators and the men who have asserted
their sexual and military capabilities are ironically by
no means paragons of masculinity. They are in human
terms failures undermined by their inadequacies and in-
sufficiencies. They are-- in keeping with the sexual
imagery of the novel-- "Schlappschwänze" (see p. 128, p.
520).

The web of sexual associations reaches out still
further, and in particular with reference to the theme of
birth. This theme shapes the novel in two ways: the
novel extends from the conception of a new life over the
nine months of pregnancy to the point when the child is
delivered; during this period of gestation the cooks are
bearing their children throughout the centuries which

Grass's 'history book' covers. The women-- the Ilsebills--
suffer from their lack of a male sexual organ, whilst the
men are envious of the women's capacity to create new
life. As a reaction to this subjectively felt sense of
deficiency the men have given birth, so the turbot claims,
to all manner of lifeless inventions. As the women began
to lose power and the matriarchal system started to dis-
integrate, "das Zeusprinzip, der männliche Samen, die
reine Idee setzte sich durch." (p. 122). These ideas
allow them to create products of the mind, their creations
take the form of "eine zeushafte Kopfgeburt." (p. 123).
The turbot develops his theory of the inadequacy of men in
the presence of the feminine tribunal: "Wie dürftig sind
dagegen die Männer ausgestattet. Was sie empfangen, sind
absurde Befehle. Was sie austragen, bleibt Spekulation.
Ihre Ausgeburten heißen das Straßburger Münster, der
Dieselmotor, die Relativitätstheorie, Knorrs Suppenwürfel,
die Gasmaske, der Schlieffenplan." (p. 500). Man's
adviser continues the imagery of pregnancy and birth to
include death as a kind of delivery into the life of the
next world and in so doing brings the list of man's mon-
strous creations right up to date: "Affären und Groß-
taten von heute: Kalkutta. Der Assuandamm. Die Pille.
Watergate. So heißen die Ersatzgeburten der Männer.
Irgendein Prinzip hat sie trächtig gemacht. Mit dem

Kategorischen Imperativ gehen sie schwanger. Immerhin
versetzt sie das einzig von ihnen beherrschte Militärwesen
in die Lage, den Tod als Niederkunft ins Ungewisse vorzu-
datieren. Doch was sie gebären-- ob Kreation, ob Spott-
geburt-- wird nie laufen lernen, nicht Mama sagen können."
(p. 501). The narrator himself anticipates the fish's
declaration when he speaks of "Zeugungswütige Männer, die
ihre Stinkmorcheln zu Geschlechtertürmen, Torpedos, Welt-
raumraketen umdachten." (p. 44). The achievements of men,
according to the fish, stem from a sense of inadequacy,
the need to prove themselves and their worth in relationship to women. Their achievements may be thus either a
substitute for sexuality or an extention of sexuality, of
the phallic principle. In both instances they regard
themselves as failures, either because of their discontent, their lack of wholeness, or their sexual impotence
(see p. 522). Accordingly the fish speaks of "tragische
Existenzbeweise" (p. 501). He maintains even that
throughout the course of history he has been concerned to
cover up man's failings and failures (p. 188).

It is especially interesting to examine why, in terms
of the novel, the divine discontent, the Faustian urge,
ever came into being. Wolf-Dieter Bach in his article on
Der Butt claims that the third breast and the turbot are
frequently equated, "halblaut beiseite gesprochen."[18] If

we examine the text carefully, then we will be able to establish that this statement is largely true, though the word 'equate' might need some qualification. The importance of the third breast is emphasised by the fact that it is the title of the first chapter, in other words, it precedes the résumé of the lives of the cooks, the description of the two occasions when the turbot is caught and the establishment of the tribunal. The suggestion that the third breast and the turbot are obliquely interconnected is contained in the chapter-- significantly entitled 'Die Runkelmuhme'. We are told that one of the three-breasted Aua priestesses visits the turbot and returns home without her third breast (p. 87). From that moment onwards the Edeks lose their innocence and they are seized by restlessness and discontent. They are filled with the desire to perform great deeds. They are overcome with Teutonic vitality, "zumal es ja, aus welchem Grunde auch immer, keine dritte Brust mehr gab, die den Freiheitsdurst des Mannes stillen, seinen Hunger nach Ferne sättigen, seinen Drang, um der Tat willen tätig zu sein, einlullen konnte." (p. 96). The narrator tries to explain the disappearance of the third breast in terms of the increasing influence of the turbot: the third breast (which is referred to later as "unsere ausgerottete Wunschrunkel"-- p. 89) vanishes, "nicht weil die Weiber

es satt hatten, uns zu stillen und nachzustillen, sondern
weil der Butt uns Edeks Gott sein wollte." (p. 87). The
third breast is replaced by the male symbol of the fish,
not without the craving for the third breast coming to
the surface in the mind of man from time to time. This
juxtaposition, if not opposition, of third breast and turbot, is reinforced by the fact that one of the first
pieces of advice which the fish gives man is that he must
deny himself the breast: "Zweitausend Jahre zu lang habt
ihr Stillzeit gehabt, habt ihr die Zeit im Stillstand
vertrödelt. Ich rate euch: Weg von der Brust. Ihr müßt
euch entwöhnen." (p. 44). Once man has broken away from
his dependence on the third breast, history can begin,
for the domination of Aua, "dieser dreibrüstige Ausbund
geschichtsloser Weiblichkeit" (p. 37), has come to an end.
Whilst Aua reigns supreme, men are incapable of producing
their own ideas (p. 30). With the "Wegfall der dritten
Brust" (p. 64) the masculine principle, as incorporated
in the turbot, gains ascendancy.

Wolf-Dieter Bach also points to the close relation-
ship in symbolical terms between the fish, the penis and
the embryo or child: "Und da meint er (= der Fisch) das
Glied letztlich nicht für sich, sondern meint 'was im
Schoß der Frau steckt'-- und Schoßsteckling ist auch das
Kind."[19] Also sind die Bilder 'Penis' und 'Kind' auf

symbolischer Ebene weithin austauschbar." He even sees a
symbolical connection between breast and penis. The dream
in which the narrator imagines himself as a woman giving
birth to a pregnant daughter who in turn produces a boy
with a fish's head (p. 615) does suggest the symbolical
link between penis, child and fish. The novel is in
effect dominated by the concept of the three. Both men
and women aspire to the possession of a third entity,
whether this be the desire of men and women to produce a
child or child substitute, or the pursuit of the masculine
principle in the shape of the fish, the yearning of women
to possess a penis-- or to destroy the male organ, and
the craving of man for the third breast. Men and women
long for this third element, as a vague, sometimes only
dimly apprehended objective or ideal, one which will bring
about an end to all desire, produce the ultimate state of
satisfaction, which existed before the "Wegfall der dritten Brust", the paradise towards which men would wish to
advance or to which they would wish to return. The narrator expresses these interrelationships and this pattern
of ideas in the first chapter: "Also gut. Zugegeben:
wenn ich ins Leere greife, meine ich immer die dritte
Brust. Geht mir bestimmt nicht alleine so... Es muß ja
nicht immer das bißchen mehr oder weniger Brust sein. Zum
Beispiel könnte ich deinen Arsch samt Grübchen genauso

schön finden. Und zwar auf keinen Fall dreigeteilt.
Oder was anderes Rundes. Jetzt, wo dein Bauch sich bald
kugeln wird und Begriff ist für alles, was Platz hat.
Vielleicht haben wir nur vergessen, daß es noch mehr
gibt. Was Drittes. Auch sonst, auch politisch, als
Möglichkeit." (p. 13).

The narrator even compares Ilsebill's expanding
stomach with a gourd such as the one in which Simon Dach
and the prophet Jonah sought refuge and viewed the horrors
of the world as though they were surrounded by a paradise
garden. Such an idyll turns out to be a false retreat,
a dream which does not offer protection from the harshness
of reality. Such happiness can only be short-lived, for
its fragility is soon smitten by the insidious worm of
destruction: "Glück, so gefährdet wie des Propheten
Kürbis, den Gott-- es hätte auch gut der Butt sein
können-- durch einen Wurm stechen ließ." (p. 119). In
this quotation the turbot and with it the worm are in
opposition to the gourd, the vision of happiness, which
is obliquely connected with the fresh hope that the new
life of a child embodies. Hence it is misleading to
claim that images such as child, gourd, male organ, and
fish are symbolically interchangeable: they preserve
their own identity and may be linked either be their affinity or by their opposition, depending on the context.

What draws them all together is the fact that all represent a third possibility-- 'Was Drittes', a dream to which
all aspire, a dream which may be false, unattainable or
which may contain a glimmer of hope for the future ("Das
Ganze ist mehr ein Traum. Nicht Wunschtraum."-- p. 12).
The ideal state, according to the poem entitled 'Aua', is
the situation in which man were to be relieved of the
necessity of having to choose between two alternatives,
and a third possibility were to put an end to all discord
and schizophrenia. Polarity would be superseded by wholeness. The women accuse the narrator of being a "Brustkind" (p. 492). By that they obviously mean that in their
opinion he has always been childish and will remain so
(p. 492). In the light of the imagery which we are discussing the word 'Brustkind' could acquire an additional,
quite different connotation: it could suggest that the
narrator has never abandoned the hope of finding the third
way, he always remains a dreamer (cp. pp. 513-14 where the
opposite meaning applies). In this sense, the history of
mankind has been a continuous failure to find the third
alternative, the escape route from the two extremes which
so far have dominated the political landscape.

The fish in Grass's novel is a multi-faceted image
in particular by virtue of its allusive links with the
third breast, the penis, the child and even with the

gourd. It has an external, independent existence of its
own in that it is an indispensible element in the fairy-
tale which forms in various ways the basis of the novel.
At the same time it may be viewed as the externalisation
of something which is revelatory of the inner life of man,
the embodiment of urges, desires and thoughts which may
belong to the conscious mind but which may lie dimly apprehended and well concealed within the subconscious mind.
The turbot exists therefore both outside and inside man.
Thus statements in the novel which suggest this double
function and this dual existence and which one is inclined
to dismiss initially as jocular, off-hand remarks may well
be more relevant than originally, on first reading,
appeared to be the case. For example, Franziska Ludkow-
iak's attempt to characterise the speaking fish when the
three lesbians first make his acquaintance is largely
accurate: "Der sei aus dem Zwischenreich des Unterbewußt-
seins gekommen. Der mache spaltsüchtig und erinnere an
Filme, in denen der Irsinn leicht versetzt aus rissigen
Spiegeln schaue." (p. 50). The turbot's description of
himself as "meine buttige, ins Urdunkel weisende Exis-
tenz" may have a broader, more comprehensive meaning in
that the word 'Urdunkel' can refer to the dark recesses
of the mind and to the remote historical past from which
mankind has emerged. The image of the turbot represents

the internal forces to which man (and woman) is subject
and yet represents the internal forces of character which
impels him onwards. The relationship between the fish
and man along with the associations attached to it em-
braces the central theme of the novel to which Wolfgang
Hildesheimer refers in the following terms: "Etwas nicht
lassen können und nicht tun können, das ist nicht bloß
ein Thema. Es ist *das* menschliche Thema, und in seiner
Behandlung und Meisterung hast Du Vorfahren in Shakespeare
und den griechischen Tragikern."[20] One might describe
the turbot as being emblematic of those forces of fate
which stem not only from the outside world but from within
the nature of man. At the same time its connection with
the child and the third breast leave open the possibility
that the vicious circle may be broken, that through new
life and new thinking man and woman may find a third way
forward which might avoid the pitfalls of the past.

History

As can be seen from the preceding duscussion of *Der*
Butt the history of the German-speaking area-- and of
Europe-- presents a sorry spectacle. As the book implies,
the unofficial version of Grimm's fairy-tale has been converted into reality: man's ambition to conquer the world
and nature has led to the greatest inhumanity. The turbot

confesses all: from the beginning of historical time he has advised men and his advice has worked to the disadvantage of women and to the disadvantage of mankind in general. War, so he claims, is the father of all things, and accordingly men have brought death and destruction to their fellow human beings (p. 658). His admissions constitute a condemnation of himself and his ostensible protégés. He even manages to accuse men of abusing the power which he had conferred upon them and of making power into an end in itself (p. 188). It has been his task, as we have noted, to divert attention from men's failures (p. 188). What men regard as their achievements, according to the fish, are intended to compensate for their incapacity to conceive and bear children, as well as concealing their failures in the personal sphere. In accomplishing such feats men are constantly posing questions about their own identity and the purpose of life (p. 501). In their search for identity they must slave away in the tread-mill of world history, "damit sie ausgemachte Männersache, datierte Siege und Niederlagen, Kirchenspaltungen und polnische Teilungen, Protokolle und Denkmäler ausspuckt." (p. 501).

Grass's novel *Der Butt* is a history of cooking and cooks, a history of emancipation, a story of the trial of a fish and of the trial of the narrator, the story of a pregnancy, and a history of mankind with particular reference to the German variety of man. From this many-sided historical narration there emerges a specific attitude to history. The turbot describes the book as "eine große historische Auf- und Abrechnung." (p. 524)-- this is perhaps a rather grandiose designation particularly if one bears in mind that the turbot is not the most reliable of fishes and adapts his statements to fit in with the inclinations of his hearers. Nevertheless, even if all allowances are made for exaggeration and melodrama, the turbot's pronouncement does contain a basic element of truth; the novel is a listing and a settlement of accounts. In coming to terms with the past-- 'Bewältigung der Vergangenheit', though this term never appears in the novel-- Grass conveys a view of history which is already suggested in the quotation at the end of the last paragraph. History appears to be a treadmill which, with monotonous regularity, allows circumstances and situations to recur whose basic similarity is not obscured by superficial differences. In this sense history is represented in the same way as in *Die Blechtrommel*-- there the image is that of the roundabout and much emphasis is placed on the imagery of circularity. In *Der Butt* historical events speak for themselves though their speech forms are amplified by the author. Many examples can be found. Danzig

at the mouth of the Vistula has exemplary significance
(p. 52) in that it has been a ping-pong ball in the game
of politics played by Germans, Poles, French and Russians
since the time the Teutonic Order began to make its mark
in that part of Europe. It has been destroyed and re-
built with sickening frequency. The internal struggles
within Danzig between those in authority and those
attempting to assert their rights have not changed, nor
has the manner changed in which the latter have been
treated (see p. 152). Grass conveys an impression of
historical immutability. The author or at least the
narrator speaking in the recent past to Ilsebill is aware
that progress and retrogression are inseparable companions: "Immerzu Rückfälle. Nach Robespierre kam Napoleon
und dann dieser Metternich..." (p. 419). Interlinking
all historical events is the continuous thread of violence.
The narrator expresses this idea in various forms. At
one stage he claims that if one takes a detached view--
he calls this "aus einer Kürbishütte gesehen", the Thirty
Years' War has never ceased (p. 118). History is described
on one occasion-- admittedly by the turbot-- as an inevitable sequence of war and peace (p. 661). The narrator
keeps his view of history in the forefront of the reader's
mind by referring to the wars and battles in which Germans
have been engaged or which have taken place on German soil:

the defeat of the Teutonic Order at Tannenberg in 1410, the battles of the Thirty Years' War (eg. Lützen, but especially Wittstock an der Dosse, the battle which Grimmelshausen's hero witnesses), the War of the Austrian Succession (1740-48), the Seven Years' War (Kolin, Rossbach, Leuthen, Hochkirch, Kunersdorf, Torgau and Burkersdorf), the battles of the Napoleonic Wars (Austerlitz, Jena, Auerstedt, Wagram), the Franco-Prussian War, the First World War (Tannenberg) and the Second World War (Tobruk, Stalingrad). The turbot recalls as well that the 'limited conflicts' of the post-war period have also caused the deaths of millions of people (p. 659). The narrator also reminds us that the hunger which affects large areas of the world is also a form of war (see p. 661). He gives expression to the continuity of violence, as we have already observed, by reference to the ways in which the individual cooks have met their death (see p. 571).

In commenting upon the constant presence of violence in the lives of the cooks Grass is interlinking the various aspects of history which we have mentioned earlier: the history of the cooks and cooking, the history of emancipation, the story of the trial, and the history of the narrator and of mankind. The pent-up aggressiveness which erupts with such frequency is represented

in quite different terms two pages before the end of the
novel, on this occasion in terms of the fairy-tale (see
p. 692 and also p. 285 of this chapter). This statement,
which is made by narrator, could be regarded as the
summing-up of the survey of history which has been undertaken in the novel. The context is significant in that
Maria has just mentioned the name of the official who
gave the order to shoot on that fateful day in 1970 when
her fiancé was killed during the uprising of the dock
workers in the Polish ports. The reader is reminded of
the imaginary conversation which Maria has with Jan as
she watches him in the crowd: "Gleich werde ich sagen:
Recht hast du, Jan. Man muß das historisch sehen. Das
hört nie auf. Auch nicht im Kommunismus. Immer die
Niederen gegen die Oberen." (p. 644). Neither communism
nor capitalism, to judge by this statement, has found the
complete answer to the latent trend towards violence
within society.

Runge's bitter comment that men tend to tolerate
only the one truth (p. 448) gives one indication of how
that violent strand in history remains unbroken. The
kind of men-- and women-- who ensure the continued existence of violence are described in a poem by Grass which
occurs in the novel under the title 'Am Ende' (p. 120).
In the poem the author asks himself, somewhat diffidently,

whether men who stop at nothing in the pursuit of their

final objective are coming to an end. Such men, however,

have been a feature of history according to the narrator

ever since they broke away from the tutelage of women,

ever since the emotional umbilical cord which attached

them to women was severed (see p. 127). Our guide through

the centuries describes them in the following terms, and

detailed examination of the passage would reveal the pro-

gression of man from the time of the Migration of the

Peoples via the Teutonic Order and the Reformation to the

twentieth century:

> Männer unter Lederkappen und Helmen mit nagelndem
> Blick. Männer mit schweifendem, die Horizonte ab-
> tastendem Auge. Zeugungswütige Männer, die ihre
> Stinkmorcheln zu Geschlechtertürmen, Torpedos, Welt-
> raumraketen umdachten. Männer mit System, in Männer-
> orden versammelt. Wortgewaltige Wortspalter. Sich
> unbekannte Entdecker. Helden, die nicht, nie und
> auf keinen Fall im Bett sterben wollten. Männer,
> die mit hartem Mund Freiheit verordneten. Durch-
> haltende, sich selbst überwindende, standhafte,
> ungebeugte, immerwieder trotzdem sagende, den Feind
> sich erfindende, grandios verstiegene, die Ehre um
> Ehre willen suchende, prinzipielle, zur Sache kommen-
> de, sich ironisch spiegelnde, tragische, kaputte,
> darüberhinaus weisende Endzielmänner. (p. 44).

The Teutonic Knights (eg. pp. 146, 686), preachers

such as Hegge at the time of the Reformation (eg. pp.

288-89), those who employ the guillotine in the name of

human progress (eg. pp. 358-59, p. 452) and finally Otto

Stubbe who assumes the now-or-never look when listening

to August Bebel (p. 548), all belong to the category of

those who pursue ideals to the exclusion of human considerations. According to the fish their entry into the
historical arena coincides with the emergence of the
principle of masculinity and "pure idea" (p. 122). Insistence upon absolute values has been reinforced by a
sense of personal as well as sexual inadequacy and failure, and thereby men have been converted into the monsters
of history (see p. 522 and p. 572). Lena Stubbe characterizes the situation accurately after having listened to
the arguments of her fellow-passengers on her way to
August Bebel's funeral. She wonders what will happen when
there is no-one who can find a compromise between the dog-
matisms of left and right, for she maintains that such
rigidity of attitude is dangerous (p. 559).

It is not only men whose minds may be blinkered and
who pursue their objectives with Coriolanus-like tenacity,
women too may be subject to the same degree of intolerance
and of inflexibility. The narrator compares Ilsebill, his
wife, with Sieglinde Huntscha and concludes that both are
very similar to Dorothea von Montau, who, intent on casti-
gating the flesh and her gaze fixed upon the crucifix,
scarcely notices that her daughter has been scalded to
death (pp. 158-59); for both Ilsebill and Sieglinde are
imbued with a rigid morality and refuse to be diverted
from their purpose (p. 170). Absolutism and single-mind-

edness are not then a prerogative of one or the other of
the sexes: both are capable of the same obsessive
devotion to principle.

As I have suggested, Grass creates the impression
that history repeats itself in thinly disguised variations:
"plus ça change, plus c'est la même chose" could be an
appropriate subtitle for the novel. Not only events be-
tray this similarity, attitudes too conform to a pattern.
Those who are unswervingly dedicated to their own version
of the truth have populated Europe from the beginning of
historical time and all men suffer from or emulate their
inhumanity. In this sense men are all cast in the psychological mould of history. All men share in the collective
consciousness which is the accumulated product of centuries. All men operate within the restrictions which
these strata of awareness impose. Grass creates within
the novel the impression of the co-existence of past and
present within men's lives. This he achieves by the insistence on a historical continuum and also by the fact
that the narrator-- and the turbot-- have both experienced
the flow of time and have been moulded by it. History
intrudes into the present and man cannot escape its all
pervasive influence. Attitudes and ideas stem from a
historical 'culture medium' which came into being centuries ago.

The period of National Socialism is rarely touched
upon in the novel: admittedly Lena Stubbe's death in
Stutthof and the battles of Stalingrad and Tobruk are
mentioned, but none of the lives of the cooks completely
spans the years from 1918 to 1945.   The turbot himself
would prefer to see the book finish with the life of Lena
Stubbe.   He is prepared to accept responsibility for all
European history including Napoleon and William II, but
maintains that Hitler and Stalin are outside his area of
responsibility.   He even dismisses the present as being
beyond his sphere of competence (p. 572).   On another
occasion it is stated quite specifically that the turbot
refuses to assume responsibility for the last two cooks,
i.e. Sibylle Miehlau and Maria Kuczorra (p. 648).   The
turbot presumably sees no connecting link between German
history before 1914 and German history after 1914.   "Was
danach kam (i.e. after William II), kam ohne mich.   Diese
Gegenwart ist nicht meine.   Mein Buch ist geschlossen,
meine Geschichte ist aus." (p. 572).   The narrator, however, is much more realistic and does not believe in
abrupt dividing lines or 'year zero':   "Da rief ich:
'Nein Butt!   Nein!   Das Buch geht weiter und die Geschichte
auch.'" (p. 572).   The narrator in effect establishes the
link between the eighth chapter and the preceding seven
chapters.   Chapter VIII forms an integral part of the

uninterrupted flow of history. The narrator thereby puts in their place those who regard the Nazi period as twelve exceptional years of temporary aberration, or those who try to date German history from the year 1945 onwards.

The characterisation and the narrative allow pessimistic conclusions to be drawn about the history of Central Europe. Yet the possibility of the vicious circle being broken, as in *Hundejahre*, does exist. The author leaves open a narrow chink through which the faint light of hope shines. And it is Grass's intention that the novel should be open-ended, as are all his narrative works.[21] Neither men nor women have established the right mode of behaviour, and this is especially so if female thinking merely operates within the strait-jacket of the male understanding of history (see p. 664). Both men and women need to be emancipated from the past and the present. The imagery surrounding the turbot points to the existence of a third alternative, a third mode of behaviour, a third entity, which will allow a new direction to be found though there is no certainty that this will be so. On this point characterisation, narrative and imagery complement each other. All elements within the novel-- narrative perspective, the story itself, the fairy-tail, the imaginative élan, the imagery and the view of history-- all combine to produce a novel which is exceptionally stimulating and may be regarded as a close rival, if not the equal, of *Die Blechtrommel*. As Wolf-Dieter Bach maintains, *Der Butt* provides the opportunity for meditating upon the relationship between the psychology of the individual and the historical process.[22] Like the Danzig Trilogy it is an unofficial historical survey which, though softened by humour, takes the form of a lament.

Notes

1. Page references are to the Luchterhand edition of *Der Butt* (Darmstadt and Neuwied, 1977).

2. *Die Zeit*, 12.5.1978.

3. Fritz J. Raddatz, "Heute lüge ich lieber gedrückt, Gespräch über den *Butt* mit Günter Grass," *Die Zeit*, 12.8.1977.

4. Rolf Michaelis, "Mit dem Kopf auch den Gaumen aufklären," *Die Zeit*, 12.8.1977.

5. Wolfgang Hildesheimer, "Butt und die Welt," *Merkur*, Vol. 10, No. 31 (1977), 966-72.

6. Manfred Durzak, "Ein märchenhafter Roman, Zum *Butt* von Günter Grass," *Basis*, Vol. 9 (1979), 71-90.

7. Peter Russel, "Floundering in Feminism: The Meaning of Günter Grass's *Der Butt*," *German Life and Letters*, Vol. XXXIII, No. 3 (April 1980), 245-256.

8. On page 41 of *Der Butt* Grass has his narrator state that his fish is a "Steinbutt" which is normally translated by 'turbot'. Hence throughout the chapter I have employed the term 'turbot' even though the English translator of the novel has used the word 'flounder'.

9. Heinz Ludwig Arnold, ed., *Günter Grass, Text und Kritik* (Munich, 1978).

10. See Heinz Rölleke, *Der wahre Butt. Die wundersamen Wandlungen des Märchens vom Fischer und seiner Frau*

(Düsseldorf/Köln, 1978). In this book the author
maintains that Philipp Otto Runge did take down two
differing versions of the fairy-tale.

11. As under note 9, p. 32.

12. Hanspeter Brode, *Günter Grass* (Munich: Beck, 1979),
p. 188.

13. Rolf Michaelis provides a table in *Die Zeit*, 12.8.1977,
indicating the interrelationships between cooks, narrators and members of the tribunal. A similar table
is also to be found in Volker Neuhaus, *Günter Grass*
(Stuttgart: Metzler, 1979), p. 144, and this includes
also the names of the narrators' friends.

14. As under note 9, p. 11.

15. As under note 7, p. 248.

16. As under note 5, p. 971.

17. As under note 6, p. 86.

18. Wolf-Dieter Bach, "Was flach fiel. *Der Butt* von
Grass: Ein Märchen für uns Kinder alle," *Die Horen*,
Vol. 22, Part 4 (1977), 128.

19. As under note 18, p. 126.

20. As under note 5, p. 970.

21. As under note 9, p. 30.

22. As under note 18, p. 130.

CHAPTER VII

Das Treffen in Telgte: *a celebratory novel*

Günter Grass states his objective in writing this
'Erzählung' on the first page of the book. He explains
that he is going to tell the story of "what began in
Telgte" because Hans Werner Richter, one of the co-
founders of Group 47, "wishes to celebrate his 70th birthday". It is in this sense that *Das Treffen in Telgte* is
a celebratory novel: it is dedicated to Hans Werner
Richter as a kind of literary birthday present.

However, Grass does not describe in his novel the
meetings of Group 47 which took place in the years between
1947 and 1967. He does not relate how the German authors
of the post-war period assembled at regular intervals in
various places in West Germany to read from their works
and to discuss the problems of literature and the problems
of their own epoch. Instead he transposes the action
three centuries back and has the literary get-together
take place in Telgte, a place of pilgrimage on the Ems, a

short distance from Münster. For reasons of mathematical
nicety he has the literary proceedings unfold, not two
years after a war, but one year before the end of the
Thirty Years' War when preparations for peace are in full
swing. The reader is quickly made aware of the similarity
of the two historical situations. The two Group 47s are
convened at a time when Germany is suffering from the
consequences of a full-scale military and political catastrophe. The reader naturally recalls a section from *Der
Butt* which anticipates one element in the basic structure
of *Das Treffen in Telgte*: "Denn im Grunde hat, aus einer
Kürbishütte gesehen, der Dreißigjährige Krieg nie aufge-
hört, weil solch eine Kürbishütte, die ja ein Nichts ist--
wie der Prophet Jonas erfahren mußte-- dennoch der geeig-
nete Ort bleibt, die Welt ganz und ihre wechselnden
Schrecken alle zu sehen. Das liebliche Jammertal."
(p. 118).

As in *Der Butt* the continuity of history is a strand
which links the various elements together in *Das Treffen
in Telgte* and contributes to the overall coherence of the
novel. Attitudes and actions recur with alarming, if not
sickening, frequency. The mould which forms the psychological, social and political environment seems to be
almost inescapable, if not immutable. The first paragraph
of the novel emphasises the inextricability, the virtual

interchangeability of past and future, with the present
enjoying a precarious existence between the two: "Gestern
wird sein, was morgen gewesen ist. Unsere Geschichten von
heute müssen sich nicht jetzt zugetragen haben. Diese
fing vor mehr als dreihundert Jahren an. Andere Geschichten auch. So lang rührt jede Geschichte her, die in
Deutschland handelt." (p. 7).

Celebrating a birthday and a literary society by
reference to a previous, ostensibly remote century, may
appear initially somewhat surprising. However, Group 47
was in no sense a unique phenomenon in German literary
history. The seventeenth century in particular saw the
emergence of a number of such societies which were dedicated to the promotion of the German language and literature. At least three spring to mind and they are all
mentioned in Grass's novel (p. 26): firstly, the 'Frucht-
bringende Gesellschaft', to which, amongst others, Opitz,
Harsdörffer, Logau and Moscherosch belonged; secondly, the
'Hirten- und Blumenorden an der Pegnitz', which was cen-
tred in Nuremberg and of which Harsdörffer, Birken and
Rist were members; and thirdly, the 'Kürbishüttengesell-
schaft', which met in Königsberg and whose central personalities were Heinrich Albert and Simon Dach. Given the
existence of such societies, reflecting the twentieth century in the mirror of the seventeenth century is not so

surprising after all. In fact as the reader immerses himself in the narrative, he will find such a transposition
to be both a genial idea and a source of great stimulation.

As was the case with Group 47 after the Second World
War, a considerable number of literary personalities-- and
to a lesser extent publishers-- put in an appearance at
the Group 47 of the seventeenth century. On a purely
superficial level Grass's imaginative construction of a
literary conference against the background of the Thirty
Years' War could serve as an introduction to the literature
and atmosphere of the seventeenth century, for during the
course of the three-day meeting the reader becomes
acquainted with both the works and what might have been
the characters of the writers concerned. Not only do the
members of the three literary societies to whom we have
referred join in the proceedings-- apart from Opitz who had
fallen victim to the plague in 1639-- but also somewhat
better known figures in the literary-- and musical-- life
of the seventeenth century make their pilgrimage in one
guise or another to Telgte: for example, Weckherlin, the
secretary to the exiled Elector Palatine in London, Paul
Gerhardt, the Protestant hymn writer, Johann Scheffler who
was later to make his reputation under the name Angelus
Silesius, Christoffel Gelnhausen who as Grimmelshausen
modelled the novel *Trutz Simplex* on the landlady of the inn

where the conference takes place, and Heinrich Schütz,
Master of Music to the Elector of Saxony. Other lesser
literary mortals include Greflinger, Zesen, Czepko, Buch-
ner, Hoffmannswaldau and Lauremberg. Each member of the
conference emerges as a differentiated individual in the
light of what he-- or she-- says or does, but also in the
light of the readings taken from the authors concerned.
The reader is regaled with a panoramic sweep over the
literary-- and to a lesser extent musical-- activities of
the seventeenth century.

Apart from Libuschka, the landlady of the Brückenhof,
three personalities stand out in particular in the course
of the narrative: Simon Dach, Christoffel Gelnhausen and
Heinrich Schütz. They emerge as the leading individuals
within the conference-- and the novel-- for at least three
main reasons: firstly, they contribute more than anybody
else to the unfolding of the plot; secondly, in quite
simple terms, they gain a good deal more attention in the
story than do their contemporaries and hence they stand
out with a clearer delineation as characters than the
other members of the conference; and thirdly, they allow
the literature and political activities of the seventeenth
century to be viewed in perspective.

Let us first examine the relationship of these three
characters to the plot. Initially one might be tempted to

think that Grass's imaginative presentation of a literary
conference would be largely static, partly because a three-
day conference consisting mainly of readings and to a much
lesser extent of the drafting of a peace manifesto does
not offer much room for narrative manoeuvre. However, our
author handles his material so skilfully that he can
appeal to his reader on at least three levels: firstly,
by introducing the reader to the literary scene of the
seventeenth century, primarily by means of the readings;
secondly, by portraying a series of clearly defined characters, that is the members of the conference, and by
showing how they interact; and, thirdly, by relating the
conference to the broader background of the outside world
by means of a series of actions, in other words a plot,
which reaches out beyond the largely petty squabbles between individuals within the conference. The intrusion of
the brutal outside world of reality into the ostensibly
pure and undefiled world of literary readings is relatively simple and yet highly effective. Simon Dach has convened a conference, having sent out a batch of invitations
to his literary contemporaries. It is to take place in
Oesede near Osnabrück. As the convener and organizer of
the assembly Dach is obviously interested in the smooth
running of the conference and is keen to reduce, if not to
eliminate, all friction between individuals and all

administrative difficulties. If one were forced to cate-
gorise, one might maintain that in his role as chairman
Dach represents the static or conservative principle.   In
short, if Grass had to rely on Dach for a plot, he would
be greatly disappointed. However, the nightmare of all
administrators, the hitch, intervenes to disrupt Dach's
well-ordered plans: the inn which was to be the haven for
literature is already occupied by Swedish troops.   The
authors who are just beginning to assemble are on the
point of despair and are already considering dispersing
when another intervention takes place, this time for the
good. Christoffel Gelnhausen, who is in charge of a squad
of imperial horsemen and musketeers, arrives on the scene,
accompanied by the literary contingent from Nuremburg.   He
recommends an inn in Telgte for their gathering, escorts
the writers to his suggested rendezvous and decisively and
amusingly evicts the occupants from the inn.   The meeting
in Telgte can and does begin. Gelnhausen alias Grimmelshausen, the military man with literary aspirations but at
that time no literary products, becomes gatecrasher and
participates in the discussions during the conference.
The soldier and regimental secretary affect the course of
events on a second occasion with the best of intentions
but with disastrously sobering results: after a short
absence from the inn he returns with the ingredients for a

royal feast. The poets are highly delighted with the banquet that follows. At this point Heinrich Schütz who,
though not a gatecrasher, certainly is an outsider amongst
the men of literature interrupts the revelry and to the
consternation of the gullible men of letters lets in the
light of reality. By his persistent and authoritative
interrogation Schütz establishes that the ingredients of
the meal which had so satisfied the palates of the poets
had proceeded from a military encounter with Swedish
troops who in their turn had plundered and murdered some
local peasants. The connoisseurs of literature are plunged
into despair and they are both horrified and disgusted.
Gradually they and their chairman recover their composure.
Gelnhausen has a quarrel with Libuschka, threatens to expose her in a novel which he intends to write, and leaves
the conference room and the inn, taking his troops with
him. The conference proceedings, including the reading
of Dach's poems, are brought to a successful conclusion,
but, military protection once withdrawn, the inn is set on
fire by an unknown hand. This brief outline of the plot
does demonstrate that Dach, Gelnhausen and Schütz are the
main protagonists and that the plot has a significant role
to play in the novel as a whole, serving to provide one of
the most substantial frameworks of the novel.

Let us now examine the character of the chief

protagonists and investigate their function within the novel. Grass constantly establishes points of comparison-- literary and political-- between the seventeenth and twentieth centuries. He does not, however, associate the authors of the Group 47 directly with the writers of the seventeenth century. The narrator himself who is a member of the literary circle in Telgte has a shadowy existence in the background of the novel, is not actively involved in the plot and is at pains to keep his identity secret. One suspects that if he were to identify himself with any particular writer he would opt for Grimmelshausen, though he does expressly deny any connection with him (see p. 115). Nevertheless it would not be inadmissable to see a close relationship between Simon Dach and Hans Werner Richter. After all the novel is dedicated to Richter on his seventieth birthday and like the occasional poems of Dach it celebrates a person and an event. Simon Dach, as the narrator recalls, owed his professorship in Königs- berg to a poem of homage composed in honour of the Elector of Brandenburg on the occasion of his entry into the town (see p. 165). Like Richter, Dach fulfills the same func- tion in the meeting of the Group 47 of the seventeenth century. Dach acts as convener, organizer and chairman of the conference. Without his initiative the meeting could not have taken place. He is involved in all the major decision-making: for example, he accepts Gelnhausen's

offer of accommodation in Telgte (p. 14);   he dispels the

reservations of his colleagues when the regimental secre-

tary supplies the ingredients for their festivities

(p. 112);   and he advocates that the conference should

continue after Heinrich Schütz has established the origin

of the food.   Like Richter, Dach presides over the indi-

vidual readings-- apart from his own-- and the subsequent

discussions.   Dach not only acts as chairman in a purely

formal manner, his chairmanship-- and leadership-- are

readily accepted by his fellow-authors (see p. 33).   Dach

sets the tone in effect for the whole of the meeting.   He

commends tolerance to all the participants (see p. 29);

acts as mediator when disputes appear to be getting out of

hand (p. 31);   readily appreciates the pros and cons of an

argument and is concerned to steer a middle course in as

conciliatory a manner as possible (p. 37);   and employs

diversionary tactics in order to avoid conflict (p. 86).

He, more than anybody else, places the smooth running of

the conference before petty wrangling, insisting that the

proceedings should be orderly (p. 106);   and applies other

elementary strategies to damp down ill-humour and conten-

tiousness.   Just as it would be with Grass himself, Simon

Dach hopes to avoid an excess of theory (p. 21).   Like any

good chairman, Dach tries to ensure that those of different

temperament and viewpoint are at home and at ease in the
midst of the meeting which is taking place 'under his
roof' (see pp. 24-25). In short he views himself as a man
of peace and acts in accordance with this self-imposed
image, employing the term "Ironiker" as an appropriate
epithet for himself.

Simon Dach is not only the organizer and chairman who
enjoys the whole-hearted acclaim of his fellows, but he
serves also as the emotional barometer of the conference.
When, for example, it is found that the conference cannot
be held in Oesede, Dach is on the verge of despair and
thus accurately reflects the feelings of his companions.
His despondency is much out of keeping with his accustomed
composure. When on another occasion the poets are horrified and sickened by the thought that their festivities
derived from the murder of the peasants and from Gelnhausen's attack on the Swedes, Dach once again mirrors the
consternation of his fellow-writers (p. 125). He participates in the lamentations and breast-beating of his companions and shares their despair and feelings of complicity. He, more than anyone else, considers that he as
chairman must bear responsibility for this state of affairs. In fact, though Dach is portrayed as being worldly
wise ("lebensklug", p. 128) and as being well-versed in
political matters, he is also subject to an underlying

melancholic disposition (see poem of Dach, p. 129).

Dach's capacity for indulging in melancholy should, however, not be viewed necessarily in a negative light. To judge by *Aus dem Tagebuch einer Schnecke* Grass would regard melancholy as an essential precondition for political action. The lecture Grass gave on the occasion of the five-hundredth anniversary of Dürer's birth is an apologia for melancholy as a springboard for an active involvement in human affairs. On the morning after Gelnhausen's disclosures Dach has retreated from the abyss of despair, resisted the temptation to wallow in melancholy and recovered his composure. Even after his colleagues have expressed doubt about their moral justification in drafting a peace appeal and after the discovery of a possible thief in their midst, Simon Dach nevertheless reasserts his authority as chairman and intellectual leader. The recovery of belief in himself and in his objectives after a period spent in doubt and in nihilism marks Dach out as having the essential characteristics of the man of action who pursues his aims with quiet determination, profoundly aware of the snail-like pace of progress and able to overcome those setbacks which lie in his path. In this sense Dach is capable of making constructive use of melancholy and has no inflated understanding of the nature of progress. In short, he accords with Grass's definition of the

man who is able to involve himself in activities which
benefit his fellow human beings: "Nur wer den Stillstand
im Fortschritt kennt und achtet, wer schon einmal, wer
mehrmals aufgegeben hat, wer auf dem leeren Schneckenhaus
gesessen und die Schattenseite der Utopie bewohnt hat,
kann Fortschritt ermessen." (Aus dem Tagebuch einer
Schnecke, p. 368).

As organizer and chairman Dach has an essential but
somewhat humdrum role to play in the proceedings and in
the novel. The fact that his poem constitutes an important framework within the novel enhances and complements
Dach's function as chairman. Gelnhausen, however, can
play his part in the activities of the conference with
panache and bravado, for he is not hemmed in by the cares
which are the province of the administrator and he can
benefit from the fact that he is on the one hand soldier
and man of the world and on the other hand would-be literary artist. In fact he tackles all the problems and situations with which he is confronted with consummate artistry
and the utmost inventiveness. It is as though the insights
he has gained as a man of war into reality enhance and are
enhanced by his boundless imaginative élan. Even though
he has not produced any literary works by the year 1647,
he does appear to eclipse many of the other writers merely
by what he says and does, in other words, by the way his

understanding and fantasy inform his statements and actions. Admittedly he can benefit from the reputation he
already enjoys in the world of literary actuality before
he joins the cast of *Das Treffen in Telgte*. Nevertheless
Grass does build Gelnhausen up as a man of stature within
the confines of the novel itself. Gelnhausen does not
rely on the fame he has acquired elsewhere.

From the outset he is represented as an individual
who rises head and shoulders above his contemporaries in
terms of mental agility and sheer inventiveness. Harsdörffer explains to Dach that Gelnhausen's fertile exu-
berance almost outsteps the bounds of literature: "Der
lüge bessere Mär, als sich erdichten lasse." (p. 12).
When it comes to expelling the Hanseatic merchants from
the Brückenhof, Gelnhausen wields his sword and his fantasy to the benefit of the poets. He presents himself as
the papal nuncio's personal doctor, who is escorting a
group of plague-ridden individuals into quarantine: "Es
seien unter den matten, wie man ja sehe, hinfälligen
Gestalten auf und vor den Fuhrwerken etliche von der
Beulenpest befallene Leichenstrohkandidaten... Die Pest--
das wisse jeder und das sage er als Arzt, der mit allen
Weisheiten Saturns geschlagen sei-- schone den Reichtum
nicht, raffe vielmehr mit Vorbedacht Kostbarkeiten und
bedenke Herren in Brabanter Tuch besonders gerne mit ihrem

Fieberatem." (pp. 17-18). The merchants request a written statement of the reasons for their expulsion from the inn, Gelnhausen draws his sword, says it is his quill and asks who is the first one to whom he should give it in writing. Under such threat the guests vacate their rooms with the utmost haste. The reader can derive pleasure from this amusing incident whilst at the same time not being unaware of the amoral nature of Gelnhausen's impudent action.

A similar combination of elements is present when Simplex puts an end to the frugality of the writers' meals: an audacious, basically crude, amoral action, humorously embellished with linguistic and imaginative extravagance, either on the part of the narrator or on the part of Gelnhausen himself. The impending banquet is announced by the commander of the imperial troops with an appropriate dose of histrionics: "Noch im grünen Wams, die Feder am Hut, sprang er zwischen die Herren, salutierte nach kaiserlicher Manier und rief das Ende der Grützsuppenzeit aus. Er habe dem schmalhansigen Elend den Schlußpunkt gesetzt. Ihm seien fünf Gänse, drei Ferkel und ein fetter Hammel zugelaufen. Mit Würsten habe man ihn unterwegs beworfen." (p. 106). The food which has so miraculously forced itself upon Gelnhausen is soon joined by cutlery, altar cloths, a canopy, five candelabras and a bronze figure of Apollo. Understandably Dach is both

amazed and apprehensive. Gelnhausen indulges in yet another flight of fancy coupled with flattery, in order to
allay Dach's fears. He claims that the ambassadors at the
Peace Conference had warmly welcomed the poets' meeting;
that the papal nuncio, Monsignore Chigi, had requested
Harsdörffer to write a dedication in his copy of one of
the writer's books; and that Count Johann von Nassau,
the Emperor's representative, had sent a golden ring for
Simon Dach, giving his official the instructions to attend
to the wellbeing of the poets (pp. 110-11). Gelnhausen's
poetic licence is not revealed until the repast is in full
swing and until Heinrich Schütz punctures the inflated
representation of what turns out to be a sordid reality.

Gelnhausen for his part is on other occasions keen to
deflate the pretentiousness of the men of letters, particularly when this takes the form of unrealistic theorising.
Sigmund Birken, for example, lays down the rules according
to which various types of people, whether they be children,
old people, women, heroes or peasants, should speak in a
work of art: the children childishly, the old sensibly,
the women chastely and tenderly, etc. Stoffel Gelnhausen
makes it quite clear that such a theory does not accord
with his understanding of reality (pp. 36-37). Unlike
some of his literary contemporaries the future Grimmelshausen is soberly aware of the fact that the poets'

conference would quickly come to an inglorious conclusion,
were the military protection to be removed (p. 43). Even
after his duplicity has been unmasked, the regimental
secretary remains amusingly irrepressible, even producing
a final trick to mark his departure from the conference.
Immediately before the final session Gelnhausen enters the
conference room by the window and expresses his pleasure
at being once again in the company of writers whom he
hopes to regard at a later date as his fellow-artists.
His arrogance arouses the indignation of the conference
participants and on behalf of his colleagues Harsdörffer
demands an explanation of Grimmelshausen's recent behaviour. The latter treats the poets to a cold douche by
relating his behaviour to the hypocritical homage which
the poets pay their patrons: "Mit seinen Reitern und Mus-
ketieren habe er zeitgemäß gehandelt, wie die hier ver-
sammelten Herren gezwungen seien, zeitgemäß zu handeln,
indem sie mit ihren Huldigungspoemen Fürsten zu loben
hätten, denen die Mordbrennerei geläufig wie das tägliche
Ave sei, deren größerer Raub als sein Mundraub mit Pfaf-
fensegen bedacht werde, denen Untreue praktisch wie ein
Hemdwechsel sei und deren Reue kein Vaterunserlang halte."
(p. 151). He rejects the poets' condemnation of his em-
bellishments of reality by referring to their departure
from the truth in their own works of art. Gelnhausen's

final act of roguishness is to throw a purse in through
the window of the conference-room, claiming that this had
been left in Libuschka's bed by one of the gentlemen.

Much of the interest of the plot centres on the personality of Grimmelshausen, in that he introduces the un-
predictable elements into the course of the narrative.
Furthermore he stands out amidst the members of the conference as the most fascinating personality as a result of
his remarks and of his rascally exploiting situations by
means of his exuberant imagination. He is presented as
the likeable rogue who is practising in real situations
what will ultimately be the techniques he employs in his
works of art. He emerges as an individual whose understanding of life is comprehensive rather than partial as
seems to be the case with many of the conference members
who, apart from Dach and Weckherlin and, of course Heinrich Schütz, appear to have isolated themselves in one
aspect of life, that is, in the artistic sphere. They may
lament the plight of their country, but their understanding of the totality of experience is defective in that
their activities are oriented exclusively towards literature. In this sense Stoffel Gelnhausen introduces a new
perspective into the conference, and like Schütz he allows
the reader to view the poets' meeting, their deliberations
and the literature of the seventeenth century from a

different angle. It goes without saying that the regimental secretary is a source of amusement for the reader on account of his knavishness and his fanciful and theatrical observations.

Another individual who attends the meeting and who is also an outsider is Heinrich Schütz. This is clear from the first moment of his appearance-- "jemand, den keine Gruppe aushalten konnte." (p. 55). Partly because of his peripheral position he provides the conference, like Gelnhausen, with a new dimension: "Sein nicht etwa herrischer, eher der vermeintlichen Störung wegen bekümmerter Auftritt hob die Versammlung der Dichter in Telgte und gab dem Treffen andererseits kleineres Maß." (p. 55). He is described as a man of distant authority and austere greatness and he asserts himself on a number of occasions in an unquestioned manner. Schütz, for example, reiterates in clear unequivocal terms what the purpose of the conference is: "Der geschriebenen Wörter wegen, welche nach Maßen der Kunst zu setzen einzig die Dichter begnadet seien. Auch um der Ohnmacht-- er kenne sie wohl-- ein leises 'dennoch' abzunötigen." (p. 94) and thus dispels the doubts of the introspective poets. On another occasion he arrogantly puts all the poets and poetry in their place by asserting the supremacy of music: "Wie die Sonne zwischen den Planeten, strahle die Musik

inmitten der freien Künste." (p. 98). He even goes so far
as to comment on the state of the German literary scene at
the time: "Wo das Vaterland daniederliege, könne die
Poeterei kaum in Blüte stehen." (p. 85), having just pronounced his condemnation of the extract from Gryphius'
Leo Armenius (p. 85). In fact only Johann Scheffler, and
to a lesser extent Georg Greflinger, comply with Schütz's
rigorous expectations of literature (p. 84). It is, however, obvious, that the other outsider in the conference,
Grimmelshausen, finds favour with this judge: "Denn jener
hergelaufene Stoffel, der freilich lustiger spinne als
etliche der angereisten Poeten, lüge sich eine Welt zu-
sammen, die ihre eigene Logik habe." (p. 119). It would
not occur to the reader to dispute the correctness of this
observation, for the poets and the reader accept Schütz
as a figure of authority. It is perhaps fortunate for
Dach that Schütz has already left the conference by the
time Dach reads his offering. And on a more practical
level it is Heinrich Schütz, not Simon Dach, who forces
Gelnhausen to admit his guilty involvement in the skirmish
with the Swedes. After having discovered the truth he
makes it quite clear that the conference must be completed
(p. 125). There are a number of occasions on which Schütz
does not fit into the otherwise generally accepted proce-
dures of the conference: for example, he addresses the

meeting unannounced (p. 83 and p. 98) and thus eclipses
Dach as chairman (this is also the case on p. 71). It is
noted on other occasions that Schütz had a sobering effect
on the assembled poets (p. 121) or that only 'Schütz retained his composure.' (p. 125). Heinrich Schütz more
than anybody else-- with the possible exception of
Gelnhausen-- has the capacity to dominate the meeting of
the writers, not because he is popular among his contemporaries, but by virtue of his authoritative manner, his
reputation as a composer and his intellectual stature.
The overall effect of Schütz's presence at the conference
is to damp down any inordinate pretensions the writers may
cherish. Furthermore he allows the literary achievements
of the seventeenth century to be viewed with greater
clarity. Without him-- and without the interventions of
Gelnhausen-- the reader might be tempted to attach too
much significance to the works of the writers concerned
and to the impact which literature is capable of making on
the world of politics.

The fact that the novel deals with the limited theme
of a literary conference contributes considerably to the
unity of the book as a whole. The coherence of the novel
is enhanced, as has just been suggested, by the non-static
nature of the conference, in other words, by the interplay
of the main characters. One other factor which binds the

novel together still further and heightens its appeal is
the similarity, so Grass would have us believe, between
the seventeenth century and the twentieth century with
regard to the predicament of Germany itself and the plight
of literature. The political and the literary crisis go
hand in hand, the one mirroring the other. The two are
inseparably interlinked, as is evident in Dach's soliloquy
about the purpose of the conference: "Dort wolle man
tagen, bis alles, die Not und das Glück der Poeterei wie
das Elend des Vaterlandes, besprochen sei." (p. 20). The
same twofold objective is stated once again when on a
later occasion the reasons for the assembly of the poets
is mentioned: "sei es, um dem zuletzt verbliebenen Band,
der deutschen Hauptsprache, neuen Wert zu geben, sei es,
um-- wenn auch vom Rande her nur-- ein politisches Wört-
chen mitzureden." (p. 26). Heinrich Schütz, as we have
already observed, adds his own confirmation to such statements (p. 94).

The similarity between the seventeenth and twentieth
centuries-- the resemblance of literary and political
situation in both these periods of time-- is constantly
in the foreground of the reader's mind, not because the
narrator-cum-author draws attention to this fact but because the reader himself automatically makes the comparison. The statements and quotations the writers make are

so obviously relevant to both centuries that the likeness
in attitude and situation just cannot be overlooked. Thus
the twentieth century is constantly present as a factor
throughout the novel, even though the present, that is the
time in which the book was written, is mentioned only once
and in fact in the first paragraph of the novel. The
novel is dependent for its effect upon the reader's knowledge of the present century and for that matter of the
intervening centuries. The twentieth century provides its
own set of criteria which come into play once the act of
reading begins. Just as in *Die Plebejer proben den
Aufstand*-- though perhaps more so-- *Das Treffen in Telgte*
relies upon knowledge previously acquired by the reader.

The desperate plight of Germany is a theme which is
continually stressed throughout the course of the narrative, either by statements which are attributed to the
various writers of by means of quotations taken directly
from their works. Opitz, so the narrator claims, wrote
to Dach from Danzig suggesting the need for a conference
and in so doing stressed the division of Germany: "Ein
treff allmöglicher Poeten, in Breslaw oder im Preußenland,
sollt vsrere sach einig machen, derweil das Vaterland
zerrissen..." (p. 24). Johann von Rist begins the Peace
Manifesto by quoting from his own work entitled *Das
Friedejauchtzende Teutschland*, thereby lamenting on the

devastation which the Thirty Years' War has wrought in
Germany: "Teutschland, das herrlichste Kaiserthumb der
Welt, ist nunmehr auff den Grund außgemergelt, verheeret
und verderbet, diß bezeuget die Warheit." (p. 91).
Andreas Gryphius also comments on the destruction to
which Germany has been subjected when he gives a reading
from his tragedy *Leo Armenius*: "In dem vnser Vaterland
sich nuhnmehr in seine eigene Aschen verscharret, vnd in
einen Schauplatz der Eitelkeit verwandelt, bin ich ge-
flissen vns die vergänglichkeit menschlicher sachen im
gegenwertigen Trawerspiel vorzustellen..." (p. 79). A
quotation from a poem by Daniel Czepko anticipates the
kind of remark which was to be made in the nineteenth and
twentieth centuries, suggesting that Germany is not necessarily a geographical entity, but rather a country of the
mind or perhaps anywhere where two or more Germans are
gathered together: "Wo Freyheit ist und Recht, da ist das
Vaterland, Diß ist uns aber nun und wir ihm unbekannt..."
(p. 158). Many of the problems of the twentieth century,
and especially those of the post-war period, are pre-
figured in other readings which the poets give. The de-
bates about the purity of the German language and the intrusion of foreign words into German are foreshadowed in
the satirical poem which Johann Michael Moscherosch cites
from his *Geschichte Philanders von Sittewald:*

> Fast jeder Schneider   will jetzund leyder
>
> Der Sprach erfahren sein   Vnd redt Latein
>
> Wälsch und Frantzösisch   halb Japonesisch
>
> Wan er ist doll vnd voll   der grobe Knoll..." (p. 38)

Rist's reference to the peasants' fear of the return of
the old political order conjures up the post-war concern
about restoration (see pp. 104-05). The Peace Manifesto
which is read at the close of the conference summarises
many of the fears and hopes for the future which have already been made evident in the course of the three days
of readings and discussions, especially the concern of the
poets for the well-being of their own country: "Es drohe
dem Reich Zerstückelung dergestalt, daß niemand mehr in
ihm sein Vaterland, das einstmals deutsch geheißen, erkennen werde." (p. 173).

One particular poem, Dach's 'Klage über den endlichen
Vntergang vnd ruinierung der Musicalischen Kürbs-Hütte vnd
Gärtens', is the final literary work to be read at the
conference and constitutes a fitting climax to the proceedings. More than any other single work it epitomises
the plight of Germany in the seventeenth century and anticipates much of what was to come. It not only forms the
climax of the meeting but provides yet another cohesive
element within the novel in that references, some direct
and others more veiled, are made to it throughout the

course of the narrative. Indeed Dach quotes from his poem
in the introductory speech to the assembled poets, indicating the need to make their voice heard above the noise of
battle and the long-winded talk of peace: "denn was wir
zu sagen haben, ist nicht angewelschtes Geschwätz, sondern
von vnserer Sprache: Wo laß ich, Deutschland, dich? Du
bist durch Beut vnd morden bald dreissig Jahr her nun
dein Hencker selbst geworden..." (p. 27). By the inclusion of this quotation Grass achieves a number of objectives: he allows Dach to re-emphasise the twofold purpose
of the assembly, i.e. to give new status and orientation
to the German language and make a modest contribution to
the solution of political problems (cf. p. 26). At the
same time Grass establishes a double perspective: the
meeting of the poets can be viewed as a reflection of the
age to which they belong; and the likeness between the
seventeenth and the twentieth centuries is immediately
conveyed. The words of Dach could readily have proceeded
from the pen of a twentieth century author. The self-same
sentiments, though obviously not in identical form, are
expressed in Bertolt Brecht's poem entitled 'Deutschland'.[1]
Quotations from other seventeenth century writers and comments by the narrator, as has already been indicated, reinforce and are reinforced by the quotations from Dach's
lamentation. The next reference to Dach's poem is slightly

more oblique. The assembled poets entertain each other
with a series of anecdotes which contain varying degrees
of bawdiness. This prompts the landlady, Libuschka, to
relate her experiences during Tilly's attack on Magdeburg,
how she profited from her plundering: "Sie prahlte mit
Körben voller Goldklunkerkettchen, die sie den hinge-
machten Weibern vom Hals geschnitten hatte. Endlich stieß
Gelnhausen sie an, damit sie verstumme. Das Elend Magdeburgs ließ nur noch Schweigen zu." (p. 52). This last
sentence is clearly an inversion of the quotation from
Dach's poem to which the narrator refers when Dach gives
his reading (p. 164). Once again the analogy between the
seventeenth and the twentieth century is abundantly obvious, for it would not be difficult to find counterparts
in the present century to the devastation of Magdeburg
during the Thirty Years' War.

A key word in the opening lines of Dach's poem is
echoed in the paragraph following the reference to Magdeburg. Simon Dach comments on the fact that people are too
easily inclined to laughter in instances where laughter is
inappropriate. He explains this situation in the following terms: "Das komme, weil selbst dem feinsten Gemüt das
Grauen gewöhnlich geworden sei." (p. 53). The word
'Grauen' recalls the beginning of Dach's poem: "Waß
grawen seh ich doch?" One might be prepared to dismiss

the inclusion of this word as coincidental, were it not
for the fact that it is repeated in another, equally significant situation in the narrative. On the morning
after Gelnhausen's disclosures the writers are still suffering from a sickening feeling of horror and disgust,
compounded by the impression that Weckherlin's purse has
been stolen. Their consternation reaches its climax in
the question: "Wohin mit dem Grauen?" (p. 143). The
writers' perturbation at having feasted on the suffering
of others and Dach's sorrow at the devastation of Albert's
garden are thus interlinked.

Dach's elegy is given its reading on the third day of
the conference as the final item. The poem is intended to
offer his friend Albert consolation at the loss of his
garden and the gourd hut situated on the island Lomse in
the middle of the river Pregel. The narrator represents
the literary and musical festivities of the friends and
their idyllic delight as "die glücklich gefundene Har-
monie" (p. 164), thus echoing Dach's description of the
garden as "ein kleines Paradieß" (line 40).[2] The destruction of the garden may be likened to the expulsion from
paradise and, as Albrecht Schöne claims, the Königsberg
garden and the gourd hut assume the role of a microcosm.[3]
The progression of the poem makes the symbolical function
of the garden quite clear. The lament at the devastation

of the garden proceeds to encompass the destruction of
Magdeburg and the dismemberment of Germany, as the narrator indicates: "Es mündet die Klage über die Zer-
störung Magdeburgs (wo der junge Dach studiert hatte) in
umfassende Trauer über das sich selbst zerstückelnde
Deutschland." (p. 164).

In the course of the poem, Dach issued a warning to
Königsberg, just as Jonah threatened Nineveh with the
wrath of God from the Biblical gourd hut, though Dach's
warning is ignored-- if one is to judge by Königsberg's
fate at the end of the Second World War-- whilst Nineveh
does not suffer at the hand of God. The poet condemns
war and ardently desires peace, hoping that a lesson could
be learnt from the suffering of others: "O würfen wir
doch klug durch frembder Noht vnd Schaden, Ohn Zweiffel
kähmen wir bey Gott hiedurch zu Gnaden!" (p. 164). Dach's
poem prefigures the course of the writers' conference as
well as the course of German history from the seventeenth
to the twentieth centuries. With hindsight Grass exploits
a symmetry which exists between poem, conference and history. The devastation of the garden and the gourd hut as
described in the poem has as its counterpart in the book
the destruction of the inn, the so-called 'Brückenhof',
for no sooner are the readings completed and the chairman's final words pronounced than the poets' temporary

retreat from the world, their literary paradise, is burnt
to the ground by unknown hand. Dach's advice to Königs-
berg-- and to Germany-- goes-- in the long run-- unheeded
just as the writers' manifesto, their appeal for peace to
the Princes, is lost in the fire: "So blieb ungesagt, was
doch nicht gehört worden wäre." (p. 180). Germany's capacity for self-laceration to which Dach refers in the
poem continued undiminished until the collapse of Germany
in 1945. The devastation of Germany-- and the division
of Germany-- which took place in the seventeenth century
are a foretaste of what happened in the twentieth century.
Dach's lament at the transience of life and of the products of man as expressed in the poem is poignantly reinforced by the fact that Königsberg is no longer part of
Germany, though this is not an observation that is made in
the book.

As Albrecht Schöne observes, "Dach's 'Klage' corresponds to the model of the 'Leichgedicht'."[4] Accordingly
his poem concludes with the consoling thought that the
works of the poets will survive and hence immortalize the
writers themselves: "Es ist kein Reim, wofern ihn Geist
und Leben schreibt, Der uns der Ewigkeit nicht eilends
einverleibt." (p. 164). These closing lines which offer
the poets comfort midst the insubstantiality of their
lives are well received by the assembled company. They

prompt the narrator to explain how rich citizens and members of the nobility like to benefit from the immortality
which poetry confers and thus employ the poets' talents
on the occasion of weddings and funerals. It is in this
sphere that the poets exercise great power: "Diese kleine,
ein wenig lächerliche Macht gab ihnen sogar die Möglichkeit, zu ordentlich bezahlten Aufträgen zu kommen." (p.
165). Dach himself earns his living, so the narrator
claims, by the writing of occasional poems for which he
is commissioned. He jocularly admits this in verses which
the narrator includes in the text: "Kurtz, bey Heyrath
und bey Leichen Spricht man mich umb Lieder an Gleich als
einen Arbeitsmann." (p. 165). The narrator recalls that
Simon Dach owed his professorship in Königsberg to a poem
of homage dedicated to the Elector of Brandenburg (p. 165).
Gryphius comments sardonically on Dach's over-productive-
ness, employing thereby a central image of Dach's 'Klage':
"Du machst dreyhundert vers eh' als ich drey gemacht, Ein
Lorberbaum wächst spät, ein Kürbs in einer nacht." (p.
165). Nevertheless much praise is lavished upon Dach's
poem and reaches its climax in Harsdörffer's exclamation:
"O, hätten wir doch gegen die schlimme Zeit eine Kürbis-
laube, weit genug für uns alle." (p. 166).

As is indicated in Grass's story, Dach's poetry was
for the most part written for specific occasions. The

same can be maintained in connection with *Das Treffen in
Telgte*: it may be categorised as an 'occasional' story.

It was written on the occasion of Hans Werner Richter's

seventieth birthday and pays homage to him in the same way

that Simon Dach paid homage to the Elector of Brandenburg

in the year 1638. There is, however, an important dis-

tinction in that the book which has been written for Hans

Werner Richter is free from that hypocrisy of which

Grimmelshausen accuses the poets in their compositions.

The person to whom the tribute is being made may well pro-

nounce himself fully satisfied with his birthday present.

To judge by the book Reinhard Lettau has edited on the

subject of the Gruppe 47 Hans Werner Richter did occupy a

role in the meetings and conduct himself in a manner which

has much in common with that of Simon Dach as portrayed

in Grass's novel.[5] Hans Werner Richter did issue the in-

vitations to the meetings (see p. 321 and p. 391), he

acted as chairman and leader of the discussions (see, for

example, pp. 48, 51) and on a number of occasions it is

attested that he did this with great skill (see p. 22 and

p. 290). Böll claims that the Group 47 would be unthink-

able without Hans Werner Richter (p. 390) and the editor

himself attributes the favourable development of post-war

German literature to the efforts of Richter, "dessen

Großzügigkeit, Initiative, Belehrung und Freundschaft er

nicht dokumentieren kann." (p. 17). Furthermore Hermann
Kesten pays tribute to the fact that Richter encouraged
the political involvement of the members of the Gruppe 47
(p. 327). If one bears such statements in mind, it is
probable that Hans Werner Richter will identify himself
with the person of Simon Dach. If he does so, he will no
doubt be highly satisfied, if not delighted, by the reflection he sees, for Dach embodies the characteristics of
a political realist whose endeavours are worthy of imitation. Hans Werner Richter will find the book to be a
fitting and touching tribute to the contribution he un-
doubtedly made to the development of post-war German
literature. He will be impressed by this unique example
of an 'occasional' novel and he may well recall that the
Gruppe 47 made Grass famous-- or so Richter would have us
believe (p. 291). In this sense Grass is expressing his
gratitude to Richter through the medium of this story.

Das Treffen in Telgte is not only the celebration of
a birthday, it is also the celebration of a literary conference, of Group 47. Despite the qualifications which
are implied within the story the conference is clearly
represented in a positive light. The writers highlight
the predicament of literature in the seventeenth and-- by
implication-- in the twentieth century, reveal their virtual impotence and yet do not fall victim to their feeling

of powerlessness: they force their impotence to make con-
cessions. More importantly, however, the reading and appreciation of literature is demonstrated as a source of
great enjoyment.

This book is equally an assertion of faith in literature, an affirmation of the significance of literature.
Both Simon Dach and Heinrich Schütz make this assertion.
The chairman of the conference expresses the invincibility
of literature in a particularly striking manner which has
special relevance for the devastated Germany of 1947:
"Und wenn man sie (= the poets) steinigen mit Haß ver-
schütten wollte, würde noch aus dem Geröll die Hand mit
der Feder ragen." (p. 178). In this sentence which provides the key to the understanding of the drawing on the
dust-cover. The book is thus a celebratory novel in a
number of ways: it celebrates a birthday, a literary group
and its meetings, as well as literature itself. *Das
Treffen in Telgte* may be regarded as a celebratory novel
in another way too: it pays observance, as does *Der Butt*,
to the continuity of German history. In the spirit of
Bach's elegy it laments the ritual of German history, re-
gretfully, realistically, but not without a glimmer of
hope. It points to the repetitive nature, the virtual
circularity, of the German continuum. It tells us sadly
what has been and what is, and thereby suggests what

should have been.   In this sense *Das Treffen in Telgte*
belongs to the pattern established by Grass's first novel,
for it is as much a threnody as is *Die Blechtrommel*
itself.   A celebratory novel indeed.

Notes

1. Bertolt Brecht, *Werkausgabe edition suhrkamp*, Vol. 9 (Frankfurt/M: Suhrkamp, 1967), p. 487f.

2. Simon Dach, *Gedichte*, Vol. II, Walter Ziesemer, ed. (Halle/Saale, 1936).

3. Albrecht Schöne, *Kürbishütte und Königsberg* (Munich, 1975), p. 32.

4. Albrecht Schöne, as under note 3, p. 60.

5. Reinhard Lettau, ed., *Die Gruppe 47* (Neuwied and Berlin, 1967).

CHAPTER VIII

Kopfgeburten oder Die Deutschen sterben aus:

an election manifesto à la Grass

Fritz Raddatz has maintained that Grass has invented
over the past few years a new genre: what Raddatz chooses
to call "den erzählenden Essay".[1] The term 'narrative
essay' is probably initially an appropriate term for cate-
gorising Grass's most recent book which was published in
June 1980. In coining this term Raddatz thinks of Grass's
two longish essays 'Kafka und seine Vollstrecker' and
'Im Wettlauf mit den Utopien' as being the natural antecedents of *Kopfgeburten*.[2] It is certainly true that there
is a narrative element in both of these essays but only
in the sense that the first essay proceeds from a discussion of Kafka's *Das Schloß*, and the second one is based
upon an analysis of Döblin's *Berge, Meere und Giganten*.
However, Grass himself is not telling the story. The
essays seem to be rather the attempt to establish a relationship between the worlds which Kafka and Döblin depict in their respective novels and our present-- and
future-- reality. In this sense they are nothing more

than relatively conventional literary essays, and do not deserve the title of narrative essay. Yet such an observation does not invalidate Raddatz's categorisation of *Kopfgeburten* as a narrative essay. If one wished to locate the ancestors of *Kopfgeburten* more accurately, then I think it would be more correct to regard it as a fairly natural progression from *Aus dem Tagebuch einer Schnecke*. At the same time it would be possible to find elements which link it with many of Grass's narrative works, more especially in terms of narrative approach, imagery and ideas, and with his essays.

Furthermore Raddatz's enthusiasm for the work also seems somewhat misplaced, for he describes it as "a masterpiece of virtuosity". However, as one reads-- and re-reads-- the book one is more and more assailed by the impression of 'déjà vu' or 'dájà entendu'. For example, the identity of author and narrator-- a gap which has been closing gradually ever since the publication of *Die Blechtrommel*-- is now total, an event for which we were prepared both in *Aus dem Tagebuch einer Schnecke* and *Der Butt*. When the author wishes to indulge in flights of fancy, he has recourse to the employment of a device called 'Kopfgeburten', a term and image with which the reader is acquainted from *Der Butt*. The idea that the democratic process is long-winded and tedious (eg. p. 160) is familiar to us from *Aus dem Tagebuch einer Schnecke*.

Admittedly the medium for expressing this idea is not the image of the snail but rather the myth of Sisyphos, of which mention is made in *Aus dem Tagebuch einer Schnecke* in which Willy Brandt is apostrophised as a Nordic Sisyphos (p. 303). The two teachers who are Grass's principle 'Kopfgeburten', Dörte and Harm Peters, are imagined as engaging in the election campaign of 1980 like Sisyphean heroes, who participated in the election campaign of 1969-- according to *Aus dem Tagebuch einer Schnecke*-- and intends-- according to *Kopfgeburten*-- to do likewise in the autumn of 1980. Other themes are equally well documented. For example, Franz Josef Strauss who gets a good deal of stick in *Kopfgeburten* has already received a fair drubbing elsewhere (see *Der Bürger und seine Stimme*, pp. 197-98, pp. 199-200, p. 232). One might be tempted into thinking that the economic interplay between the Northern and Southern hemispheres is a fresh theme which will titivate our jaded palates. However, this is not so, for Vasco da Gama in *Der Butt* is very much aware of the problems of over-population and starvation in Asia and, like Dörte and Harm Peters, visits a slum during the course of stay in India (p. 224).[3] And the comments Grass makes about the Germans and Germany are all ones which have appeared elsewhere in various forms whether this be

in *Aus dem Tagebuch einer Schnecke*, *Der Butt* or essays
such as 'Begegnungen mit Kohlhaas' from the collection of
essays entitled *Der Bürger und seine Stimme* (1974).
Kopfgeburten, it seems to me, is largely eclipsed by
Grass's previous works, obviously by the major novels but
also by the semi-autobiographical and semi-narrative work,
Aus dem Tagebuch einer Schnecke, Grass's earlier experiment in the sphere of the 'narrative essay'. Perhaps one
ought to introduce oneself to the works of Grass by reading *Kopfgeburten* first and then these disconcerting and
negative criteria would not hamper one's capacity for enjoying the book.

The ostensible starting-point for the book was Volker
Schlöndorff's proposal that Grass should write a script
for a new film for him. Accordingly references to the
production of the film and the adaptation of the text to
the film abound throughout the book. In this sense one is
reminded of the Fathers' Day episode in *Der Butt* in which
the characters behave as though they were taking part in
a film or of the situation in *Örtlich betäubt* where the
patient can observe events of past and present on the
television screen in the dentist's surgery. Günter Grass
draws attention to the fact that *Kopfgeburten* could be a
film or a book or both at the same time (p. 8).

Before looking at the structure, themes and imagery

of the work, it is perhaps appropriate to understand the
time scale within which the book operates. Grass tells
us that he is writing his book in November 1979 and intends to complete it on New Year's Eve of the same year
(p. 85). In other words, he is writing his book several
months before the federal election campaign of 1980. On
another occasion he provides additional information about
the chronological framework: he states that he and his
wife Ute returned from their Asiatic tour (by kind permission of the Goethe Institute) in the autumn of 1979.
His two teachers, however, the figments of his imagination, "fliegen im Vorgriff: Ende August achtzig" (p. 133),
in other words, between the 'Landtagswahl' in North-
Rhine Westfalia at the beginning of May and the federal
elections of October 1980 (p. 43). One other date also
has an important role to play in the book, and that is the
seventh of December 1979, the day on which Nicolas Born to
whom the book is dedicated died in Berlin from cancer
(p. 144). Having neatly located his book in time, Grass
proceeds to turn time topsy-turvy by recalling a narrative
technique to which we are accustomed in *Der Butt*: "Es
soll nämlich (wie in meinem Kopf, so auf dem Papier) alles
gleichzeitig stattfinden." (p. 106). This time scale is
an important factor in coming to an understanding of the
book and appreciating its significance. The book was

published in June 1980 and describes a trip to the Far
East which two young teachers make and during the course
of which we are given some insight into the way they think
and behave and the way they intend to pursue the Sisyphean
task of influencing the course of political events by
participating on behalf of the S.P.D. and F.D.P. in the
election campaign. They are to be regarded in many ways
as being exemplary. Grass treats them sympathetically and
it could be justifiably claimed that the author regards
their behaviour as being worthy of imitation by those who
are concerned about the democratic welfare of their country. An apologia of the book is at hand. It is certainly
not a novel, it could be regarded as a narrative essay,
but it seems to me that it is first and foremost a guide
for the good citizen, an election manifesto, a piece of
political propaganda, an attempt at political education.
Herein lies the vital difference between *Aus dem Tagebuch
einer Schnecke* and *Kopfgeburten*: the former, published in
1972, reviews a previous election campaign and explains
why the author became involved, whilst the later book reviews a future election campaign and tells the good citizens of West Germany why they and the author should support their own democracy against any danger which may
threaten it. In short, preventing Strauss gaining power
is more sensible-- and more likely to succeed-- than

fighting Strauss and his allies once they are in power.
The vision of what happened in 1933 might not have been
far from Grass's mind. At the end of the book Günter
Grass places his book (or film) in relationship to the
events of the future: "Der Film muß jetzt schließen.
Nur die Schule und der Wahlkampf gehen weiter (p. 179).
Kopfgeburten prepares the citizens for their future activities. The praeceptor Germaniae-- and the two teachers
who are his brain children-- tell us, not what what we
should have done, but what we should do.

Having isolated what to me seems to be the central
purpose of the book-- and having explained in effect why
it is futile to condemn the book by relating it to previous narrative works of Grass (other than *Aus dem Tagebuch
einer Schnecke*)-- it is important to emphasise that
Grass's contribution to the process of political education
takes place against a broad background of fact, fiction
and fantasy. Strauss and the problems of population and
hunger in the Far East exist as political facts; Dörte
and Harm Peters do not exist, they are fictional characters who exercise a representative function; Nicolas Born
did exist and no longer exists, but lives on as a source
of inspiration. The world of fantasy clusters round that
nodule to which Günter Grass has given the label of 'Kopfgeburten'. Indeed Grass's political manifesto plunges

immediately within the first few lines into a completely
fanciful idea, a speculation which recurs throughout the
whole length of the book, and which occurs to him amidst
the teeming population of Shanghai: "in Zukunft habe die
Welt mit neunhundertfünfzig Millionen Deutschen zu rechnen,
während das chinesische Volk, nach Zählung der in zwei
Staaten lebenden Deutschen, mit knapp achtzig Millionen
Chinesen zu beziffern sei." (p. 5). After introducing us
to this piece of fantasy which could easily have been
hatched by a Hitlerian head, Grass then acquaints us with
the equally fanciful contrary notion that the Germans are
a dying race, "ein Raum ohne Volk" (p. 7), a fear which
besets the 'Christian' opposition in the context of West-
German political reality. Having named two of his brain
children, he then mentions Zeus as the original father of
all such creations: "Zeus... aus dessen Kopf die Göttin
Athene geboren wurde; ein Widersinn, der männliche Köpfe
heutzutage noch schwängert." (p. 8). As in all births,
the creatures produced from the mind of man may be healthy
or unhealthy, wholesome of unwholesome, well-proportioned
or misshapen.

Grass then continues to list his series of brain-
children, some of which are dear to him and some, the products of other minds, fill him with fear and horror, like
the "Ausgeburten" which he mentions in *Der Butt* (pp.

500-01). One notion which particularly appeals to him and which he categorises as 'eine Kopfgeburt' at a later stage in the book (p. 156) is the proposition that literature is the only bond which links the two Germanies (p. 8 and p. 154) and that cultural links should be strengthened by establishing "eine Nationalstiftung" (p. 154), an idea which Brandt suggested in his governmental declaration of 1972: "es soll ja kein museales Monstrum, sondern ein Ort geschaffen werden, der jedem Deutschen geeignet wäre, sich selbst, seine Herkunft zu suchen und Fragwürdigkeiten zu finden." (P. 155). He intends to try and popularise this idea during the course of his election campaign (see p. 154), partly because he feels that he owes it to Nicolas Born (p. 157). Günter Grass mentions also the modest attempts which he and other writers have undertaken to maintain contacts between writers from East and West Germany, how he and Nicolas Born and others visited East German colleagues in East Berlin: the Schädlichs, the Kunerts, Sarah Kirsch, Sibylle Hentschke, Brasch until the 'Ausbürgerungen' began (see p. 57, pp. 80-81). Grass constantly rebels against Franz Josef Strauss's denunciation of writers as 'rats' and 'blow-flies' (see p. 56 and elsewhere) and refuses to allow the voice of protest to be quelled by political authority: "Keiner der Mächtigen kann mir das Wasser reichen. Lächerlich sind sie und

Pfuscher obendrein. Hochmütig spreche ich ihnen Kompetenz ab, mich beim Schreiben zu stören." (p. 105). One is reminded of the drawing of the dust-cover of *Das Treffen in Telgte*: the hand with the quill rising undaunted from the rubble-- or are these Sisyphean stones? Grass does in fact refer to an essay which appeared in *Die Zeit* under the heading: 'Wir werden weiterdichten, wenn alles in Scherben fällt' (p. 19).

Having mentioned the theme of population and the unifying role of literature in Germany, Grass now turns to 'Kopfgeburt' Number Three: his 'Lehrerehepaar' (p. 11), who, he tells us, comes from Itzehoe. The wife, Dörte, was born in 1948, whereas the husband Harm Peters in 1945 (p. 21). Both are products of the 1968 student protest movement: "Vor zehn Jahren wollten sie mit vielen Wörtern 'kaputtmachen, was uns kaputtmacht.'" (p. 11). Now both of them are active members of political parties, Harm belongs to the S.P.D. and Dörte to the F.D.P. (see p. 19). Like Günter Grass they intend to engage in the election campaign and whilst they are abroad, Harm practises his election addresses, pronouncing on many of the issues which affect modern society and the world as a whole: nuclear energy, disarmament, the poverty and over-population of the Third World (see pp. 107-08). Already his diary is full of political engagements for the weeks

following his return to Germany (p. 107). Like their mentor we must presume that they wish to be involved in the
election campaign in order to ward off "bedrohlich Kommen-
des, das notdürftig mit dem Namen Strauss benannt wird."
(p. 61). Like the praeceptor Germaniae, they do not intend to be idle bystanders, for "es könnte zu viele Leute
geben, die sich ihre kleine Lust am Untergang bestätigen
lassen wollen." (p. 18). One assumes that they share
Grass's assessment of Strauss as "eine fehlentwickelte
Begabung." (p. 174). Harm's comments on Strauss are just
as damning: "Der, der ist auch nur von vorgestern. Der
will noch immer Stalingrad halten." (p. 84). And Dörte
Peters frequently threatens that she will not bring a
child into the world if Strauss is in power (see p. 59
and elsewhere).

Apart from their political involvement, one of their
constant preoccupations is the problem of whether they
should have a family. In this way Grass crosses one
'Kopfgeburt'-- his couple of teachers-- with the 'Kopfgeburt' of the population explosion. The result of this
crossbreeding is that the Peters' debate about having a
child unfolds against the background of their trip to Asia
and their experiences there. Grass projects this juxtaposition of the two 'Kopfgeburten' onto the screen in the
following fashion: "Und so könnten die 'Kopfgeburten' als

Film anfangen: Totale der Landkarte des indischen Subkon-
tinents. Sie, in Brusthöhe angeschnitten, verdeckt halb
den Golf von Bengalen, ganz Kalkutta und Bengla Desh,
nimmt wie beiläufig die Pille, klappt ein Buch zu (trägt
keine Brille) und sagt: 'Wir können davon ausgehen, daß
im Bundesstaat Indien die Geburtenkontrolle, im Sinne der
angestrebten Familienplanung, gescheitert ist.'" (p. 13).
The dust-cover of Grass's book, which once again has been
designed by the author, presents us with two pictures of
the original Zeus-like 'Kopfgeburt': the one shows the
head of a man with an egg, or egg-shaped embryo resting
upon his forehead, whilst the other shows the embryo as
having developed into a foetus. If Grass had not chosen
to make the image of the 'Kopfgeburt' into the focal point
of his book, then this positioning of Dörte against the
background of the Indian subcontinent would be next in
rank as a possible substitute for the present drawing on
the jacket of the book. Or perhaps it would be more appropriate to regard Dörte's projection onto the film
screen as being the pictorial representation of the second
element within the title of the book, i.e. 'Die Deutschen
sterben aus'. For the to and fro of the debate between
husband and wife as to whether they should add to the already excessively large population of the world by producing a child is a constant theme throughout the book and

takes place against the backcloth of the population explosion and the starvation in India and in other parts of
Asia, especially the island of Bali. Their discussion is
also conducted in an atmosphere which is populated by
fears, fears for the future of our planet because of the
failure to contain this population growth and fears for
the future because of recent-- and impending technological
discoveries-- the new 'Kopfgeburten' which dehumanize men
and women and may encourage global confrontation: comput-
ers, fast breeders, intercontinental rockets, early warning systems, micro-processors, data banks and last but not
least atomic energy for use in peace or war. As our
author comments, we have come to rely on such inventions:
"Wir sind schon zu abhängig von unseren sich selbsttätig
weiterentwickelnden Kopfgeburten. Seit Zeus: sie pflan-
zen sich ohne Eisprung und Samenguß fort." (pp. 162-63).

　　　The child of Dörte and Harm remains something which
is purely notional, in this sense it is nothing more than
the rest of Grass's 'Kopfgeburten', products of fantasy
rather than reality (see p. 136 and also p. 53). As Dr.
Wenthien, the teachers' guide during their tour of Asia,
remarks in commenting on the increasing number of people
in Asiatic countries, "die werden sich ordentlich und
nicht mittels Kopfgeburten vermehren." (p. 111). It is
he who provides Harm and Dörte with information in

mathematical terms about the population explosion in Asia
(see p. 55 and p. 110), could arrange for them to stay the
night with a family living in the Cheetah-Camp slum near
Bombay (pp. 45-48), tells them its history, and describes
the effects of the Western economic system on the countries of the Third World: "Landflucht und Verslumung,
Raubbau und Verkarstung, Unterernährung und Hunger, Luxus
und Elend, staatliche Willkür und, alles überragend:
Korruption..." (p. 50). He also emphasises the interde-
pendence of East and West and paints the future in grim
terms: "von hier aus (i.e. from Asia) wird sich die Zukunft unseres Planeten bestimmen. Von hier aus werden
uns, den von Menschenrechten faselnden Plappermäulchen,
die neuen Menschenrechte diktiert werden." (p. 52). In
short, Wenthien guides them, not only on their tour of
Asia, but also guides them through the Brandt-Report and
the Papers of the Club of Rome, so much so that both Dörte
and Harm can quote from these two documents at election
meetings (see p. 158 where reference is made to Brandt's
"Neue(r) Weltwirtschaftsordnung"). So much emphasis is
placed upon the problem of over-population and the relationship between North and South that *Kopfgeburten* could
also gain the title of the 'Brandt-Report à la Grass'.
It is still true to say, however, that Grass's book is an
essay in political education. The two teachers are taught

by Grass himself, by Wenthien, and their experiences in
Asia, to view Germany and the Germans in global terms.
They are subjected to a process of preparation for the
election campaign so that they in their turn may teach
others. The praeceptor Germaniae gets the desciples he
deserves.

Fritz Raddatz has described *Kopfgeburten* as a narrative essay. However, even the word 'narrative' is a
relative term, for in comparison with Grass's novels the
story-telling does not grip the reader's attention, though
it could be claimed that the tale he tells is not supposed
to be in the same class as what one has come to expect
from novels such as *Die Blechtrommel* or *Der Butt*. For
example, Günter Grass states apologetically that nothing
much happens between husband and wife apart from the
'child' dispute: "Nur Verstörungen und Ortswechsel,
welche Handlung sonst hätten Harm und Dörte zu bieten?
Außer dem Kind Ja, dem Kind Nein spielt sich zwischen den
beiden nichts Aufregendes ab." (pp. 34-35). Our author
also playfully suggests that some narrative mileage could
be made out of a liver sausage which Harm Peters wants to
present to a friend of his on the island of Bali but Grass
creates the impression that he does not intend to be taken
seriously on this matter. The friend concerned, Uwe
Jensen, could be involved in arms smuggling and partisan

warfare, and his activities could produce, according to
our author, a kind of sub-plot, "als eine gegen Dörtes
Wunschkind gerichtete Kopfgeburt." (p. 65). However, the
sausage proves to be less 'handlungsträchtig' than he had
originally supposed (p. 101). Our author teases the reader and plays a narrative game of cat and mouse, but it is
not his intention to entertain us with a series of anecdotes.

Apart from Brokdorf which is added to the list of
'Kopfgeburten', figuring in the first chapter of the book
and gaining this appellation at a later stage in the book
(p. 77 and p. 136), Grass also introduces us to another
'Kopfgeburt', the inclusion of which is an essential ingredient in his political manifesto. The 'Kopfgeburt' in
question, that is, the myth of Sisyphos, is not referred
to directly as such but Grass comes close to giving it
this label. On one occasion, for example, Grass obliquely
conjures up the idea that Sisyphos may be regarded as one
of his 'Kopfgeburten' by stating that all of them are absurd (p. 162). Quite apart from this circuitous and perhaps fanciful argument and given the fact that Grass's
attempt to predate his own career (pp. 23-26) and to re-
model Strauss's career (pp. 173-78) are both described as
being 'Kopfgeburten', a myth could easily claim to being
regarded as 'eine Kopfgeburt' though not Grassian in

origin. Certainly the idea of giving the name of Sisyphos
to the tourist agency with which Dörte and Harm visit Asia
is a fanciful notion, in the best tradition of Grass's
'Kopfgeburten' (see p. 32). The prospectus advertising
the tour of Asia introduces the theme of Sisyphos from
the outset: "Wer den Stein wälzen will, wer die Kraft
hat, zu sehen und begreifen, was uns tief innen beunruhigt,
wem es um Tatsachen, auch um harte Tatsachen geht... steht
dort in sachlicher Maschinenschrift vor knapp gehaltenen
Informationen, die über die Säuglingssterblichkeit in Süd-
ostasien, über Bevölkerungsdichte und Pro-Kopfeinkommen
auf Java Bericht geben." (pp. 32-33). At the same time
the author tells us that he will explain the reasons for
this name later (p. 32). The prospectus does give an outline of the purpose of the tour of Asia-- it is to be concerned with fact-finding which will lead to the formation
of new ideas and attitudes and could also be said to provide a commentary on the book as a whole, for the book is
intended to stimulate a reorientation of ideas and attitudes in all spheres as a preparation for victory in the
election campaign. Like Rudi Ditschke in the sixties,
Günter Grass is attempting to sensitize, in his case, his
election campaigners and the electors about the problems
of the Third World and the problems of Germany against a
global background (see p. 168). Like all political work

this is a Sisyphean task. After christening the travel agency Günter Grass has his hero explain at a much later stage in the book what Sisyphos means for Dörte and Harm, for he compares the labours and spiritual attitude of Sisyphos with the tasks and ethics of democratic socialism (p. 101). Each political problem, whether it be the reform of the pension system or Brokdorf and the disposal of nuclear waste, presents itself to his mind like a stone which has to be pushed up the hill and which then rolls back down into the valley. The labours are many and interminable. Grass makes it quite clear that he regards Harm-- and his wife for that matter-- as being exemplary: "Und Harm hört auf Dörte und auf Camus. Ihn kann Orwell nicht schrecken. Harm ist der absurde Held wider das Absurde, er ist der Held der Geschichte." (p. 102). The image of the snail as the symbol of democratic progress (see p. 141) has been replaced by the myth of Sisyphos as interpreted by Albert Camus (p. 103). Ultimately Grass produces his credo: the stone can take on various forms for him: a book as one of a series, freedom for 'absurd' heroes, or justice, "dieser so leichthin talsüchtige Brocken" (p. 103), but he claims that his stone gives him a sense of purpose: "Er enttäuscht mich nie. Er will von mir nicht, ich will von ihm nicht erlöst werden. Menschlich ist er, mir angemessen und auch mein Gott, der ohne

mich nichts ist." (pp. 103-04). Harm's and Dörte's journey through Asia is emblematic of the voyage through life:
"Mit Sisyphos lässt sich werben. Mit dir lässt sich
reisen." (p. 104). Grass even goes so far as to quote (in
German) the final words from Camus's 'Le Mythe de Sisyphe'
in order to express his sense of content. "La lutte elle-
même vers les sommets suffit à remplir un coeur d'homme.
Il faut imaginer Sisyphe heureux." (See p. 106 in
Kopfgeburten). The word 'Kopfgeburten' is an umbrella
term which allows Grass to gather together in playful and
scurrilous manner numerous ideas and fancies calculated
to stimulate his electioneers and his readers, the potential voters, whilst the myth of Sisyphos supplies the
momentum, generates the energy necessary to convert ideas
into political reality.

Sisyphos does not stand alone as the only source of
inspiration for Grass. In eulogizing Nicolas Born, to
whom the book is dedicated, Grass establishes a link between Born and Camus, quoting once again from the final
paragraph of 'Le Myth de Sisyphe': "Du kennst das: den
Stein wälzen. Als wir dir nachriefen, hat dich Ledig-
Rowohlt, dein alter Verleger, mit Camus verglichen. ('Ich
verlasse Sisyphos am Fuße des Berges! Seine Last findet
man immer wieder.') Das ist heroisch. Weshalb mir Harm
und Dörte Helden sind." (p. 148). The tribute that Grass

pays to Nicolas Born, who died on 7th December 1979 is the tribute of one friend to another ("Freunde(n), die befreundet bleiben, weil keiner des anderen Freundsein durch Annäherung verletzt." (p. 147). It is the homage paid by one writer to another, by one idealist-- with its English meaning!-- to another. Grass quotes from one of Born's poems, which reveals him as a dreamer and a visionary, a person who aspires to Utopian ideals but is united with Grass in his understanding of the absurd. Both of them produce 'Kopfgeburten' (see p. 146) and in this they both inhabit the same realm of the spirit. In church Grass acknowledges his indebtedness to Nicolas Born but trusts that he can turn to him as a source of inspiration: "Nicolas Born ist tot. Trost weiß ich nicht. Wir könnten versuchen, ihn weiter zu leben." (p. 147). One of Grass's final 'Kopfgeburten' (see p. 148) is to take Nicolas Born with him as companion into Orwell's decade and observe Dörte and Harm Peters as they engage in their Sisyphean political task (p. 148) in accordance with the principle: "Der absurde Mensch sagt Ja, und seine Mühsal hat kein Ende mehr." (p. 162).

Kopfgeburten is not a fully-fledged narrative work and those who compare it with Grass's earlier fiction will be disappointed. Like *Das Treffen in Telgte* it is a touching tribute to a friend and fellow-writer. Like many of

Grass's works it is bound together by the cohesive effect
of one central image and achieves a stimulating impact
through the associations which stem from it. Like *Aus dem
Tagebuch einer Schnecke* it deals with an election, not,
however, retrospectively. It outlines, not a past election, but a future election. In this lies its originality.
As Goethe is quoted as saying in 'Le Mythe de Sisyphe,
"mon champ, c'est le temps."[4] This is certainly true of
Günter Grass in *Kopfgeburten*. He would probably classify
his sphere of time as "die Vergegenkunft" (p. 130).
Having said that, however, one ought to recall that Grass
acknowledges his special indebtedness to the future in the
book itself: "O Zukunft! was täten wir ohne ihn? Wer
könnte seine Wortwörtlichkeiten ersetzen? Mit wem ließen
sich fortan unsere Alpträume bebildern? Wie soll ich
meine 'Kopfgeburten' ohne ihn weitertreiben?" (p. 44).
The book, his attempt at political education, his night-
mares, his brain-children, his fanciful notions, his
dreams, in short his 'Kopfgeburten', would be a nothing-
ness, "ein Rauch von Winden" (see p. 152), without the
able assistance of the future.

Notes

1. Fritz Raddatz, "Der neue Grass: heitere Groteske, ernster Nonsense," *Die Zeit*, 16.5.1980.

2. Both essays are to be found in Günter Grass, *Aufsätze zur Literatur* (Darmstadt and Neuwied: Luchterhand, 1980), though both of them were published originally in 1978.

3. Page numbering refers to the Luchterhand edition of *Kopfgeburten oder die Deutschen sterben aus* (Darmstadt and Neuwied, 1980).

4. Albert Camus, *Le Mythe de Sisyphe* (Gallimard, 1942), p. 93.

By way of a conclusion

Auf was lasse ich mich ein? Auf Gegenwart. Als ich
aus den fünfziger Jahren in die sechziger Jahre hinein
weitläufig über Vergangenes schrieb, riefen die Kritiker:
Bravo! Vergangenes muß bewältigt werden. Und zwar aus
Distanz: Es war einmal.

Als ich Ende der sechziger in die siebziger Jahre
hinein über Gegenwärtiges, zum Beispiel über den Wahlkampf schrieb, riefen die Kritiker: Pfui! Wie kann man
sich distanzlos auf die Gegenwart einlassen. Und obendrein so deutlich politisch. So wollen wir ihn nicht.
Das wird von ihm nicht erwartet.

Als ich Ende der siebziger Jahre (abermals weitläufig)
die Steinzeit (und was ihr folgte) mit der Gegenwart
verquickte, riefen die Kritiker: Na endlich! Da ist er
wieder. Offenbar hat er resigniert und die Flucht in die
Vergangenheit angetreten. So gefällt er uns besser. Das
war er sich und uns schuldig.

Wenn ich mich nun, kurz vor Beginn der achziger Jahre,
wieder (distanzlos) in die Gegenwart verbeiße-- obgleich
Strauss ein Relikt der fünfziger Jahre ist--, werden die
Kritiker-- na was schon-- rufen: Klar doch! Sein Beitrag
zum Wahlkampf. Er kann es nicht lassen. Und was heißt
hier Kopfgeburten! Der hat Kinder genug in die Welt
gesetzt. Der kann gar nicht mitreden. Der wird Kinder-
losigkeit als gesellschaftliche Tendenz nie begreifen.
Das ist ein Thema für junge Autoren. Der soll lieber
bei seiner Vergangenheit, beim Eswareinmal bleiben.

Günter Grass, *Kopfgeburten oder die Deutschen sterben aus*,
pp. 129-130

In the GERMAN LANGUAGE AND LITERATURE MONOGRAPHS series the following monographs have been published thus far:

1. *Ingeborg Henderson:* Strickers Daniel von dem Blühenden Tal: Werkstruktur und Interpretation.
Amsterdam, 1976. viii, 206 pp. Bound.

2. *Peter Mollenhauer:* Friedrich Nicolais Satiren. Ein Beitrag zur Kulturgeschichte des 18. Jahrhunderts.
Amsterdam, 1977. viii, 267 pp. Bound.

3. *Rolf R. Mueller:* Festival and Fiction in Heinrich Wittenwiler's *Ring*. A Study of the Narrative in its Relation to the Traditional Topoi of Marriage, Folly, and Play.
Amsterdam, 1977. viii, 155 pp. Bound.

4. *Gayle Agler-Beck:* Der von Kürenberg: Edition, Notes, and Commentary.
Amsterdam, 1978. xii, 230 pp. Bound.

5. *David Artiss:* Theodor Storm. Studies in Ambivalence.
Amsterdam, 1978. xix, 215 pp. Bound.

6. *Heinz Bulmahn:* Adolf Glassbrenner: His Development from *Jungdeutscher* to *Vormärzler*.
Amsterdam, 1978. x, 153 pp. Bound.

7. *David B. Richards:* Goethe's Search for the Muse.
Amsterdam, 1979. iv, 112 pp. Bound.

8. *Ingeborg Hinderschiedt:* Zur *Heliand*metrik. Das Verhältnis von Rhythmus und Satzgewicht im Altsächsischen.
Amsterdam, 1979. vi, 144 pp. Bound.

9. *William E. Jackson:* Reinmars Women. A Study of the Woman's Song (Frauenlied and Frauenstrophe) of Reinmar der Alte.
Amsterdam, 1981. xxiv, 374 pp. Bound.

10. *Helene M. Kastinger Riley:* Das Bild der Antike in der Deutschen Romantik.
Amsterdam, 1981. xvi, 288 pp. Bound.

11. *Irene Stocksieker Di Maio:* The Multiple Perspective. Wilhelm Raabe's Third-Person Narratives of the Braunschweig period.
Amsterdam, 1981. iv, 149 pp. Bound.

12. *Noel Thomas:* The Narrative Works of Günter Grass - A Critical Interpretation.
Amsterdam, 1982. vi, 370 pp. Bound.